UNDER THE RAINBOW

Also by George Mair

The Eagle and the Dragon
Braceros: The Helping Arm
The Jade Cat Murders
Bridge Down: America's Collapsing Infrastructure
How to Write Better
Inside HBO: Cable TV vs. VCR
Lethal Ladies: True Stories of Women Who Murder for Love
Family Money: Inheritance Battles of the Rich and Famous
Star Stalkers
A Woman's Guide to Divorce
Oprah Winfrey: The Real Story
Bette: An Intimate Biography of Bette Midler

UNDER THE RAINBOW

The Real Liza Minnelli

George Mair

A Birch Lane Press Book
Published by Carol Publishing Group

A Birch Lane Press Book
Published by Carol Publishing Group
Birch Lane Press is a registered trademark of Carol Communications, Inc.

Editorial, sales and distribution, rights and permissions inquiries should be addressed to Carol Publishing Group, 120 Enterprise Avenue, Secaucus, N.J. 07094

In Canada: Canadian Manda Group, One Atlantic Avenue, Suite 105, Toronto, Ontario, M6K 3E7

Carol Publishing Group books may be purchased in bulk at special discounts for sales promotion, fund-raising, or educational purposes. Special editions can be created to specifications. For details, contact Special Sales Department, 120 Enterprise Avenue, Secaucus, N.J. 07094.

Manufactured in the United States of America
10 9 8 7 6 5 4 3 2 1

Library of Congress Cataloging-in-Publication Data

Mair, George, 1929–
    Under the rainbow : the real Liza Minnelli / George Mair.
       p.   cm.
    "A Birch Lane Press book."
    ISBN 1–55972–312–2 (hc)
    1. Minnelli, Liza.   2. Actors—United States—Biography.
3. Singers—United States—Biography.   I. Title.
PN2287.M644M35   1995
782.42164'092—dc20
    [B]   95–19243
                                                          CIP

To the two newest stars in my firmament—
Granddaughter Shannon Mair
and
Grandson James Abroms

Thanks to...

My editor

Hillel Black, whose patience and guidance made it possible to create this story of an incandescent star, *LIZA*.

My agent

Natasha Kern, and her assistant, Oriana Green, whose savvy and sensibility got me started and kept me going to the successful ending. When a writer has a good agent, he doesn't need much else.

Contents

UNDER THE RAINBOW

1

The Defining Moment

It happened the night of November 8, 1964. In September Judy was preparing for a concert at one of her favorite halls, the London Palladium, before her favorite audience, the British. The mail brought a copy of *Liza! Liza!*, her daughter's new record that included the song "Try To Remember" from *The Fantasticks*. Liza's rendition overwhelmed Judy. She immediately phoned Liza. "How would you like to sing with me at the Palladium?"

"Oh, no, Mama," Liza replied. "It's too much, Judy and her kid. Why don't you just do it yourself?"

Envisioning a sensational show with the two of them together, Judy exercised her maternal prerogative and said she wasn't listening to any negative talk. Liza *must* do it. Judy hung up, called the London newspapers, and announced the duo's performance for November 8. Tickets sold so fast the promoters quickly scheduled a second performance. Again the house seats sold in hours. Another call to Liza in the United States. "We're sold out! Isn't it great?"

Daughter acquiesced to mother, but the mother didn't realize what she had done. If there was ever a classic illustration of opening Pandora's box, it was Judy insisting Liza appear on the same stage with her at the Palladium.

Before coming to London, Liza asked her old classmate from the New York High School for Performing Arts, Marvin Hamlisch, to create her solo arrangements. On September 9 Liza flew into London's Heathrow Airport and was met by Judy's then husband, Mark Herron.

November 8 arrived, and for the first time in their adult lives, Liza and Judy appeared onstage together performing before a packed audience. One English critic summarized the electricity of this performance: "At times one had the incredible sensation of seeing and hearing in Liza the Judy Garland of twenty-five years ago."

Liza sang eight numbers on her own and Judy ten. They performed twelve songs together with Liza singing a variation of "Hello, Dolly" to her mother: "Hello, Mama, you're still growing...You're still going strong." Liza's performance of "Who's Sorry Now?" brought the audience to its feet.

Everyone was stunned by the electricity of the performance, including Judy, who realized she was being replaced in the hearts of the audience by a younger woman, her own daughter. Liza, confused, exhilarated, and scared, suddenly had the same revelation. She was confronting her forty-three-year-old mother with a performance that declared the older woman obsolete. Judy reacted defensively by trying to upstage Liza, stepping on her lines, and at one point deliberately trying to push Liza off the stage.

"Life was always speeded up in my family," Liza would say a quarter of a century later. "We went through in two hours what most mothers and daughters go through for years. It was funny because when that show started, I'd never done anything. So, I hear her say, 'Ladies and Gentlemen, Liza Minnelli' in a great proud voice. And, I come on and I sing and the audience really likes it and I hear her backstage going, 'Yeah, baby! Go, baby, go! Yeah, baby!'"

But through Liza's solos and the duets with Judy, the relationship between mother and daughter changed forever. When they came offstage at the end, Judy sent her daughter to her dressing room. As she turned to go, Liza saw her mother was going back alone to take the star's last bow. Something welled up inside Liza and she ran toward the audience to take the bow with her mother. The two had been mother and daughter. Now they were tough competitors. It was the end of one life and the beginning of another.

"When I was a little girl," Liza remembered, "and I jumped onstage to dance while Mama sang, it was an unrehearsed, amateurish, and spontaneous thing. But at the Palladium, Mama realized she had a grown-up daughter and I wasn't a kid anymore. I'm sure this happens with almost every mother and daughter. But it happened to my mother in front of eight thousand people. Mama became very competitive with me. I wasn't Liza, but another woman in the same spotlight."

Each woman had met her destiny, and they never again performed together.

2

A New Star Is Born

The first person to visit Liza in her life was Frank Sinatra. That was a mark of the life ahead. It began at 7:58 on the morning of March 12, 1946, in Hollywood's Cedars of Lebanon Hospital. Liza Minnelli, star to be, was born to two other stars, Judy Garland and Vincente Minnelli. No one in this family was prepared for what would happen to their lives after that.

Liza was born by cesarean section and weighed six pounds ten and one half ounces. Despite Vincente's fear that any child of his would look like him, the infant Liza was beautiful, with her father's big brown eyes and Judy's beautiful skin. A few days after Liza entered the world, she and her mother went home to their Evansview Drive house where a $70,000 nursery had been created for Liza. It was the beginning of what life would be like growing up in Hollywood! For Judy, already a star, Liza's presence marked a substantial change in her life, even more than for most new mothers.

Liza's godparents were Kay Thompson, a close friend to Vincente for ten years, and her husband, Bill Spear. Kay would continue to play an important role in the lives of Vincente, Judy, and Liza. A piano prodigy at four, she played the music of Franz Liszt with the St. Louis Symphony at fifteen and became a singer with a local band at seventeen. In 1939 Kay got a spot in a CBS radio show

.in New York where she met Judy Garland and their friendship began. Kay would become the friend who was always there when she was needed.

Kay helped the pregnant Judy get ready for the new arrival. As Vincente said, "Judy was making last-minute arrangements for the cesarean scheduled for March 12. The remodeling [of the nursery] was complete, the layette installed, and the godparents selected. They would be Kay Thompson and Bill Spear, who'd been my friends for ten years."

Liza Minnelli was born into a waiting and welcoming world. Kay gave Judy a bracelet the day Liza was born. Later, Judy and Liza would exchange wearing that bracelet for good luck. "If I go before you go, I want to be wearing this," Judy said. "I don't care what dress you put me in [to be buried], but I'd like to be wearing this bracelet."

If she had been a boy, she would have been called Vincente, but since she was a girl, Judy and Vincente called her Liza in tribute to their good friend Ira Gershwin, who wrote a song about a Liza and May, Vincente's mother.

Liza immediately established herself in the world, as her doting father noted at the time: "Soon after, I was allowed to see Liza. She was, of course, the most beautiful baby in the nursery. As for those other wrinkled babies around her, all they needed was a cigar in their mouths to look like Eddie Mannix at the studio. There, alone on a table, was a perfect child, with absolutely no wrinkles, letting out a healthy cry—projecting!"

3

Growing Up Liza

During her early childhood, Liza was rarely left alone and there was no competition between her parents other than to see who could be nicest to her. In the process, Liza became part of her parents' show business life. She played with the children of other show business stars such as Dean Martin, Oscar Levant, Lana Turner, Lauren Bacall, and Edgar Bergen, some of whom would grow up to be entertainment stars in their own right.

Liza was fortunate to have a well-read, literate father. She recalled, "Daddy would read me all kinds of bedtime stories from Colette to H. G. Wells. He'd tell me about the Bois de Boulogne in real little details. Daddy was ethereal while Mama was more adamant. I loved Daddy more than anyone in the world."

Vincente recalled with warmth and love the joy of coming home to his infant daughter: "Liza was a darling baby, a great beauty and much loved. We couldn't wait to get home each night to tell her. Her seriousness and highly determined spirit were funny and touching in one so young. Liza was only a few months old when she learned to climb the stairs of the nursery and she'd make her arduous way to the upper level to join Judy and me while we had our predinner martini. She was still crawling at the age of two. Liza would navigate her way so rapidly you'd swear she was moving on wheels."

Growing up the daughter of a movie star and a director was different because they were so far removed from the lives of ordinary people. Still, like most ordinary people, movie stars and directors love their children and lavish gifts and good times on them. The good times in the Minnelli household included having the police block off their street so they could run a small train around to entertain their children. It also meant clowns, jugglers, magicians, circus performers, donkey rides, and puppet shows.

A curious but understandable metamorphosis began with the birth of the cute, precocious Liza and dramatically affected Judy's life from then on. Judy Garland worked very hard, made many sacrifices, and finally became one of America's biggest movie stars—particularly after *The Wizard of Oz* and *Meet Me in St. Louis*. It was impossible for her to go out in public without being immediately recognized by her adoring fans. She was their friend, the girl next door, their favorite daughter—they called her "Judy," never "Miss Garland"—and it became impossible for her to walk in public without being mobbed by autograph seekers. She had to be driven even if her destination was within walking distance. When she tried to dine in an empty restaurant, it would soon be filled with fans coming over to say hello and asking her to sign their menus or napkins.

All that attention came before the arrival of Liza. Suddenly, the baby was the center of attention and the movie-star mother was assigned the role of supporting actress. She had help with yucky things like changing diapers, but she was there to play mommy and she was determined to be different—more loving and sensitive— than her mother Ethel.

The relationship between Ethel and Frances Gumm (Judy's name until it was changed to Judy Garland at the suggestion of entertainer George Jessel) transformed from a close mother-daughter union into a mean, demanding manager-performer arrangement. Ethel directed and relentlessly drove Frances while her daughter tried to win the audience's approval, which was all Ethel seemed to care about. Years later Judy née Frances summed up the pathetic story of her early childhood: "I was always lonesome. The only time I felt accepted or wanted was when I was onstage performing."

Judy's upbringing was in sharp contrast to how Liza would grow up. Liza was the adored focus of her father's life, and both Judy and Vincente lavished everything on their daughter. Also, when Liza was still quite young, she began assuming a mothering role toward Judy.

Later, Judy would imitate her mother with her treatment of her other two children, Lorna and Joey. It was a strange divergence of parental behavior with Judy treating Liza as a grownup while viewing her other two offspring as troublesome children.

When Frances didn't behave as expected, Ethel had ensured her obedience with a particularly cruel and emotionally damaging form of punishment. No matter what strange city they were in, Ethel would pack her suitcase, tell Frances she was a bad girl, and leave her locked in the hotel room alone. Eventually Ethel would return, and the terrified, abandoned little girl would sob her repentance and beg her mother never to desert her again. It was a lacerating form of torture and mind control that, along with the drugs Ethel would later give her, destroyed her daughter emotionally. It also set the stage for her emotional dependence on her husbands and Liza.

One chronicler of Judy Garland's life, Jim Spada, thought Judy was a pitiful victim of her mother's overbearing stage ambitions and that this behavior was imposed in turn on Liza.

Liza the child—a joy and fulfillment, to be sure—was also a problem that made Judy's life physically and emotionally more difficult. Judy and Liza started out competing with each other for attention, although as a baby Liza was not aware of it.

Judy's worries as a new mother were made worse by her drug dependency. Following a long-established pattern, prescription drugs were often ordered by MGM-sanctioned doctors. They were supposed to look after Judy but were mainly looking after the financial fortunes of the studio. At different times Judy had trouble waking up or going to sleep or suffered from colitis, so she took sleeping pills and the amphetamines Dexedrine and Benzedrine.

"We were happy with each other," Vincente Minnelli reminisced about that time. "There were the sad times, to be sure, but they were so minor compared to what we usually had. I'd learned to accept those aspects of Judy's makeup that couldn't be changed. She was a Gemini, so her frequent swings from exuberance to moodiness were understandable as part of her sun sign's twin personality."

In addition to considering the astrological influence on Judy's personality, Vincente also believed that she possessed a hair-trigger temper because she was left-handed. He generally perceived actresses as insecure and unstable. Vincente endured Judy's behavior as long as he could because he, too, was insecure and felt Judy, the quintessential movie star, was better than he deserved and he should be willing to pay any price to have her. In the end, the price was too high. The drugs exacerbated the trauma of their bad times.

He once described how he tried to appeal to her will as a professional actress and her duty to her audience, following another drug-generated despondency: "It was after one of these episodes Judy confessed, 'I think I might be taking too many of those pills.'

"'I know,' I answered. She waited for me to go on. 'I can't put my foot down and tell you to stop,' I said. 'I know there are times when you're tired and when things don't go well at the studio. There are several actresses around who are doing the same thing. And, I can always tell when they're on Benzedrine. Just as I can with you. You think you're doing wonderfully, this is the best performance you've given. But you're not nearly as effective as you think you are.'"

He went on. "Judy became a great star, like many others, by manufacturing her own adrenaline and filtering it through a relaxed approach toward performing. But she'd made twenty-three pictures in her nine years in films. The demands on her natural vitality were excessive."

Vincente repeatedly asked Judy to stop taking the pills, and she promised she would try. But, she was up against a powerful group of people who cared only about getting one more performance out of her. The cycle began with her own mother, who wanted to please MGM head Louis B. Mayer more than anything else in life.

Judy never forgot how her mother punished her when she was a child. Judy felt her mother would betray her in an instant if it meant getting her a good booking or a starring film role and thus making Mayer happy. Vincente got along well with Ethel, even though she initially objected to his relationship with her daughter. But he couldn't help but notice the hostility between Ethel and Judy.

Judy felt her mother robbed her of her childhood and the father she loved so much. Since her mother kept Judy and her two sisters on the road touring, Judy hadn't been with her dad very much. His absence may have created an illusionary image of how wonderful her father was, but the image was there to haunt her all the same. All this, along with Judy's other insecurities—rational or not—pushed her to the nirvana of drugs.

Vincente's father died in 1947, further contributing to his depression over all the other problems coming down around him. Then Judy became upset over his sexual inclinations, thinking he was paying more attention to her costar in *The Pirate*, Gene Kelly, than to her. She was convinced Vincente was having an affair with Kelly. Whatever the cause, Judy started missing shooting dates and everybody knew something was wrong.

Vincente remembered those times unhappily: "Judy, in her paranoia, became jealous of the time Gene Kelly and I were spending together. We would be so concerned with getting the choreography right we excluded Judy from our discussions. I'd felt it wasn't necessary for her to have to deal with such problems. But she felt neglected."

The tensions were never left at the studio, but followed Judy and Vincente home to be expressed in loud arguments that often resulted in somebody leaving to sleep on Ira and Lee Gershwin's couch. Judy and Vincente would make up and shoot another scene or two, then go home and have another fight. This domestic turmoil was seriously affecting the shooting schedule and Louis B. Mayer ordered Judy to see Dr. Frederick Hacker, his Austrian psychiatrist. Unfortunately, Dr. Hacker couldn't effect the cure he, Vincente, and Mayer wanted.

"Judy's mood was unaltered and our spats and bickerings became more magnified," Vincente said. "I tried to control my own volatility, but occasionally failed. The lashing out left raw scars."

Liza was two but would become increasingly aware of the turmoil between her mother and father as she grew older. After they finished *The Pirate,* Vincente took Judy on July 10, 1947, to Las Campanas, a private sanitarium near Long Beach which specialized in treating emotionally troubled rich people for $300 a day. It was the first of many times Liza's mother would be taken away from her. To Judy, Las Campanas was simply "the Nuthouse" where she occupied one of the special bungalows—not unlike the special bungalows at the Beverly Hills Hotel, but with a more expensive day rate.

Judy looked back later and said: "It didn't take me long to realize my bungalow was next to Ward Ten, the violent ward. I met some of the most charming people there—sensitive, intelligent, humorous people. As far as I could gather, none of them were demented in the common sense. Most of them were too highly strung for reality. I realized I had a great deal in common with them."

Vincente handled Judy's absence with gentle dissembling when Liza wondered where her mother was. "I told our daughter her mother would be back very soon," he said. "I'm thankful Liza had a very capable nurse during those years. Between the two of us, we hid the unhappy truth from her until she was old enough to cope with it."

But they couldn't hide Judy's absence completely since she insisted on seeing Liza and Dr. Hacker thought it good therapy for Judy to keep her connection with her family.

Judy spoke of Liza's visits to her at Las Campanas: "Liza would toddle into my bungalow and into my arms. I just held her and she just kept kissing me and looking at me with those huge, helpless brown eyes. I didn't know what to say to her. After they took Liza away, I lay down on the bed and started to cry. It was physical pain, pure torment at not being able to be with my baby. I almost literally died of anguish."

As Liza looked back on her childhood, she assessed what happened: "I had a crash course in growing up. I learned too much, too soon, too fast. I remember going through a period of my life when, if anyone laughed at me, I'd burst into tears. There were all these pressures going on around me: the broken marriages, the court appearances, the suicide attempts. Somehow I seemed to thrive on them. People think it's easy because Judy Garland was my mother. Boy, I've got news for them! Sure, it was tough being her daughter, but Mama was a friend of mine, a trying friend, but a friend. She never denied me anything and once she cried because she said she had no money to leave me, but Mama left me her guts and integrity."

Surely it was obvious to many that Liza was not having a healthy childhood. Some people even thought she wasn't *allowed* to have a normal childhood. In retrospect, most blamed the explosive relationship between Vincente and Judy. In the end Liza was the most hurt by the combustible marriage although in time, as she grew older, she discovered many other people had divorces, suicides, hard times, and trauma. Her childhood wasn't all that different even if it was a bit more dramatic. And as a mark of Liza's growing maturity, she began to discriminate between her mother's suicide attempts and determine which were serious and which were cries for attention.

Consistent, however, was Liza's constant and careful protection of her mother's public image for as long as Liza knew Judy's image was important. It all made for a rollercoaster kind of childhood for Liza in many ways. Certainly it was different in the sense of where her mother and father worked. To Liza, her parents worked in a dream factory called a movie studio.

"MGM seemed like a factory to me," Liza remembered. "I loved it. I got to know every inch of the studio, all the shortcuts to the different stages, and all the underground passages. And all the people knew me there. I would run around and chat with everyone. What really interested me the most was watching people dance. The musical numbers were so wonderful and I wondered if I could do them." It turned out, of course, she could. She copied and learned from what she had seen stars like Fred Astaire and her mother do. And she became obsessed with becoming a dancer.

Vincente Minnelli described driving home from MGM one day with his five-year-old daughter after a long day at the studio. Liza said, "Daddy, I want you to direct me!" Vincente, not understanding Liza's words at first, assured her he would direct her in a scene when they got home. But Liza protested, "No, I want you to direct me! I want you to get mad at me and shout! Just like you get mad at other people."

It was the expression of a childhood dream that would be fulfilled twenty-three years later when Vincente directed Liza in *A Matter of Time*. Liza remembered that drive home from the studio clearly: "I used to be at the studio so much. I especially loved the musical numbers. I didn't quite understand the drama…but the music numbers I thought were wonderful. I used to see how people would change after Daddy talked to them. I wanted to know if I could do that and to show off for him. Of course, I always wanted to be perfect for him."

From her mother Liza learned dancing and singing and storytelling. As Liza said, "Mama would always change her stories to suit the company. I would hear one story maybe twenty-nine different ways and I asked her once which one I was supposed to believe. Mama told me, 'Whichever one you like the best, whichever one made you laugh, believe that one.'"

Liza learned—first from her mother and then from her peers—people want to be entertained. They do not want to be depressed. Both Judy and Liza were brought up to understand their role in life was to elate people, not make them unhappy.

Thus in their presentation of their own lives, the two dismissed their sadness. For example, Liza showed her ambivalence when she told columnist Rona Barrett, "I had the best life. I really had a weird life, but I really had a great life. We laughed. Nobody wants to hear about that." And she later commented, "I know some people who think reality must be constantly depressing, but I think reality is something you rise above."

Judy learned all the world expected her constantly to be the sweet teenager who found happiness somewhere over the rainbow. Liza learned the same lesson. They were rewarded well, these stars of the American heart, but they earned it with long hours, arduous performances, and suppressed personal traumas. Making *somebody* happy was not their credo. Instead, their credo was to make *everybody* happy, as Jimmy Durante used to say. And when the body or mind wasn't up to making everyone happy, there was an agent, manager, or mother—in Judy's case, all three—standing in the wings with amphetamines to hype the performance or barbiturates to calm the star down between appearances.

Like many successful show business parents, Vincente Minnelli and Judy Garland worked long hours and traveled a lot. While Vincente often let his daughter hang around the set in the early years, Judy couldn't do that as easily with her travel schedule. A better solution was to have the whole family go to the studio together as they did when Vincente directed Judy in *The Pirate,* a romantic farce in which the wife of a boring mayor in the West Indies is secretly in love with a dashing pirate. Vincente even worked out an appearance for Liza, so she made her film debut at fourteen months.

In the past, Bill Spear and Kay Thompson were helpful in smoothing some of the rough spots for the Minnellis, but they were having their own problems. In 1947 Kay finally went to Las Vegas to divorce Bill and marry, professionally at least, the Williams Brothers Quartet. One of the brothers, Andy Williams, eventually went solo. Kay was pregnant in her mind with an imaginary daughter, Eloise, who would ultimately inspire a series of books about a six-year-old who lived at the Plaza hotel. Some suggest the character was based on Liza because she spent so much of her childhood in hotels with her mother, just as Judy had.

4

Suspension of Movies
and Marriage

S oon after the problems on *The Pirate* and Judy's release from
the sanitarium, another even bigger movie was launched.
Called *Easter Parade,* it was set to star Judy and Gene Kelly,
with Vincente Minnelli directing. This time, however, Judy's psychiatrists intervened and convinced Louis B. Mayer the health of one
of his most important stars hung in the balance. Mayer ordered
Kelly replaced by Fred Astaire and Vincente replaced with Charles
Walters because Judy couldn't take the pressure of working with
Vincente. This was a harsh blow to Vincente's ego, both professionally and personally.

Through 1948 Judy's condition worsened, but she continued to
work and Vincente did not. He wasn't allowed to direct a major
picture during this period. As he said: "I had no paranoid feelings
the studio was out to get me, that I was being kept idle because I
was now anathema to many. Never was I made to feel the studio
wrote me off as a director and relegated me to being Judy's
caretaker and, since I wasn't doing too good a job at it, I shouldn't
have expected anything more from 'them.' Never was I made to feel
that, and though I disclaim any symptoms of paranoia, I admit the
possibility crossed my mind more than once."

The new arrangement worked in some ways, but Judy was still

popping amphetamines to keep herself in semi-starved shape. Her behavior continued to be erratic, costing the studio extra money in overtime for the rest of the crew who had to wait for Judy to show up or get ready to perform. *Easter Parade* was released in July 1948 and turned out to be a smash.

Things calmed down a bit in the Minnelli household, with Liza demanding and getting more and more attention from both her parents, although their interest in each other was waning. Judy's doctors were prescribing more rest. Translated into everyday life, this meant more time away from Vincente, and inevitably, Liza. Judy at this point was a shadow of herself, weighing only eighty-five pounds.

In a cruel twist, the studio that put Judy in the care of a doctor who prescribed drugs for her decided that her behavior on *Easter Parade* and *The Pirate* was expensive and troublesome. So on July 19, 1948, the studio sent a registered letter suspending her for three months. Judy was warned she'd better straighten out or she would be fired.

Liza was two years old and began noticing the tension around her. Liza's parents decided to stay married but live in separate houses. Judy moved out of the house on Evansview Drive and into a house of her own at 10000 Sunset Boulevard. Liza began to see more of "Nanna," her pet name for grandmother Ethel.

Judy finished her suspension and went on to her next film performance as a replacement for the pregnant June Allyson. *In the Good Old Summertime* brought the long-awaited cameo appearance of almost-three-year-old Liza when Judy's costar Van Johnson picked her up while walking along with Judy at the end of the picture. It was a brief appearance in more ways than one as Liza described it years later. "I dressed myself and wore a pretty white outfit. But when Van picked me up, I remember feeling his cool hand on my rear end. I forgot to wear underwear!"

In the Good Old Summertime, a remake of *The Shop Around the Corner,* directed by the legendary Ernst Lubitsch, concerned a music store clerk, played by Judy, involved in a pen-pal romance with someone she has never met. Her irritating coworker, played by Van Johnson, also is in a pen-pal relationship. Eventually, the two discover they have been writing to each other, fall in love, and get married.

It bothered Judy that her character was a nice, average American girl. She felt at her advanced age—twenty-five—she should be playing more sophisticated roles. Certainly she was playing more sophisticated roles in real life, having married twice (she had previously been married to David Rose for several years), borne a child, and reveled in a variety of love affairs with rich and famous men. She wanted to be the femme fatale instead of Mickey Rooney's girlfriend at the soda fountain.

The point was underscored when Vincente became the director for *Madame Bovary,* the kind of picture she wanted to do. This was a remake of another old movie, based on the nineteenth-century novel by Gustave Flaubert. It is a moving period drama about a woman who sacrifices her marriage for love and meets a terrible end. It was first filmed in this country in 1932 under the title *Unholy Love.* Judy became even more frustrated watching her husband make the movie.

Judy and Vincente stayed married two more years but the break was approaching. "This time I couldn't hide my feelings," Vincente said. "We'd been through so much pain together. I'd exulted with Judy as she emerged into renewed periods of triumph. Why couldn't she do the same for me? I was deeply hurt." They announced to the world the marriage was dead.

Meanwhile, *In the Good Old Summertime* got good reviews and Louis B. Mayer wanted to build on that success with the $3 million production of *Annie Get Your Gun,* a musical based on the life of famous frontier woman and crack rifle shot Annie Oakley, starring Judy. Mayer asked Judy to postpone her vacation plans "a day or two" to record one of the film's key songs, "Doin' What Comes Naturally." Then he cajoled her into recording the entire score, which took six weeks and left her totally exhausted and covered with rashes. She was also losing her hair. Confronted with what he had done to his star, Mayer dumped her from the production and got Betty Hutton from Paramount as her replacement.

Toward the end of this period, Judy's doctors resorted to electric shock treatments to snap her out of her depression, but they didn't work. In 1949 three-year-old Liza made her first appearance in a movie en route to becoming a star, and in that same year her mother was first given electric shock treatment *because* she was a star.

Concerned about keeping Judy going long enough to use her in future films, Mayer consulted several people, including his advisor Carleton Alsop, who would later become Judy's agent. They decided to send her to Peter Bent Brigham Hospital in Boston, where she arrived May 29, 1949, on the eve of her twenty-seventh birthday. The hospital staff was to get her off drugs and bring back her old vivacious self. Part of her treatment was having electroencephalograms to see if her brain was functioning properly. It was.

At Peter Bent Judy was placed on a rigid schedule requiring her to eat healthy meals (she normally loved to subsist on peanut butter sandwiches and canned tomatoes) and go to sleep at nine o'clock. She suffered painful drug withdrawals that often had her hiding behind furniture or under her bed screaming in pain. After four weeks at Peter Bent, Judy was pronounced clean of drugs and released with the admonition she must live a disciplined life of good, regular meals, plenty of sleep, and not too much booze. She returned to Los Angeles, to Liza, and to her husband.

Judy and Vincente postponed the divorce for Liza's sake. This was important in some ways because Liza was particularly dependent upon the approval of her father, who treated her as far more mature than her three years warranted. She reveled in that.

Judy was accepted back into the good graces of Louis B. Mayer and went right into another picture, *Summer Stock*, with Gene Kelly. The plot involved Kelly's theatrical troupe taking over Judy's farm and Judy becoming stage struck and turning performer. MGM wanted *Summer Stock* to follow *In the Good Old Summertime*.

When *Summer Stock* was finished, MGM rushed Judy into another movie just three weeks later.

But Judy returned to her old behavior and MGM removed her from the picture on June 19, 1950. She didn't handle it well. At home two nights later she raced into the bathroom screaming, "I want to die!" over and over. She slammed and locked the door and slashed her throat with a broken glass. The paramedics were called and she was rushed to a hospital where the doctor pronounced the wound superficial. Word got out to the press about the suicide try and the studio immediately suspended Judy.

The migraines and temper tantrums returned, and Judy began to turn for comfort to the only person willing to actually sit and listen to her—her daughter Liza. Liza was hardly five years old and her mother was pouring out her troubled heart to her. Liza was bewildered but gave her mother the one thing Judy couldn't get from anybody else, sympathy. Liza wasn't old enough to understand about the drugs. That would come later.

More dramatic were the suicide attempts which were beginning to become a regular and dangerous scenario for Judy when she was distraught or not getting the attention she needed. All this was made worse because of Judy's perverse jealousy over her husband's career as he made a series of successful films, including *Madame Bovary, Father of the Bride, Father's Little Dividend,* and *An American in Paris.*

And it all affected young Liza's life as Judy's friend Evie Johnson saw Liza covering up for her mother's drunkenness or drug disability. Johnson said later, "Liza was a godsend to Judy. She was a very good, charming little girl. When things were going well for Judy, Liza would be a little homebody, clearing the table when we went for cocktails."

Now Judy turned on everyone, including Vincente and her mother, who she once ordered out of the house with the warning she should never come back to visit her grandchild. Even after this bizarre behavior, Judy and Vincente continued to stay together in their curious way until Christmastime. It was then Vincente concluded a lot of the tension in their lives came from Judy playacting and manipulating people, just as she would make up stories about phony incidents in her life for the press. Judy told Vincente she regularly manipulated the psychiatrists and studio executives who tried to control her life. For some reason this outraged Vincente. As he described in his autobiography years later: "It was damn near impossible for me to forgive Judy for this."

After this, Liza was told Mama had to "go away" again for a while, which Liza learned to expect, but this time there was an unexpected twist. Mama was going to leave her daddy forever. Though Vincente and Judy were still occasionally affectionate, they realized their marriage was unhealthy for them and for Liza. On December 7, 1950, the two officially announced they were separating in preparation for a divorce. As usual, Judy was the one who left, two weeks later, three days before Christmas. Vincente temporarily remained in the Evansview Drive house.

This time Vincente believed they were divorcing for Liza's benefit rather than staying married for Liza's benefit. As he said, "I opted for sanity. Liza's well-being would be better served if she had one stable parent living apart from his mate rather than having two emotionally wounded parents living together. Judy kissed Liza goodbye, gave me a friendly hug, and walked out. Our life together was over."

Liza would never enjoy Christmas after that and was known to break down crying if she heard her mother's recording of "Have Yourself a Merry Little Christmas."

Fourteen weeks later, Judy stood before Superior Court Judge William R. McKay and said her second husband Vincente Minnelli cared nothing about her and shut himself entirely out of her life. The divorce was granted with Judy gaining legal custody of Liza, subject to Liza seeing her father half of the time. Vincente gave both their homes to Judy—the one on Evansview Drive and the one in Malibu—and said he would pay her $500 a month alimony. The divorce left both of them emotionally drained and Vincente almost broke. Even so, he went out of his way to make life wonderful for his daughter whenever she was with him. He was like many divorced fathers who, out of guilt or love or both, try to make life with Father unrealistically special for their children.

He said, "If I spoiled Liza outrageously, it was done to achieve a balance with the starkness of her life with Judy. Much as Liza loved her mother, Judy represented duty and worry. I required nothing. As a result, I shared Liza's most carefree times."

5

A New Daddy for Liza

Judy went to New York and Liza stayed with her father in Los Angeles, where she adapted better to Vincente's bachelor life than he did. As Lee Gershwin said: "Vincente, I love her dearly, but Liza is very spoiled. It's your fault, you know. Judy's the disciplinarian with her and tries to instill some character in her. But you, you give her everything—you're nothing but a puddle of love. For her own sake, Liza should be disciplined. If she's not, you mark my words. She's going to grow up being a commuter to an institution."

To which Vincente could only respond, "I know I should, but you see, I just can't help myself."

Regardless of his shortcomings as a parent, Vincente handled his daughter with respect. As Liza herself often said, "He really understood me. He treated me like such a lady. Even then, he dealt with me on a feminine level. To do that to a little girl is probably the most valuable thing that can happen."

According to the custom at that time, custody was awarded to the mother. But Judy was an emotional and professional mess. She needed someone to guide her. Mayer dumped her. Her relationship with her own mother was a disaster. And the father of her child was estranged from her.

Judy was trying to jump-start her floundering career. She wasn't getting movie offers, and stage appearances were not pouring in, either. Her finances were tenuous, and she had a little girl to care for. Life became a series of tricks to dodge process servers, hotel managers, and repossessors. Strangely, Judy, who despised her own mother, was now becoming like her. Ethel used to pretend she was abandoning her daughter, locking Judy in hotel rooms and leaving. Now Judy was locking her own daughter out of hotel rooms for hours or even an entire day until Liza's complaints brought neighbors knocking on the door.

Judy didn't think she was a fit mother, and soon it became evident she did not much care for her firstborn. Before, Liza may have reminded Judy of happy times at MGM with Vincente. Now she was a burden. Things eased in the fall of 1951 when Judy got a nineteen-week, record-breaking stand at the New York Palace, but she was still hurting from the divorce and lonely for a supportive person in her life.

While in New York, Judy ran into Sid Luft, who she had met before at a party for Jackie Gleason. Nobody was exactly sure what Sid did, but whatever it was it kept him busy and away from home a lot. Michael Sidney Luft was a tough, macho man who attracted a lot of women and led the life of a rugged adventurer, knockabout, and con artist. He was a swaggering man's man who often carried a gun and grew up in the New York suburb of Bronxville, where he was into bodybuilding as a kid. After high school he ended up in Hollywood with an old classmate from Bronxville, actress Eleanor Powell. He became her personal secretary. Later he married actress Lynn Bari, who he was divorcing when he met Judy.

Many of Judy's friends warned her against Sid because he was a hustler, but she wasn't in the mood to heed advice. Vincente, however, sensed Sid was good for Judy. "She was now leaning on Sid," Vincente said, "who'd seemingly discovered the secret to keeping Judy sane and healthy." Sid quickly made himself her manager, convinced her to pursue a new career on the stage, and launched her with a booking at the London Palladium. It was a smart move because Judy captivated the audiences, who were already in love with her on the screen. It would be the beginning of a new career for Judy, but she was plagued by the same insecurity, stage fright, and fear of not pleasing people that had haunted her for years.

In March 1951 Judy was in London starting rehearsals for her premiere stage concert and feeling uneasy because Sid Luft had decided to stay behind in the States. However, five-year-old Liza was soon with Judy, and Sid eventually arrived to tend to the details. Actually, Liza was there because Judy sent for her and because Vincente anticipated Judy would be a hit with the British and thought it would be healthy for Liza to see her mother in good times.

"They had been apart far too long," Vincente would later write, "and though I selfishly wanted Liza to myself, now was the time she should be with Judy—during the period of one of her mother's greatest triumphs. This way Liza, who had lived through so many of Judy's down periods, could begin to understand her mother's staggering talent. Liza would also know, though her parents couldn't live together any longer, her father would always be a Judy Garland fan."

Judy's concert was a great success with adoring critics and audiences cheering her every night for four weeks. She was extremely uneasy before she started this initial concert series and endured a bad time before opening night. "I kept rushing to the bathroom to vomit," she recalled. "I couldn't eat, I couldn't sleep, I couldn't even sit down."

Judy's appearance was a smashing success and led to Sid arranging other bookings around the United Kingdom. More important, it gave Judy the feeling she achieved something on her own without Mama Gumm or Louis B. Mayer arranging things for her. It was also a wonderful feeling of maturity and freedom. It was a magical experience for Liza to see the stirring performances by her mother and the loving reaction as the audience sent waves of applause over the footlights. Those days were a special time of bonding and love for Liza and Judy. Ironically, this was the very stage where the defining moment in their relationship and in Liza's career would take place thirteen and a half years later.

After a time, Judy asked Liza to start calling Luft "Papa Sid," which Liza did. After Judy completed her English tour and returned with Sid and Liza to New York on the liner *Queen Elizabeth,* Judy shipped Liza back to her father in California. Sid and Judy remained in New York while Sid made the rounds of agents to search for bookings in America. But in the heat and humidity of the summer of 1951, the reception he got was chilly. Agents were aware of Judy's recent box office failures and of her being considered a difficult star. Major theater owners didn't need an expensive star who might not show up or, worse, appeared, but in no condition to perform.

Whatever people thought about Sid, he was imaginative and persisted at getting Judy's new career started in America. He finally convinced Sol Schwartz, a vice president of RKO which owned the Palace Theater in New York, to book Judy for a concert in October. This served everybody's purposes because it was part of the rehabilitation of a rundown star and of a rundown theater. The Palace, once the crown jewel of the vaudeville circuit, had become a dilapidated theater running five acts and a movie for a handful of customers. Schwartz wanted to refurbish and revitalize the Palace, but he needed a major star who would bring in paying customers to make it a profitable operation.

Judy worked hard on creating a good stage act in which she not only sang and danced but also reenacted scenes from some of her movie hits. She put together her new act in Hollywood and was so busy she didn't see much of Liza. Finally the October performance came, and Schwartz hedged his bets by running the five vaudeville acts and then putting Judy on afterward for what turned out to be a stunning performance for a packed, enthusiastic audience. Schwartz was ecstatic about the reception Judy received and extended the concert run to four months, longer than any other show at the Palace. But the grueling schedule of thirteen two-hour shows a week was too much for Judy and she collapsed during a performance in the third week. After a few days' rest, she cut back to ten performances a week to the end of the run on February 24, 1952.

After the Palace, Judy and Sid took a two-week vacation in Florida then headed back to Los Angeles for a March appearance at the Philharmonic Auditorium where her old friends and former colleagues could see the new Judy in concert. She dazzled them before heading for San Francisco where Sid booked another appearance. Being in Los Angeles, of course, gave Judy time to be with Liza.

Liza was with her father in Los Angeles watching the evening news in early June 1952 when—to their amazement—the anchor announced Judy Garland had married Michael Sidney Luft in Hollister, a ranching community in Northern California. Judy was four months pregnant. This pregnancy was much tougher than the one that produced Liza, and Judy relied on her old standbys to see her through: pills and more pills. Luft would search the house and the car and every place she could hide Dexedrine, Seconal, and other drugs.

In her own eyes, Judy seemed to get fatter and uglier with this pregnancy than she had with Liza. She also had a short bout with total numbness in her right arm, so she felt she needed her pills to survive. Her physical distress was compounded by the viciousness of her fights with her mother. She still refused to see Ethel, and Ethel, not a woman accustomed to being thwarted, was pressed to bring her errant daughter to heel. She couldn't lock her in or out of a hotel room anymore, but there were other hurtful things in her arsenal. She sued Judy for support. Ethel claimed Judy owed her a decent stipend, given Judy had so much money and Ethel was reduced to being an assembly line worker at $61 a week. Judy said in court Ethel had squandered the thousands of dollars she received from Judy's movie earnings.

Then Ethel trashed her daughter with bad publicity which could affect Judy's attempt at reviving her career. In an exclusive interview, Ethel told gossip columnist Sheilah Graham, "Judy has been selfish all her life. That's my fault. I made it too easy for her. She worked, but that's all she ever wanted: to be an actress. She never said, 'I want to be kind or loved,' only 'I want to be famous.'"

Liza's half sister arrived in Santa Monica's hospital to the stars, St. John's, four days before Thanksgiving 1952. She weighed six pounds, four ounces and was christened Lorna. At the time Judy said something that portended uneasiness ahead: "Lorna's birth was the only bright spot in the first year of my marriage." Judy refused to see her mother and banned Ethel from visiting her new granddaughter.

They moved into Sid's home at 144 South Mapleton Drive in Holmby Hills, adjacent to Beverly Hills. Judy stayed mostly in bed crying and popping pills. Then she tried suicide again, locking herself in the bathroom and slashing her throat. Sid broke down the door and was horrified at the sight of Judy lying in her own blood. A doctor was summoned immediately and treated Judy on the spot, stitching her throat wound closed.

The unsuccessful suicide attempt seemed completely inexplicable because Judy had just completed her stand at the Palace and Sid was producing a remake of the movie *A Star Is Born*, in which Judy would play the lead. She was just married, had a new baby, and Liza was with her. So why the depression and suicide attempt?

Liza's retrospective of these incidents was probably close to the truth: "Everything became so exaggerated because Judy was doing it. My mother did everything she wanted to do including those suicide attempts. They were just silly things to attract attention. Mama really wouldn't have killed herself in a million years. She'd come in, take two aspirins and say, 'Oh, Liza, I can't take it anymore.' Then she'd run into the bathroom and hold her breath. I'd catch on after a while, borrow the gardener's hedge clippers, snip a hole in the screen and crawl into the bathroom. Mama's suicide attempts weren't hysterics. It was acting. I tried to help her over so many pitfalls. Sometimes I could help, but sometimes I couldn't. I just couldn't cope with the legend."

When Christmas came people were all over the place. Liza was with her natural father; Sid Luft's son by his marriage to Lynn Bari, Johnny, was with his natural mother; and, Judy, Sid, and Lorna went to New York, where Judy was to perform at a charity benefit. A week and a half later, Judy's mother was on her way to work at the Douglas plant when she suffered a heart attack and slumped to the ground. Ethel Gumm was found dead next to her car.

When Sid carefully broke the news to Judy, it triggered hysteria and he had to calm her enough so she could fly—she was terrified of flying—back to Los Angeles where the three Gumm sisters were reunited once more as they buried their mother. The conflict between Judy and Ethel would continue for years in guilty memories Judy would hash over with anyone who would listen and, when there was no one to listen, with herself. Ethel Gumm Gilmore would reach out from the grave and continue to torment the little girl she originally tried to abort.

Sid Luft's frequent absences from their Holmby Hills home deeply affected Liza's life. Although Judy was the chronological grownup on the premises, Liza had become the emotional adult who increasingly took care of her mother. Beyond helping Judy, Liza also had the responsibility of looking after her siblings, including stepbrother Johnny. He was Liza's junior by only a year and a half and had an unpleasant temper that drove adults to distraction. In essence they abandoned the child to Liza's care. Liza later justified her role in managing things for her mother by saying her mother was often too naive or sensitive to cope with ordinary life.

"I worried about Mama," Liza said later. "She would put too much trust in somebody, then they'd do something and she'd take it as a slap in the face. Mama and I talked a lot. The thing I tried to get through to her was none of it really mattered. Yet, I never saw Mama in a situation she couldn't handle—even if she were having a tantrum or hysterically crying. When she'd get in a temper, it was frightening because she'd yell a lot and I'd freeze. Now I avoid people who are screaming at all costs."

Still, Judy kept going, working on *A Star Is Born*, another remake of a picture originally done in 1937. It is the story of an actor bent on self-destruction who marries a young actress who dreams of Hollywood success. The original film was based in part on a 1932 script *What Price Hollywood?*, about two actors who marry when the husband is on his way down, the wife is on the way up, and the tension that erupts between them because of this disparity. In the 1954 version Judy costarred with James Mason under the direction of George Cukor. The script by Moss Hart was based on the 1937 script by Dorothy Parker. The Hart version was written as a musical with songs by Harold Arlen and Ira Gershwin, all of which worked well for Judy.

On *A Star Is Born* Judy strove to prove she could be a star outside the MGM umbrella. But the pressure caused her to fall into her old pattern of being late, refusing to come out of her dressing room, or being temperamental on the set. Even so, Jack Warner loved the daily rushes and thought *A Star Is Born* would be a hit.

Meanwhile, Sid and Judy's marriage was faltering. Judy said, "From the beginning Sid and I weren't happy. I don't know why. I really don't. For me it was work, work, work and then I didn't see much of Sid. He was always dashing off to places lining up my appearances."

Despite the separations, scrapes, lawsuits, and slugfests Sid and Judy stuck it out eleven years. The relationship continued because Sid was largely absent. During these times Liza did a lot to hold things together for her mother such as taking care of her when she was sick, doing household chores, supervising servants, and seeing to the shopping. Once Sid Luft came home to a deserted house with everyone—except the servants who knew nothing—gone and no note or sign of what happened. Frantic, Sid called everybody they knew but no one had heard from or seen Judy or the children. After a sleepless night, Sid was notified Judy had filed for divorce, but then it was canceled and she and the children returned home.

Judy explained to gossip columnist Louella Parsons in a version much different than that of Sid and the servants. "We didn't even have a fight. I was gone exactly eight hours. We had a silly misunderstanding. I thought something that wasn't true. I love Sid and he loves me and I don't think we were ever so glad to see each other in our lives."

Meanwhile, Vincente's *An American in Paris* was nominated for eight Academy Awards, including Vincente for Best Director. Though he lost, he drew satisfaction when the film was awarded the Oscar for Best Picture of 1951. In 1953 he tried romance again and became involved with Georgette Magnani, sister of Miss Universe Christiane Martel and under contract with Universal Studios. On February 16, 1954, they were married, and in April 1955 Christiane gave birth to Christiana Nina "Tina Nina" Minnelli. Nine-year-old Liza, now competing for her father's love, didn't like Georgette or Tina Nina, but she wouldn't show her feelings in front of her father.

Georgette recalled: "I tried to treat Liza as if she were my only daughter. When her father was around, she was very sweet to me, but when he was out of the room, she would say terrible things to me. I wasn't thin. Liza would look at me and say, 'You aren't really as fat as everyone says you are.' She was not nice."

Liza would act out her anger about her father having another daughter. That was, in Liza's mind, much different than her mother having another daughter because her mother was a woman and someone Liza took care of. It was not the same relationship as Liza had with the father she adored, the most important man in her life.

Georgette said when Liza was with them she would refuse to eat with the rest of the family because she would not share *her* father with interlopers Georgette and Tina Nina. She demanded to have her meals in her bedroom. Georgette described what happened: "Liza's room was decorated all in white and Liza would eat all the food with her hands. When she finished, the wallpaper was smeared with grease, the bed cover drenched in ketchup, with chocolate stains everywhere. I think she did it on purpose."

Georgette felt nine-year-old Liza was putting on an act to get her father's attention and monopolize his time. "Vincente always treated Liza like a star. He saw her as a star because she really was very talented. He gave her everything he could. But when she couldn't get what she wanted from Vincente, she would cry and scream. I think most of the time she was acting."

Later, Vincente and the family went to France, Georgette's homeland, to make a movie about Vincent Van Gogh, *Lust for Life,* after which they returned to America. A year and a half later, he returned to France to shoot *Gigi,* but in the time between visits to France the marriage began to crumble. In fact, Minnelli eerily echoed Judy's thoughts about Lorna and Sid: "Our two-year-old daughter [Tina] was the brightest spot in our marriage."

When Vincente returned to the United States once more, Georgette remained in France to ponder what she wanted to do. Months later, she finally came back to the United States to take custody of Tina and move to New York. It was no surprise to anyone that Tina and Liza were destined to be lifetime rivals for Vincente's affection.

Soon another child was added to the Luft home. Liza's caretaking responsibilities expanded with the addition of half brother Joseph Wiley Luft, called "Joey." The child arrived March 29, 1955, and was delivered by cesarean amid much consternation because his left lung wasn't working and doctors feared he wouldn't survive. The tension was overlaid by the anticipation of the Academy Awards ceremony two days later. Judy had been nominated as Best Actress for her role in *A Star Is Born.*

The following forty-eight hours brought joy and disappointment. The joy came from Joey's lung correcting itself and the child's life being assured. Earlier Judy promised Liza, "They tell me Joey's going to die, but he's not going, Liza. I promise you that. I won't let him."

Heavy stuff for a nine-year-old to handle, but it was a common experience for Liza. The disappointment came from the television set tuned to the Academy Awards when it was announced Grace Kelly won for *The Country Girl.*

For Liza and three-year-old Lorna, Joey's arrival was unwelcome since Judy focused all her attention and love on her new son, to the detriment of her daughters and Liza's stepbrother Johnny. Lorna, sensitive to the attention showered on Joey, did things to show her displeasure and was punished by Judy, thus reinforcing Lorna's certainty Joey was more loved than she.

Still, Lorna sensed she came ahead of Liza in her mother's affections. It's hard to know about what was true because confusion seemed normal in the family and because the drugs altered Judy's moods from day to day. However, some evidence indicates Liza was not Judy's favorite. When at age ten Liza was sent to summer camp for eight weeks in the San Bernardino mountains above Los Angeles, Vincente visited every weekend while Judy came twice.

Naturally, all this fed the sibling rivalry among Joey, Lorna, and Liza. However, this distrust didn't last as the children grew a little older and Judy became more and more erratic, more like her own mother. Joey and Lorna relied on their older sister to provide them shelter and care. By the time they reached their teens, the bond between them and Liza was very tight, and it seems to have remained that way.

"One day I was making tuna salad in the kitchen and I lashed out at Mama," Liza once said. "'You're so full of sympathy and self-pity,' I told her. 'Why don't you stop it?'"

Her mother came back with an accurate self-assessment: "Liza, sympathy is my business."

Liza concluded the self-pity, the suicide attempts, and the sympathy ploys were Mama's survival techniques. Liza, instead, would run from confrontation, which is why she avoids psychiatry—a haven of her mother. Liza seeks protection in privacy.

"I'm not putting psychiatry down, but there are doors I don't want opened," she said. "I don't want to find out if I have serpents on my brain. If I go to a shrink, he might tell me things I hadn't thought of. I don't want to get lost wandering through the labyrinth of all the roles I play."

One day while Judy was still married to Sid Luft and they were living in their Mapleton Drive home, Liza and a friend were watching TV when Judy dramatically announced to them everything was over for her, she was going to kill herself. Before the girls knew what to do, Judy raced into the bathroom and locked the door. The children ran to the door and began to bang on it so Judy would open it. A pathetic, terrified Liza began to sob, "Mama, don't kill yourself."

The butler came in response to all the commotion, forced open the door, and they all stared in amazement as Judy emptied a bottle of aspirin into the toilet. She just wanted the attention a suicide attempt would bring her. "Life with her," said Liza later, "was theater of the absurd."

Growing up with her mother, Liza experienced the indignity of being kicked out of many of the finest hotels in America and Europe. Judy always insisted on staying at the best hotels wherever she went, and if she were broke, she would find various ways to stiff the management. This happened for years as her fortunes waxed and waned. Liza was a participant—usually a bewildered and unwilling one—who, when they were caught by the police or hotel management, suffered the humiliation along with Judy. It may have helped them bond in some way, but it was something Liza would have just as soon forgone.

Judy openly described the drill in a 1957 interview with *McCall's:* "When my marriage to Vincente was over, Liza and I moved into a seven-room suite at the Beverly Hills Hotel. When we were there a few weeks and they started asking about the bill, I packed a couple of suitcases and dashed down to the desk. I told them I was called to New York and would they save my suite for me? It was a big bluff which they never thought to question. Liza and I flew to New York and did the same thing at the St. Regis Hotel."

Judy would sometimes wake Liza and the other children in the middle of the night and they would all sneak out without paying. They would sometimes leave luggage behind to give management the impression they were still occupying the suite, or they would put on layers of clothes and walk out without luggage as if going on an errand.

Meanwhile, Vincente's life changed again as *Gigi* won nine

Academy Awards, including one for him as Best Director, at the Oscar ceremonies April 6, 1959. While on vacation in Italy during the spring of 1959, Vincente met Denise Giganti, a Yugoslavian beauty divorced from her Italian husband. The two fell in love, courted, and married on New Year's Eve at Anne and Kirk Douglas's house in Palm Springs. About this time his contract with MGM expired and a new arrangement was made that included the formation of his own production company, the new trend in Hollywood as the moguls and hierarchical studio structures faded into history. Directors like Minnelli formed their companies in cooperation with a studio. In Minnelli's case it was Venice Productions, for Vincente and Denise.

By then Liza had a stepbrother, a stepfather, a stepmother, a half sister from her father, an ex-stepmother, and another half sister and half brother from her mother.

6

Another Star Is Born

What was not glamorous about Liza's life were the screeching arguments between her mother and Papa Sid, her stepfather's mysterious long absences, and the new arrangement in the family that left Liza in charge of her stepbrother and half sister when she could barely take care of herself. Not that Liza objected to caring for the two younger siblings. To the contrary, she embraced them because they needed her. They gave her somebody to love and be loved by since she wasn't able to be with her father much and did not get that love from her mother or stepfather.

Liza's and Lorna's recollections about each other seem conveniently blank or twisted. Lorna seems to prefer remembering nothing and Liza seems to prefer remembering what no one else remembered. Liza, in fact, adopted her own terms for the fantasizing she used to improve her life experiences. "Wafting," she called it, as in fluttering or swirling in a turbulent wind.

"Wafting is when you pretend you're not really you," she said. "You're like a cork bobbing on the ocean. No matter how rough the water is, the cork stays afloat. Nothing can stop it."

Her mother was often drugged, drunk, and suicidal and no one seemed willing to deal with it except Liza. By the time Liza was twelve, she was actively engaged in a suicide watch over her mother, trying to control her access to pills and ever ready to call the ambulance to rush Judy to the emergency room. At the same time, Liza made scattered cameo appearances in the Lucille Ball–Desi Arnaz movie *The Long, Long Trailer* in 1954, on Art Linkletter's *Kids Say the Darnedest Things* in 1955, and on the stage of the Palace Theater with her mother in 1956.

The 1956 Palace appearance when Liza was ten probably launched her show business life. There was the cameo at the end of *In the Good Old Summertime,* but Liza's stage debut really began when Rock Hudson lifted her out of her seat when her mother beckoned her up onto the Palace stage and Liza danced to the accompaniment of Judy singing "Swanee." She did so well she was rewarded by the stage manager with a $5 bill. She saved this bill as a good luck charm because it was the first money she ever earned as a performer.

Later, at thirteen, Liza was coaxed to sing at a party at Lee Gershwin's house to which Vincente took her and Gene Kelly. The partygoers were astonished at how good she was, and Kelly immediately asked her to sing a duet with him on his next TV special. He had in mind their doing "For Me and My Gal" because he and Judy had done the song together years before in 1942.

Liza did the show with her father and mother's blessing, and while she gave a good performance and gained important experience, neither the critics nor the public were particularly taken by her. She would make several other appearances during this period, none of which seemed to capture the attention of the public. These included hosting a TV showing of *The Wizard of Oz,* something she would do again more than three decades later in 1996.

By 1958 Sid and Judy separated again. Judy banned Sid from coming near her or the children and left for some engagements in the New York area. Judy had her entire brood with her—Liza, Lorna, and Joey—but she depended on twelve-year-old Liza to look after all of them, including herself. Soon after, Judy was fired and her salary attached by New York State for unpaid taxes. Judy returned to Los Angeles with the children. She reunited with Sid once more, dropped the divorce suit, and after months of rest, was able to perform on a limited basis although there wasn't much demand for her. Liza continued to take care of chores around the house such as shopping, answering fan mail, and tending to Judy's personal needs because Judy couldn't manage. Liza adored her mother though she was always fearful of her erratic moods.

At the end of the 1950s Sid was trying to get Judy off drugs and back into good health so she could raise the money needed to pay off all the bills. The recuperation was long and slow as they moved into the 1960s. Liza finished the eighth grade and was ready for high school when Judy decided she ought to experience a different life and culture. She arranged for her fourteen-year-old daughter to spend the summer in a small town in the south of France along with half a dozen other girls; the mother of one of the girls was to tend to them all.

Judy wanted a change of scenery, too, and she gravitated to her favorite city, London, in July for a rest with her friend Kay Thompson. From this came a plan Judy sold to Sid: namely, to get out of the United States and settle the Luft family and Liza in London.

Liza would later say, "She wanted to leave all the unhappiness behind in America and live in the city she dearly loved. She was wonderfully funny and whimsical about it and she made me roar with laughter. I told her I would love to live in London."

And so they did.

To Liza it was the most wonderful fall of her life with her mother. It seemed the horrors, tensions, and bad times slipped away. Liza and Judy got along like sisters, with Judy completely off drugs. During those months, Liza saw the love other people had for her mother. Wherever they went—shopping, to the theater, walking in the park, out to dinner—it was always the same: adoring fans eager to get a glimpse of their Judy.

The rest and change of environment proved a tonic for Judy, as were her two successful performances at the Palladium. At one of them Liza was seated next to the Duke of Windsor, one of her mother's fans, as he hummed along while Judy sang. After the Palladium, Judy gave several other concerts in England and Europe, but successful as they were, they didn't completely solve the money problems that hung over the Lufts.

Short on money and living in expensive London, the Lufts decided to move back to New York in 1960. Lorna and Joey enrolled in public elementary school and Liza enrolled in the High School of Performing Arts, one of the fourteen schools her mother put her in during her teen years. There she fell in love with two things. The first was the stage and the second was Robert Mariano, another student who wanted to become an actor. She also became close friends with classmate Marvin Hamlisch, and together they made an unsuccessful demonstration record. They have maintained a successful friendship ever since.

Liza was left on her own because her mother and stepfather were busy with their own projects. Liza would spend days studying and practicing theatrical skills and would go out at night. She was a freshman in high school and already involved in the Manhattan night scene.

Judy didn't worry about Liza being on her own in New York City. "Liza I'm not worried about. She's practically a pro already. Very hip to show business. She's in the New York School for the Performing Arts, where she's majoring in the dance. She'll do well."

The one show Liza loved was *Bye Bye Birdie,* which she compared with making movies. "It wasn't the tedious process I saw at Metro. I could see it happening before my eyes," Liza said enthusiastically. "The chorus of *Bye Bye Birdie* fascinated me. It had kids in it and a camaraderie I recognized. It seemed like an answer to the kind of loneliness I felt. Just friends kidding around with lots of laughter."

That summer Liza and Judy took a summer place opposite the vacation home of John F. Kennedy in Hyannis Port, Massachusetts, where Judy and the president frequently spoke in person and on the phone. Meanwhile, Liza got a summer job at $60 a month painting scenery and working as a general gofer at the Melody Tent Theater. She also won bit parts in the choruses of *Flower Drum Song* and *Wish You Were Here* plus a part in the musical *Take Me Along*.

Judy and Vincente, along with his wife Denise, saw one of the performances which they attended without fanfare so as not to take attention away from fifteen-year-old Liza or the cast. Judy was stunned to see her daughter smoking and acting like a grownup. It was a reality check: Liza was not a little girl anymore. Vincente was less surprised, but it brought back some youthful memories for him.

He said: "We had dinner at Judy's. The three of us, with David Begelman from Creative Management Associates, would fly to Hyannis Port the next day. Judy and I were both very excited about our daughter's appearance. Liza hadn't told us how serious she was about a show business career, but Judy and I agreed it was a good way for her to spend the summer. We arrived at the theater in the round. It was housed in a tent. As I walked in with Denise and Judy, it was as if my life came full circle and I was back at the Minnelli Brothers Tent Theater. Liza, of course, was marvelous. Denise and I flew home and I was delighted Liza had done us so proud."

For Judy, the occasion brought back different, less happy childhood memories: "The only reason I'm letting Liza do this now is because she has been longing to do summer stock. When summer's over, she'll go back to school. I think it robs a youngster of too many things. It's too competitive. I don't think children should be thrown into it at all. They should have proms and football games and all the fun of growing up. I missed a lot. It's a very lonesome life."

When fifteen-year-old Liza began menstruating, she and her mother toasted the occasion with cooking wine since Sid had locked up all the whiskey and drinking wine.

In September 1961 Judy decided the performing arts school was too tough for Liza and she moved to Westchester County north of New York City so Liza could go to school there. The house was at 1 Cornell Street and technically in Mamaroneck but was considered part of Scarsdale. Liza attended Scarsdale High School for about six months. This home was close to where Sid was born and grew up in New Rochelle.

Scarsdale was a very cliquish place where most of the children came from wealthy, professional homes and had known each other since infancy. Liza was the classic new kid on the block. Though she was rather chubby, many people were impressed she was the daughter of a movie and stage star. However, some faulted her for being from "show business people."

They were taken by Liza's involvement in the school's drama department and particularly by the way she handled the title role in the production of *The Diary of Anne Frank*. Drama teacher Robert P. Haseltine wanted to produce the play but couldn't find a student he thought right for the Anne Frank role. He postponed the project until one day a colleague told him of a new girl in school who was perfect for the part. After interviewing Liza, Haseltine agreed the project could get under way. Haseltine had no idea who Liza's parents were—only that she was already a trouper.

"She worked very hard and always knew her lines," he recalled. "She was never a problem. Oh, she could play the devil—she loved playing practical jokes on the cast—but Liza always acted like a lady in front of me."

Later, when Haseltine discovered the identity of the girl playing Anne Frank, he was amazed. And he wasn't entirely pleased. As the production date approached, the school theater sold out. People were vying for the fourteen hundred seats not because they wanted to see Liza in *The Diary of Anne Frank*, but because they assumed Judy Garland would be there. She was, and cried throughout the play.

Because of the significant Jewish population in the Scarsdale area, some families stayed away from the play because it was the story of their own family tragedies. However, Mrs. Murray Silverstone, wife of a major executive with 20th Century-Fox, thought the play's message was one of courage of the human spirit as well as being a reminder of what happened to Jews under Nazi rule. She offered to underwrite the cast's trip to Israel to perform the play there.

This plan worked out well for Liza since Judy had returned to England, leaving Liza with relatives in Scarsdale. Liza visited Judy, then flew to Israel to join the rest of the cast at the beginning of July 1962. The cast performed *Diary* for a month in Israel and Liza and some other Scarsdale students also performed two other works for smaller communities in less populated areas of the country. For Liza, the summer was capped with a return trip by way of Rome and Florence.

By now the Luft family had moved back to Hollywood because film director Stanley Kramer talked Judy into taking a starring role with Burt Lancaster in *A Child Is Waiting*. This opportunity grew out of an earlier role Judy performed which, like Liza's play, had a World War II context. It was *Judgment at Nuremberg* and it garnered Judy an Oscar nomination for Best Supporting Actress. She was on her way back to Hollywood and was going to take all her children with her.

"My children are the most special thing in my life. They are very portable," Judy said. "I've uprooted them, dragged them from one country to another because I'll never leave them in the care of servants. They are happy only as long as their mother and daddy are with them. You try to keep them as long as you can and prepare for the day when they'll leave. You have to be ready not to be an idiot about it when they do leave, because they will. They must have a life of their own."

That reality was closer for Liza than Judy imagined.

7

The Career Decision

eturning to Hollywood had become routine for Liza because during her time in Scarsdale her father would bring her to the West Coast to see him. It was a regular reminder of the exciting world of entertainment in which Liza grew up. The Lufts settled in a rented house. While the marriage was still shaky, Judy's fortunes were improving with money earned from recording her Carnegie concert, some TV work with Frank Sinatra, and her work in the Stanley Kramer film.

Liza was fifteen and in the tenth grade but anxious to put school behind her and get into show business, particularly after the success of *The Diary of Anne Frank*. In her eagerness, she even took an ill-advised voice-over job impersonating her mother in a cartoon remake of *The Wizard of Oz*. Called *Return to the Land of Oz*, it also used the voices of Mickey Rooney, Milton Berle, and Ethel Merman. It proved a disaster. Some said it should have been called *Return to the Can*. Liza also had her first love affair with a twenty-one-year-old singer named Tom Cooper, who she met because of his obsession with *A Star Is Born*.

Cooper was a Kansas boy so fascinated by the plot of *A Star Is Born* that when he got to Hollywood he shot his own eight millimeter version of it. Somehow Judy heard about it and contacted Cooper for a screening to see what he had done. This led to Sid and Judy taking an interest in Cooper.

In January 1962 Sid and Cooper ran into each other at a Golden Globe Awards party. As Cooper said, "I was chatting with Sid and I had seen Liza's picture in a movie magazine so I mentioned it." Sid urged Cooper to call Liza because Liza didn't have many friends. Liza laughed about it when Cooper first phoned, then became excited to learn that he was a singer appearing at the Hilton Hotel.

She loved to hear him sing because, she told him, she also wanted to get into show business. On their dates, they would often sing songs to each other. Cooper said, "She was not your normal fifteen-year-old who can hardly articulate two intelligent words. Liza was so much fun, so eager and she was so enthusiastic about me singing." They dated for five months. The preponderance of evidence suggests that they never became lovers, which made this first brief romance of Liza's almost unique for her.

In April Judy returned alone to New York where she suffered a throat infection that put her in the hospital and brought Sid and the children flying to her bedside. She told Sid she was going to London and once again said she wanted a divorce. There followed a series of maneuvers by both Sid and Judy over possession of the children. Judy flew their brood to London. Sid followed and Judy got the authorities to keep him from taking the children back to the States.

Meanwhile, Judy was doing a movie, *I Could Go On Singing,* costarring Dirk Bogarde. At this point Judy thought it would be good for sixteen-year-old Liza to enroll in some special courses at the Sorbonne in Paris and sent Liza to France. Liza thought Paris stuffy compared to the life she experienced when she was going to school and living in Manhattan.

She said: "I enjoyed the Sorbonne despite the fact I didn't get much schooling done there. However, I did learn French, which later was helpful for my concerts. I knew what I wanted to do and I had it out with myself. I wanted to live in New York on my own and take lessons in singing and dancing and acting and see if I could do anything."

So at the end of the term in 1962 Liza telegraphed her mother who was back in the States and appearing in Las Vegas. Liza told Judy she was coming to Vegas because she had something important to tell her. Then she got on a plane and flew to New York where she met with her father. "I want to quit school, come back to New York and go on the stage," she told him. Vincente's response may have surprised Liza. "Yes," he said, "I think it's about time. You have so much energy you might as well start using it."

Her stepmother Denise encouraged her to move to New York and study theater arts. This advice coincided with Liza's desires because she preferred New York to Hollywood. "I wanted to be on Broadway," she said. "I didn't want to be a movie star. It was kind of virgin territory, the theater; not Hollywood, not the movies."

Then it was on to Las Vegas to talk to her mother about her goal. She told Judy she wanted to be just like her. As soon as Judy got word Liza was coming, she knew what was transpiring even though she didn't think it was the right thing for Liza to do.

Judy once talked about her show business life to Peter Evans, a writer she knew. "I've lived off applause ever since [I started in show business]. The trouble is, you can't put a big hand away for a rainy day. There's no interest on bravos, baby. I pray neither Liza nor Lorna is condemned to mama-repetition. I've always had such a tragic talent for fame."

But that was what was about to happen and Judy sensed it. As Liza would say, it's impossible to be the daughter of Vincente Minnelli and Judy Garland and end up in insurance or real estate.

"I knew what it was immediately," Judy recalled. "I think she decided to go into show business when she was an embryo, she kicked so much. When the wire [telling her about Liza's forthcoming visit] came, all I could think about was this child flying half the way around the world, all the time rehearsing what she would say. Then, I started rehearsing what I would say, all sorts of motherly things about going back to school. Liza was off the plane practically before the door was opened. She charged right up to me. I shot the works, 'Liza, darling, why don't you go into show business?' Then, we both started crying right there at the airport and it got very messy and happy."

The warm feeling between mother and daughter was also heightened with tension because their relationship would undergo a major change. Liza was saying she no longer needed her mother just when her mother realized she did need her daughter. Wanting to be strong, Judy made a bargain with her oldest child. "Okay, if that's what you really want to do, go ahead. Just one thing: no more money from me again—ever again. You're on your own, baby."

Baby was sixteen.

The point was a sharp one and reflective of Judy's mood at the moment. It hurt Liza, but she was determined to go ahead. Besides, she secretly thought Mama would always be there for her if the times got too rough. Judy remembered what she endured to attain princess status in the hearts of ordinary Americans by playing the innocent girl wandering down the Yellow Brick Road with her faithful dog Toto. She remembered, for openers, Shirley Temple was first choice for the role because Judy looked too mature. When they gave it to Judy anyhow, they bound her ample breasts tightly against her chest with wrappings of gauze so she appeared prepubescent. She also remembered the viciousness of her costars, who hated the little scene-stealer. The reality was trying and tiring, but the illusion worked and she was embraced by families the world over.

Now her sixteen-year-old biological successor was beginning her professional career when Mama was within months of turning forty. Judy felt herself fading as the young, vibrant personification of Dorothy. In fact, a new Judy Garland was born on the Carnegie Hall stage a few months before, on April 23, 1961. The Dorothy persona was transformed into the cult figure who would dominate Garland's remaining years. As a concert performer she would become the darling of America's gays just as Bette Midler and Jane Olivor did later. She would acknowledge this deep and curious loyalty later when she said, "When I die, they'll fly the flag at half-mast on Fire Island." It would be a love affair between Judy and her audience that would last the rest of her life.

But as one love affair was beginning, another was ending, and with the ending came a bitter fight over custody of Lorna and Joey, including the character assassination necessary for the courts to deny a woman custody of her children. It would be a dark four and a half years for Judy while Liza began her climb to stardom. In a curious way, the two were reenacting the *Star Is Born* roles.

Sid claimed in a sworn statement that Judy was an unfit mother because she was "an emotionally disturbed and unbalanced person" who tried suicide some twenty times during their marriage. "On at least three occasions during 1963 and on numerous previous occasions, she took overdoses of barbiturates. On six occasions she has attempted suicide by slashing herself on her wrists, elbows, or throat."

The pain and humiliation continued with a parade of ex-servants and others who spoke of Judy's drunkenness, abusive behavior, and drug use. One witness claimed Judy stripped naked before the employees of one hotel at which they stayed.

In response, Judy said Sid was violently abusive and she was in fear of her life. Finally, at Thanksgiving of 1965, Judy was granted a divorce and custody of the two Luft children.

Meanwhile, sixteen-year-old Liza settled into New York, living with a variety of friends starting with Tanya Everitt, with whom she shared an apartment, an acting class—and Tanya's brother Tracy, a dancer in the production of *How to Succeed in Business Without Really Trying*. She had $100 in savings and the lucky $5 bill she received from her appearance on the Palace stage while her mother sang "Swanee." The start was rough for Liza, but she was determined to make it even when she got tossed out of the Barbizon Hotel and had her luggage seized for not paying the bill. That night Liza ended up sleeping in Central Park, but she intended to succeed without Mama and Papa's help. The first person to visit her hours after she was born, Frank Sinatra, quietly sent her $500 to tide her over, but pride foolishly made her send it back.

Liza wasn't strikingly beautiful, she didn't have much money, but she did have the Judy Garland–Vincente Minnelli names. She began the dual track of supporting herself with modeling jobs for magazines like *Seventeen* and developing her stage career. There was the usual round of voice, acting, and dancing classes while seeking out stage roles. The modeling jobs began to earn her enough to pay the rent and class fees. Luckily, the "pixie look" in adolescent fashions at the time conformed with Liza's appearance. She was the subject of a big story in *TV Guide* about "the Liza Minnelli Look."

As for acting and dancing, Liza, like many children of stars, learned her name opened doors but wasn't enough to keep her inside if she didn't have talent. As she recalled, "It wasn't my great talent that got me my first few jobs. It was simply my mother's name and the curiosity factor."

It soon became clear she did have talent. One of the first to see it—painfully—was Judy, who heard her at a Robert Frost poetry reading in February 1963. Judy normally stayed away from Liza's public appearances because she didn't want her presence to create a distraction. After hearing the Frost reading, Judy had another reason: She didn't want to be reminded how good her daughter, now her budding competitor, was. Critics labeled the Frost reading a stunning display of Liza's delivery and power. It was a talent Liza tried to sharpen by taking lessons from instructors such as voice coach David Soren Collyer and acting mentor Herbert Berghof, who watched a lot of young hopefuls, including Bette Midler, pass through his classes.

Judy was wise in trying not to disrupt Liza's career, but there were promoters who wanted the notoriety she would bring to a Liza performance. These included the producers who cast Liza as the lead in a revival of *Best Foot Forward* to be staged in a small room called Stage 73, adjacent to a New York bar. They figured to capitalize on Liza's ambitions and Judy's name, and both fell for the plan.

"Mama was so great when I told her," was Liza's reaction. "I called her in California and you should have heard her. She got so nervous and she started telling me to relax and remember my poise and not to get nervous and what was I going to sing and should she fly out special arrangements? Wow, she was funny. She was a nervous wreck." Liza was paid $45 a week.

Liza's best foot forward became her worst when she broke it in rehearsals. They postponed the opening and she spent her seventeenth birthday in the hospital. Finally, when the show opened on April 2, 1963, the publicity created a mob scene and police had to control traffic. Three of the front seats were held for the arrival of Judy, Lorna, and Joey. They remained in the Palace Hotel opening night, but they did send a bottle of champagne.

Judy's absence did not daunt the promoters because anticipation of the great star coming did as much for bookings as if she actually came. The mob scene was compounded the second night when she did appear, engulfed by photographers, press agents, reporters, and an assorted entourage. Judy said, "I cried and cried, I was so proud of my baby. She worked so hard and did it all alone." It wasn't Broadway, but it was great publicity, and even though reviews were mixed, the producers were happy.

Although pretending not to interfere, Judy couldn't resist a little stage mothering. She quietly helped promote the show by asking her friend Jack Paar to invite Liza on the *Tonight Show,* which he hosted.

In his usual zany and clever style, Paar introduced "Dyju Langard"—an anagram of "Judy Garland"—as an Armenian singer. Liza's singing brought the audience to its feet. Only then did Paar unmask his mystery guest as Liza Minnelli. This was her first major TV appearance and it went well. It also hyped the stage show.

The high point of the stage show was Liza's solo of "You Are for Loving," written for her by Hugh Martin and Ralph Blane. The rendition went so well it later sold half a million copies as a single released by Cadence and had Liza's phone lighting up with offers for bookings.

The passion of her singing "You Are for Loving" was described by *Women's Wear Daily* reporter Martin Gottfried: "About five minutes before the final curtain, Liza Minnelli stands alone on the stage singing a new song called 'You Are for Loving.' If you close your eyes you would swear it was the young Judy Garland, and if you keep your eyes open, you will still have those chills running through you. Nothing else in the show can match those few minutes for sheer intensity of talent."

Ironically, *You Are for Loving*, Liza's first commercial album, did better than any recording she has made since because recordings don't seem to communicate the power of Liza's stage personality. The song underscored the axiom that show business is a small world. Hugh Martin and Ralph Blane also wrote songs for Judy in *Meet Me in St. Louis*.

Even though the cast on her leg initially restricted her to walking through the dance numbers, the critical reaction to Liza's performance was generally glowing. From Robert Coleman of the *New York Mirror* came the simple comment, "Liza is great! Liza sparkles." James Davis of the *New York Daily News* recommended seeing the show for a different reason. "*Best Foot Forward* is worth seeing if only to remember back some day to having witnessed a Broadway star in her professional debut."

And George Oppenheimer, a little more tempered in his assessment, wrote for *Newsday:* "Young Miss Minnelli, barely out of school, cannot belt out a song the way her mother does, but I feel fairly confident it will come, too. In other respects, Liza resembles Judy, not only in appearance and mannerisms, but in that intangible quality of vulnerability. You want to get up on the stage, take her in your arms and tell her how good she is."

This was a very insightful analysis of both Judy and Liza in at least two ways. First, Oppenheimer pinpointed a critical characteristic both Liza and Judy conveyed in public performances and an integral part of their personal lives: *vulnerability*. This is central to

(Above) Two veteran stars with a new star: Mother and father admire their most recent production, newly born Liza, 1946.

(Right) Little Liza with even better littler Liza: At her fourth birthday party, little Liza plays with a doll that is dressed exactly as she is, 1950.

Just pony and me: The birthday child rides a pony at her fourth birthday party.

(Below) Papa and baby sharing: A tender moment between father, Vincente Minnelli, and his beloved young daughter, Liza.

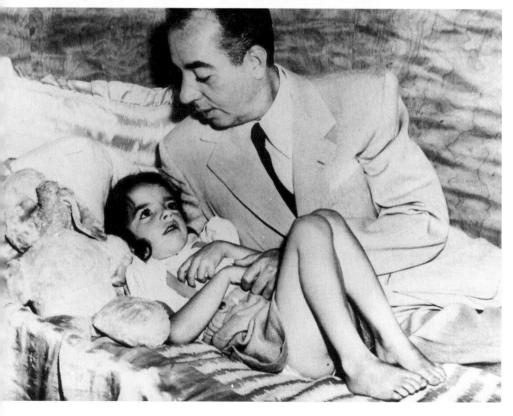

Come to Mommy, Joey baby: Judy Garland with her three children playing in the yard of their Los Angeles home and teaching the youngest, Joey to walk. Left to right: Liza Minnelli, Joey Luft, Lorna Luft, and Judy Garland. Boy in background unidentified, September 17, 1956. (Brown Brothers Photo)

A golden-voiced quartet: Judy Garland joins in an informal songfest with her three kids, Lorna, Joey, and Liza.

(Above) May I have this dance? Teenage Liza dancing with her father, MGM movie director Vincente Minnelli.

(Left) Mama and baby together: Liza with her mother Judy Garland.

(Above) Getting ready for the defining moment: Judy and Liza rehearsing for their momentous October 1964 concert at the London Palladium. (Globe Photos)

(Right) In love and late for the plane: Engaged Liza, 18, holding hands with new fiancé, Australian singer-composer Peter Allen, 21, as they drive off to the airport two days after Christmas, 1964, so that Liza can return to New York to try out for a new musical, *Flora, the Red Menace.* They missed the plane, but she got the part. (Globe Photos)

Manhattan meets Down-Under: Liza with her first husband, Australian composer and singer, Peter Allen. (Photo by Tom Caffrey, Globe Photos)

(Right) A guiding hand from Dad: Famous MGM director Vincente Minnelli working on set of *The Sterile Cuckoo* with his daughter Liza.

(Below) Launching her movie career: Liza playing the role of secretary to Albert Finney in her first movies, *Charlie Bubbles,* on the drive from London to Manchester, England, 1968. (Globe Photos)

Family support at a big opening: Lorna and Joey show up at Liza's 1968 opening at Waldorf-Astoria to lend support and cheer.

understanding their private lives. Both women were vulnerable and both women learned to use vulnerability to their advantage in relationships. Judy referred to it as sympathy, saying she was in the sympathy business. She was actually using her vulnerability to elicit sympathy to get what she wanted.

Second, this is one of the earliest comparisons of mother and daughter which would plague Liza for the rest of her career. Liza knew she looked, sounded, and acted like her mother, but she desperately wanted to be accepted for being Liza and not Judy's daughter. She would scream that need for her own identity over and over in scores of different ways for the next thirty years, but it was a legacy—or curse—that would remain hers for a lifetime.

Walter Kerr, one of the most influential theater critics in New York, saw Liza as her own person as much as a mirror image of her mother: "Liza Minnelli is certainly appealing and would be even if she wasn't Judy Garland's daughter, with something of her mother's faintly scratched tremolo clinging to her—and with a fading half-laugh that trickles away after lines. She is easy and confident and accomplished and winning and also, I would think, a person."

Judy's own assessment of her daughter's performance was proud and wistful at seeing a child with even greater potential than the parent. "You know," Judy said, "Liza's the first one of us to do this. I never had a Broadway show."

Best Foot Forward ran seven months, closing on October 13, 1963, after 244 performances. It achieved what the principals wanted. It was a money-making show for the producers and launched Liza's career even though she left the show a month before it ended. She was featured in magazine articles and received one of the Promising Personality Awards given out by *Theatre World* magazine. Just weeks before the show closed, she signed with Creative Management Associates and, more important, met Fred Ebb, who would become indispensable to her future success as her friend, mentor, professional guide, and frequently, stage director or writer.

But suddenly, she wasn't in a show, there were no new

recordings or bookings in view, and seventeen-year-old Liza was experiencing the financial terrors her mother knew after leaving MGM and Vincente. She was being turned out of hotels and, the story goes, spent one night sleeping by the fountain in front of the Plaza Hotel.

The next night a friend from *Best Foot Forward*, Paula Wayne, took her in. Liza had crashed at Paula's place at other times after late night partying, but this was more serious. Meanwhile, her mother pulled strings and burned up the telephone lines trying to get Liza another gig without her daughter knowing about it. Liza made nonpaying and low-paying appearances on popular radio shows like Arthur Godfrey's, but she needed paying jobs.

Part of Judy's motivation was she wanted Liza to do guest shots on her new TV program based in Los Angeles, *The Judy Garland Show*. Earlier, Liza hadn't wanted to return to Los Angeles because she was doing well in *Best Foot Forward*. She had also become involved with Tracy Everitt, the dancer boyfriend who set Liza's heart dancing with love. When Judy realized Tracy was keeping Liza in New York, she hired Tracy to dance on her show and brought them both to Los Angeles. As a result, Liza was able to make guest appearances on *The Tonight Show* (June 3), *Talent Scouts* (July 2), and an NBC special, *April in Paris Ball* (October 27).

Finally, Liza appeared November 17, 1963, on Judy's own ill-fated Sunday night show opposite *Bonanza*. Judy liked the show, but the network decided to cancel it because of low ratings. Judy became disconsolate because she viewed her TV show as the financial security she longed to have, but the show couldn't make it against the most popular program in America.

A few days later, however, the cancellation meant nothing when the news flashed from Dallas the president of the United States—Judy's friend—was dead. Kennedy's assassination depressed Judy because it seemed to be another tragedy in a life that alternated tragedy and exhilaration from week to week. She was giving great performances interspersed with terrible shows and had wonderful relations with family and friends interspersed with bad ones. At the time of Kennedy's assassination in November 1963, Judy's life became more barren and joyless. Judy responded by turning on the people around her.

Nineteen sixty-three was not a wonderful year for Liza either. It began with her breaking her foot in *Best Foot Forward* and ended with Liza in the hospital suffering from a debilitating illness doctors identified as a hereditary kidney problem. Liza woke up one morning in November in agonizing pain. She recalled, "My fever was raging and my legs felt like wet noodles." After three days of testing, the doctors decided she had kidney stones. Judy suffered problems with her kidneys and three years earlier was taken to the hospital in severe pain. Doctors discovered Judy apparently had contracted hepatitis at some earlier time. She was in such distress one doctor mistakenly thought her career was finished.

After recovering, seventeen-year-old Liza accepted a role in *Carnival*. The musical opened at the Mineola Playhouse on Long Island on January 28, 1964, and moved to the Paper Mill Playhouse in Millburn, New Jersey, on February 11. It was the first bright spot in months and meant she would be back performing onstage, which she loved. *Carnival* was a derivation of the MGM movie *Lili*, in which a carnival waif brings happiness to a group of misfits. Despite Liza's success in *Best Foot Forward*, Judy insisted Liza not play the role because she was too young and theater life was too sophisticated (she meant too sexually loose) for her daughter. Many people thought Judy's real motivation was that she wanted Liza back in California so she could take care of Judy.

In any case, Judy told Liza she would do everything she could to stop her from appearing in *Carnival* and called the newspapers to announce she was forbidding her daughter to appear in the musical. It seemed Judy, who had let her teenage daughter go nightclubbing in Manhattan, was suddenly afraid Liza would be exposed to sophistication. This was also the mother who told her child she could get into show business but not to expect any help from Mama. Everyone was confused by Judy's irrational reaction.

"Mama went into a rage at my refusal [to quit the show]," Liza recalled. "I was so frightened. I knew Mama could pull a lot of strings against me—regardless of everything, Mama's power is considerable."

The press agent for the production, Pat Hipp, described the bedlam Judy caused: "We were selling lots of tickets for the month's run [during which they were promoting Liza's appearance]. And, then, whammo! Judy Garland's lawyer called. She was pulling Liza out of the show. 'Too young. Much too young to be in the theater. Not now—and maybe never' was the word from Ms. Garland. Then began the coast-to-coast calls, the begging, the hysterics. We didn't know from minute to minute if we had a show."

Carnival opened January 28, 1964, as scheduled. Liza would soon be eighteen and Vincente interceded with Judy, arguing Liza was entitled to her chance. She got her chance and made the most of it. Pat Hipp recalled Liza's performance: "Liza walked on. How truly a waif she was. She'd been crying backstage before the performance. She was gorgeous. Not in the sense of beautiful, but of real, of lost, of heartbreaking, of needing. And her voice reached out and loved us. It was beautiful."

Hipp knew it would be that way because of how Liza performed earlier at dress rehearsal. "I was standing in back of the house as she was singing 'Love Makes the World Go Round.' Liza knocked me over because she was so brilliant! So divine! So magnificent! Her voice was absolute magic. My breath stopped. I honestly cannot even tell you who else was in the show. All I remember is Liza."

Hipp also remembered her impression of Liza when she first met her during the upheaval caused by Judy's objection to Liza appearing in the show. "The first time I met Liza she was sitting in an office, near the switchboard. She was wearing jeans and lots and lots of long hair. She was also crying. Judy just called her and was giving her another hard time. I took one look and wanted to wrap my arms around her."

Carnival was a critical and box-office success and marked Liza as a talent in her own right. Her sound and her body movements reflected her mother and the comparisons were made by everyone. Most thought it was wonderful she seemed to be a younger Judy Garland. From the start, Liza didn't like the comparison because, as noted earlier, she sought her own identity and would fight for it for years to come. She wanted respect for her own talent and not just as a young imitation of the little girl from *The Wizard of Oz*. She wanted to make her own name and impress everybody she was Liza, not a clone of Judy.

"I tried so hard not to sound like her that I wasn't singing well at all," she said. "It wasn't like anything—I was floundering out there in front of everybody, which was interesting." At least one critic thought she succeeded. Mike McGrady wrote in *Newsday*: "The comparisons to Judy Garland are inevitable—the tremulous voice, the respect for the lyric, the wide eyes, the clenching hands, the eyebrows never still. Yet, by the time Liza sings her second number, 'Yes, My Heart,' the applause belongs to her alone; from that point on, forget to make comparisons."

Trying to duplicate the success of *Carnival*, she accepted more parts in regional theater, including *Time Out for Ginger* with Chester Morris at the Bucks County Playhouse and *Mr. Broadway*. Neither were great productions and certainly didn't match her success in *Carnival*. In between came the touring company of *The Fantasticks*, costarring another performer in the shadow of a great star, Elliott Gould, who was then married to Barbra Streisand.

Gould's first impression of the young Liza was positive: "Liza was all manic and wild and unbelievable. She always had her heart out there. We had only two weeks to rehearse—I remember Liza's dad stopping by the Sullivan Street Theater to catch us—but they were two fun-filled weeks. But what really turned me on was Liza wasn't selfish. She was as interested in my work as she was in hers."

She got on well with Gould, which was more than she was doing with her creditors. She was simply not earning enough money to live in New York City.

"The lights in my apartment went out and I figured, oh well, it's a power failure," Liza said. "So I went down to the deli to buy some food and the owner said, 'I'm sorry, Miss Minnelli, your credit isn't good anymore.' The next morning I found my electric bill hadn't been paid. It was like a sledgehammer coming down on my head. I couldn't believe this was happening to me. I was so distraught I went to Cartier's and bought a watch!"

It sounded like Judy, but unlike her mother, Liza realized managing money was not a family talent and wisely turned that part of her life over to an attorney who began to bring some order to the chaos.

Meanwhile, Judy continued trying to help Liza, but given the brouhaha she raised in the *Carnival* incident, Liza would just as soon not have had the help. Judy made a very generous peace offering by inviting Liza to costar in her next London Palladium appearance set for November 8, 1964. The offer was appealing because Judy was beloved by British audiences and the performance was bound to be a success. In fact, it sold out in two days and a second day was added to the schedule. Still, it is hard to imagine they didn't realize they would be compared with each other, as indeed they were, by the critics and the audience.

8

Two Days That
Changed Their Lives

T he Palladium appearance was the defining moment of Liza's
life as she shone in her own light with her mother onstage,
dazzling the audience with her rendition of "Who's Sorry
Now?" It was a question Liza seemed to direct at her mother, and
the audience was cheering as Liza built the song from an easy
opening into a passionate, frenzied closing. The bravos and applause
from the audience transformed the duet into a duel. This thrust at
her mother was followed by "It All Depends on You" sung in a
manner insulting to Judy.

Whatever the harried and exhausted Judy thought about those
two nights at the London Palladium, she kept uncharacteristically
quiet about it. But Liza, in her youthfulness, did not. She realized
their relationship dramatically changed and they were no longer
only mother and daughter, but true competitors.

It was like Carly Simon's feelings years later when she heard
the first record made by Ben Taylor, her son by singer James Taylor.
"Is there a word in the English language that means both being
proud and jealous?" Simon asked. "I realize most people would be
very embarrassed to be envious of their children, but as soon as you
admit it, it becomes utterly dissipated."

In the Palladium performance, however, there was an edge

between the two women even the audience detected and didn't like. To some, it appeared Liza was more vicious in those performances than she said she was and it was a bad-tempered assault on the stature and authority of her mother.

As previously noted, the audience came to see and hear Judy. After Judy sang several of her ballads, she proudly announced, "Ladies and gentlemen, Liza Minnelli," and with those five words opened that Pandora's box.

The audience received Liza respectfully and she positioned herself center stage while her mother gracefully withdrew. Liza, in contrast to her mother's softer selections, ripped into "The Traveling Life," "Pass That Peace Pipe," and "Gypsy in My Soul" with an enthusiasm that set the audience toe-tapping and hand-clapping even before they realized they had fallen under the spell of this youthful version of Judy.

Stunned by the bravo-filled reaction to Liza, Judy returned to the stage and the rest of the evening sang ballads alone or in conjunction with Liza. But Liza was clearly electrifying the adoring Brits while Judy was producing a good but disappointing performance made worse by comparison to Liza's high energy display.

In almost pathetic frustration, Judy kept pushing down Liza's mike-holding arm as a way of telling the audience she was trying to train Liza how to hold the mike and perform. It was like a fussy mother adjusting her little girl's dress before she goes onstage. She was trying desperately to assert her control over her child and it wasn't working. Liza was behaving as Judy would were the roles reversed. There were signs of the mother's forlorn attempt to regain control through the concert that night and the concert the following night. What happened, to everybody's astonishment, was Liza inadvertently upstaged her mother.

Liza remembered that night later when she told *Good House-keeping:* "When I was a little girl and jumped onstage to dance while she sang, it was an unrehearsed, amateurish, spontaneous thing. Working with her was something else. I'll never be afraid to perform with anyone ever again after that terrifying experience. She became very competitive with me. I wasn't Liza. I was another woman in the same spotlight. It was just too hard for me to try to cope. And it was *her* night. I *wanted* it to be her night."

Liza's professional feelings warred with her personal feelings and left her conflicted during and after the performance. Before the Palladium performance, Liza was frightened of appearing with her mother because Judy was so much better than Liza, or at least, that's what Liza thought. During the performance, Liza transformed from Liza the daughter to Liza the performer just as Judy became the performer when the spotlight hit her. Afterward both she and Judy reverted to daughter and mother, vowing never again to perform on the same stage.

Thirty years later, long after Judy was dead, Liza still remembered this defining moment in her life, telling an interviewer, "The first time I saw a tape of the show, I watched it with Robert De Niro. He said the funniest thing of all. He said, 'God, you had such chutzpah! You were so brave, at that age, to just go out there and do it. What had you done before?' I said, 'Nothing.'"

Liza went on: "[Beforehand] I kept saying, 'Mom, I'll sit in the front row. Honest, I really don't have to be up there.' She said, 'I don't want to do it alone. Please do it with me.' She was frightened of the comeback and she didn't want to be alone up there. And we were so close—not only mother and daughter, but also good friends. In two hours, we went through what most mothers and daughters go through over years and years—which was a daughter's discovery she has a force in herself to be dealt with and a mother's reaction to a daughter growing up. It's all up there, all that stuff.

"I was relieved the audience liked me and I could feel she was relieved the audience liked me. And then, I felt the competition from her. Remember the little business she did with the microphone, tossing it back and forth? I remember thinking: 'Well, far out! You never did *that* in rehearsal, Mom! This is very interesting.' By the end of the show, I knew I'd never be afraid to be onstage with anybody. If I held my own with my mother, I'm not gonna be afraid of anything!"

Peter Allen showed up in Liza's life the first night at the Palladium, courtesy of her mother, who met the Australian singer in Hong Kong while on vacation at the end of May 1964. Judy accepted an Australian tour in the spring of 1964 and took her new love interest, Mark Herron, with her. Mark had been a big fan of Judy's for years and finally became involved with her after they met at a party in Hollywood given by costume designer Ray Aghayan. Judy was recovering from the failure of her TV show and having a relationship with a good-looking man ten years her junior proved a wonderful tonic.

The Australian tour was a disaster, with Judy forgetting words and songs and finally being booed off the stage in Melbourne. Dumping the tour, Judy and Mark fled to Hong Kong to recover and have a little vacation. They saw Peter Allen and Chris Allen (no relation) performing in the Starlight Room of the Mandarin Hotel and thought they were terrific. In Hong Kong Judy came down with another bout of too many pills and Mark kept a vigil by her bed. When she recovered, she announced to the press she and Mark had been married aboard ship on June 6.

When Judy and Mark left the Far East for London, she arranged for the Allen Brothers to come to London, got them gigs in some of the clubs, and used them as her warm-up act. Moreover, she was so charmed by Peter she wanted to bring him and Liza together. "I have met the most divine boy," Judy told Liza. "You two have the same crazy sense of humor." With that, she introduced them and the two began dating around London.

Peter Allen was born Peter Woolnough on February 10, 1944, in Tenterfield, Australia. He was raised in a small town by women— his grandmother, mother, and three aunts—which may have affected his gender preference for men. He began performing as a small boy and mastered the piano at ten. He was definitely a child prodigy.

As his mother Marion Woolnough recalled: "Once when he was seven years old, we went to visit some friends and they had a piano. Peter wandered over to it and we hardly took notice of him.

Half an hour later we heard a perfect rendition of 'Put Another Nickel in the Nickelodeon.' He just played it! He knew how to sing every popular song of the day and somehow he was able to play them by ear.

"When this happened I thought 'Well, I must get him a piano.' When he started lessons, three teachers said they couldn't teach him because he would take the pieces home and come back for the next lessons and play them beautifully. But he would forget to turn the pages and the instructors would realize Peter learned to play them by ear and he wasn't going to bother and learn to read music."

At eleven, Peter started playing the piano on the family side of the local bars. (English and Australian bars are divided into a men's side and a family side.) The men would drink and the women would sit around Peter's piano singing. By the age of twelve, Peter was earning a regular wage playing at the bars. This was important since his father apparently hadn't held a job since he returned from serving in World War II. The following year—his thirteenth—was a bad year for Peter and he unexpectedly did some serious growing up.

His mother described part of it: "When Peter was thirteen, we had a dreadful year. My mother died and Peter was heartbroken. She helped me raise Peter while his father was in the service and he loved his grandmother more than life itself. When she died Peter began a nervous habit of wringing his hands that stayed with him for a couple of years."

Then there was Peter's father Dick and Peter's stormy relationship with him. The same year, Dick shot himself in their bathroom and Peter cleaned up the splattered brains and blood.

Even in death the father cast a curse on the surviving family, as Peter's mother told it: "Dick was a mean, brutal man, the town drunk, and Peter always had a bloody nose from being battered by him. Dick was fired for drunkenness from every job he ever held. He treated Peter and Lynne [Peter's sister] terribly. When he was drunk he would stagger around saying he had taken poison, and I used to wish it were true because he was just so awful. When Dick shot himself, it was the scandal of the town and we were shunned by everyone. No one in the town would help us. We couldn't even find anyone to act as pallbearers to carry the coffin! It was awful! My hair turned gray that year."

Worst of all, Peter and his family became outcasts in this small Australian town. Peter couldn't get work to support his family. His memory of their straits was bitter: "Lynne, my mother, and I stuck together as best we could because the people who owned the house we lived in gave us two weeks to get out and move out of town. I could no longer go to the pub and play piano because people would just point and stare. We left town after auctioning off the furniture because there was no money. Half the town turned out to watch the bus leave. We never went back."

Eventually Peter joined the resort circuit where he got his big break with an act called the Two Shades. They were booked to perform on *Australian Bandstand,* a clone of Dick Clark's *American Bandstand*. One of the Two Shades quit before the show, and that's when the father of the other thought of teaming his son with Peter. Peter Woolnough and Chris Bell got together, changed their professional name to the Allen Brothers, and soon became regulars on *Australian Bandstand*. At sixteen, they were household names down under.

They began opening for a hot Las Vegas–Miami act, Frances Faye, who had boundless energy. She packed them in to the popular club Chequers with a very successful show held over for three extra weeks. Everybody wanted to see and hear this brazen, brassy lady audiences either hated or loved as she performed dozens of songs she interrupted with double entendres and sexual suggestions.

Peter was inspired by this free-wheeling lady who would sit around totally naked talking serious philosophy and show business gossip while smoking joints. She also guided Peter in some of the nuances of being a successful, sophisticated performer, and before long the Allen Brothers swept Australia with their first hit recording, "My Secret." This success spurred Chris's father to send them on a tour of Asia, which led to a booking at the Crow's Nest in the Hong

Kong Hilton Hotel, where they met Judy.

Judy and Mark came back night after night to see the Allen Brothers act and to party with Peter, making the rounds of the after-hours places.

As Peter described a typical night: "When we arrived back from our tour of the after-hours clubs, Judy sent for her limousine so we could go and watch the sunrise. Later we went to the Repulse Bay Hotel (the fanciest in town) to get a drink. Mark said he would wait in the car. Judy and I were still in evening clothes and the hotel wouldn't serve us a drink. So Judy ordered the whole breakfast just to get a sherry. It was so hysterical, staring at the table of food, and they still wouldn't serve us a sherry because it was too early. We left the hotel, only to find the car gone, so the two of us were sitting in the gutter at nine in the morning, with all those people passing by on their way to work staring at this woman in her sequined gown and wondering if it was Judy Garland."

"Finally," Peter continued, "Mark turned up and on the way home talked about acting and how you must be true to yourself and Judy started yelling he didn't know what he was talking about. She stopped the car, got out, and started yelling. 'These are the people you have to reach! This is the audience! These are my people! You must appeal to the masses!' And thousands of Chinese folks are staring at her without the foggiest idea who she was. So, I thought, 'Well, Judy certainly has a sense of the moment!'"

Judy insisted she would take over management of the Allen Brothers and make them stars. Neither they nor Chris's father objected. Judy's first step was to have them come to Tokyo from Hong Kong with her on the ship *Roosevelt,* where the Brothers and Judy put on impromptu performances to the delight of management and passengers. Peter was at the piano as always, and Chris was on guitar, with Judy singing.

It was a kind of bonding between Peter and Judy professionally and personally. As Peter would later describe it: "Late at night, after everyone would go to bed, Judy and I would go for a swim, dry off, open the lounge ourselves, and sit at the piano singing songs together. She was the first person I ever met who knew as many songs as I did, and we shared a mutual delight in well-written melodies and good lyrics. That is really how we became friends, sitting up late at night, working out new arrangements for songs. She really did love music more than anything. I think she liked the fact I wasn't terrified of her, but I was in show business. I knew so little about her reputation I really wasn't in awe of her. She liked that."

Judy insisted the Allen Brothers follow her to London in six weeks when their appearance at the Tokyo Hilton was finished. They agreed, said good-bye, and assumed it would all be forgotten before Judy's plane set down at Heathrow Airport. But it wasn't, and several weeks later she telephoned Peter in Toyko. She was sending plane tickets and had lined up some engagements for them. Judy wanted Peter to do two things. One was open her act when she was on tour. The second, which she didn't tell him, was to meet Liza in London for whatever might happen. The first of these objectives was Judy the business manager at work. The second was Judy the mother taking care of parental business.

Judy announced the arrival of the Allen Brothers to the English press with glowing words: "I heard them and liked them when they were singing at the Hilton Hotel in Hong Kong. They are going places, these boys. They are a wonderful pair. Peter and Chris are without a doubt the best act I have ever seen. They have such vitality, exuberance, and warmth I find quite irresistible. If you need one word which sums them up it is simple: talent!"

Coincidentally, Peter and Chris arrived in London the day of the big concert at the Palladium. It was the first time Peter experienced Judy onstage in other than a club environment as she was in Hong Kong and Tokyo. Colleagues said Peter was surprised by what he saw. One friend of Peter's said, "What astounded him most was the unabashed competition going on between mother and daughter. Liza was no longer the little girl Judy could just bring onstage for a moment of motherly indulgence. In fact, this London opening marked Liza's first performance as a show business adult."

And true to being a mother, Judy pushed Liza to meet this wonderful man she found for her. Judy said, "This is the boy I've been telling you about. Peter, this is my daughter I've been telling you about. You'd be perfect for each other."

Peter was overwhelmed by Liza's incredible talent and may have fallen in love with her then, even though they were just introduced. Judy brought Liza and Peter together as a possible love couple even though she suspected Peter was gay or bisexual. But then again, Judy always gravitated toward effeminate men such as Liza's father Vincente. Liza would sometimes do the same.

The evening of the Palladium concert marked the beginning of a high-octane star-swirl that left Peter dizzy. This was the London of 1964 when the new rock 'n' roll madness epitomized by the Beatles swept the country. After Judy and Liza's first performance, they all adjourned to the hot disco of the moment, the Ad-Lib, run by future best-selling author Jackie Collins, where they were in the company of the Beatles, Rudolf Nureyev, and Dame Margot Fonteyn. Stellar company or not, Peter suffered from jet lag and, to everyone's amusement, fell asleep at the table.

But it wasn't the end. The good times kept pumping as Peter remembered: "We all went out together in this huge social whirl. One night we went to actor George Sanders's country home and I played the piano while Judy and Vivien Leigh traded chorus after chorus of 'Hello Dolly.' But soon Liza and I were sneaking off on dates of our own and one weekend we went off to Paris so I could meet her father, Vincente Minnelli, who was directing *The Sandpiper* there. Vincente invited us to lunch and, since they were also shooting *What's New Pussycat?* at the same studio, we sat down to lunch with Richard Burton, Elizabeth Taylor, Peter O'Toole, Woody Allen, Paula Prentiss, and Ursula Andress. I was getting a crash course in celebrity."

Clearly, Peter was in love with Liza, and of course, Liza was in love with him because he was cute and talented with a sense of humor. They were out every night and attended every "in" party in London, besides having their own private parties together. Three weeks after Peter landed at Heathrow Airport for the first time, they double-dated at London's Trader Vic's with Judy and Mark and Peter's performing partner Chris.

While Judy was in the powder room, the talk turned to Peter and Liza's romance and Peter said he wished he could go steady with her. Mark said they would have to be engaged for it to happen and Peter instantly turned to Liza and said, "All right, let's be engaged then. Liza, if you'll marry me, I'll never stop trying to make you happy." Liza happily responded, "Yes, Peter, I want that."

Whereupon Peter took a diamond ring off his little finger and slipped it on Liza's ring finger to the excitement and delight of Judy as she returned to the table. Peter said, "We'll get married in New York early next year. I didn't ask Judy's permission. We just told her and she was so happy she nearly cried. The wedding cannot be too soon for her. She can hardly wait to be a grandmother. It has been all so quick I can't believe Liza's wearing the diamond ring I gave her."

About then *Flora, the Red Menace,* came into Liza's professional life. It was a play satirizing communism, in which Flora Meszaros, an outgoing artist, is convinced by her boyfriend to join the Communist Party. Liza wanted to play the lead but was having a difficult time convincing director George Abbott and producer Hal Prince to cast her even though Fred Ebb, one of the show's composers, felt she was the perfect Flora. Even while she was in London rehearsing for her appearance with her mother, she was also practicing some of the songs from *The Red Menace* so she would be ready when the time came to sing for the director and producer.

She kept after Ebb to get her an audition. "Whenever there's something I want, really want, I persevere until I get it. I really hounded Fred."

Ebb was captivated by her waiflike quality and gave his approval for the role, but Abbott remained unconvinced. So the day after her engagement to Peter, Liza left her fiancé to fly to New York and try out again for *Flora, the Red Menace.*

Fred Ebb and his musical partner John Kander had met Liza in the early sixties while they were creating *Flora*. Liza was performing in *Carnival* when a friend of Kander's brought her by his New York apartment. Liza was thinking of making an album, and the friend thought Kander and Ebb might have some material that would work for her. In a 1979 interview, at which Liza was present, with *People* magazine's Barbara Rowes, Ebb recalled his first impression of Liza. "I took one look at her and thought, 'Well, here she is, Miss Raggedy Ann....She was dirty, awkward, and wrinkled. I wanted to throw her in the bathtub."

Liza was unimpressed with the team until she heard some of the songs for *Flora*. "When I heard the music, I got up and asked if I could sing those songs now." She did. Kander and Ebb were hooked.

This time the tryout was before tough old—he was in his seventies—producer George Abbott. It didn't go well. Part of the problem was the status and personality of George Abbott.

Martin Gottfried, chief drama critic for *Women's Wear Daily, New York Post*, and *Saturday Review*, described Abbott in his biography of Bob Fosse, *All His Jazz:* "The only good [musical] was a hit show; that was the conventional wisdom. An audience might be convinced it was supposed to enjoy a lofty-minded play because it was being culturally nourished in the process; an audience could be chided for missing the point of something intellectual or abstract. But not the audience for a musical. There, the crowd was the judge, its laughter and cheers had to be won or else the show was given the hook. Abbott was the crusty old grandpa of the Broadway musical who decided what would work and what wouldn't.

"George Abbott was a successful director of drama and farce, who turned to musical comedy in the 1930s and was equally successful. Successful? His record was astounding. He was Mr. Broadway Musical. He was also 'Mr. Abbott.' It was suspected even his mother called him Mr. Abbott, and the respect wasn't a matter of his imposing height [six feet six inches] or even his imperious manner. It was because, like his shows, George Abbott had no nonsense about him. He was in the business of making entertainment, not philosophical statements or art. He was brisk, he was unsentimental, he was unemotional, and if these were shortcomings in the man, they were strengths in the director."

Liza was determined, and high school friend Marvin Hamlisch was directing the pit orchestra. But Abbott didn't like her audition. He thought she was just some star's brat trying to break into show business on her mother and father's fame. It put Abbott off even before she opened her mouth. He told a colleague in a loud voice while Liza was onstage, "This is a waste of time. She's not right for *Flora*. She's not what I have in mind, and I don't think she'll be able to carry it."

Liza didn't make it on that audition, but she kept talking to everybody about how much she wanted the role and she came back to audition time and again. It finally came down to Liza or Eydie Gorme, Abbott's first choice. But Gorme was unavailable, so three days before rehearsal started, Liza was cast in the lead role.

"I guess they couldn't find anybody else," she said. As it turned out, her performance made Liza the youngest performer ever to win a Tony as Best Actress in a Musical. This was the beginning of a partnership between Liza and Kander and Ebb that still thrives today.

Abbott changed his attitude toward Liza after he saw how cooperative and hardworking she was in rehearsal. He remarked that Liza took directions as fast and as well as Helen Hayes, and producer Hal Prince also seemed happy with Liza's performance. She was cast opposite Second City comedian Bob Dishy, and Fred Ebb did much to mold her into the leading lady she was supposed to be in her first real Broadway show. Liza was eighteen and partly because of her youth, partly because she was sensitive about her family links, she wanted to prove herself.

"I've had to prove myself to some extent and that's kind of rough," Liza told Joanne Stang in a May 1965 interview for the *New York Times*. "People keep expecting you to live up to a legend, but if you keep thinking about it, you're dead. You can't put that responsibility on yourself. Anyway, your famous parents can open a lot of doors for you, but between 8 and 11 P.M. there's no pull. First of all, people aren't going to put $40,000 behind a name if there's nothing to back it up, if it's just a curiosity thing. Mr. Prince was not about to do that. And Mr. Abbott has never once referred to my family. He's never once referred to, you know, my mother. He's always respected me for myself."

Although not as well-known to the public as, say, Marvin Hamlisch, lyricist Fred Ebb, together with composer John Kander, is responsible for such Broadway classics as *Cabaret, Zorba the Greek,* and *Kiss of the Spider Woman.* Ebb has managed to keep his private life completely out of the public eye despite his close friendship with Liza. In 1962 Ebb was introduced to Kander by publisher friend Tommy Valando, who suggested the two might consider collaborating. Ebb said of the meeting, "We came to each other fresh from our failures."

Kander had just composed *A Family Affair,* which lasted six days on Broadway and was notable only for being the producing debut of Harold Prince.

"I remember I liked [Kander] right away," Ebb recalled. "Our neuroses complemented each other. It was instant communication and instant songs."

Nearly instant success followed. Before the end of 1962 they had a hit song, "My Coloring Book," sung on *The Perry Como Show* by Sandy Stewart following an introduction by Kaye Ballard. This marked the beginning of the Kander and Ebb legacy. Stewart, Kitty Kallen, and Barbra Streisand each recorded popular versions of it. The next year Kander and Ebb followed their success with the Streisand hit, "I Don't Care Much."

Kander and Ebb also collaborated with Richard Morris on the musical *Golden Gate,* which was to open in San Francisco on April 18, 1963, to commemorate the fifty-seventh anniversary of the 1906 San Francisco earthquake. Although the play never opened, material from it caught the attention of producer Prince, who immediately contracted the team to write songs for a musical he was developing, *Flora, the Red Menace.* Regardless of *Flora's* success or failure, Harold Prince had already contracted Kander and Ebb to work on his next project, a musical treatment of John van Druten's play *I Am a Camera,* which was to be called *Cabaret.*

Liza evaluated musical mentor Ebb: "Fred is the only person I've ever loved and trusted. He knows me better than anyone else. He makes me decide to be a little better than I've ever been before. He reminds me I'm not great unless I'm great."

Meanwhile, Judy and Mark returned to America after a short vacation in Greece and brought with them Peter and Chris, whose American careers Judy planned to launch through her expansive show business connections. In December 1964 the Allen Brothers made their first major appearance at the Diplomat Hotel in Miami Beach. Liza was there to share the holiday with Peter just before she took *Flora* on the road.

When Peter and Liza returned to New York, they decided to get an apartment together on Fifty-seventh Street. Soon they were the most sought-after young couple in Manhattan, running from party to opening to reception to performance and being hailed as the adorable new lovebirds. Still, show business kept them apart with Liza working in *Flora* and Peter and Chris making appearances in Toronto, Miami, and Las Vegas or going on the road as Judy's opening act.

As grateful as the Allen Brothers were to Judy and as much as Peter regarded her as a friend and future mother-in-law, they soon discovered Judy was an offstage pain of the first order. One main problem, Peter noted, was the giant star had terrible stage fright. Peter and Chris would play a set of warm-up numbers and wait, but Judy still wouldn't appear. They would play another set and wait again, but Judy didn't appear. And so it would go interminably until the audience became so unruly Peter and Chris would have to retreat from the stage. Finally, a doctor would announce Miss Garland was too ill to perform and the audience would become furious.

In Cincinnati the audience surged over the footlights, across the stage, and into the dressing rooms, demanding either a performance or an immediate refund. As Peter said: "She was, if you can imagine, terrified of going onstage; she felt she needed all manner of help to get out there. But once she was actually on the stage it would usually be all right. For a while she would be hypnotized to go on and it worked. It helped her overcome some of her tremendous fear."

Meanwhile, out-of-town tryouts for *Flora* began April 3, 1965, in New Haven and then Boston, with mixed reviews often accusing Liza of attempting to imitate her mother. Still, that's why some people went to the show—they wanted to see the new Judy Garland. There was one way Liza was *not* like her mother: the way she treated Lorna and Joey. In the midst of rehearsals, the hotel manager where Judy was staying in New York called Liza to say Judy had locked her children out of the room again. This time they were locked outside on the freezing terrace. Liza, having lived through the same hurtful experience many times herself, rushed over and rescued her siblings.

However, no matter how hard Liza tried, nothing could rescue *Flora, the Red Menace*. It opened May 11, 1965, in the Alvin Theater. Opening night was a sellout, with people hoping to see Vincente Minnelli and Judy Garland at their daughter's first Broadway show. Both came and played the proud parents. At the cast party afterward, Judy hugged her daughter and whispered in her ear, "You're standing in stardust." It must have been a bitter-sweet, whimsical moment for Judy, reminding her of her own early days.

Still, *Flora* was not destined to last long. It struggled through eleven weeks and eighty-seven performances before it closed July 24, 1965, losing $381,000 for its backers. But much good came of the project. Liza won the Tony, and the other three nominees that year—Elizabeth Allen in *Do I Hear A Waltz?*, Nancy Dussault in *Bajour*, and Inga Swenson in *Baker Street*—were also in short-run shows.

Critics of Liza's performance couldn't agree. Howard Taubman of the *New York Times* wrote, "The voice is not yet distinctive, but she can keep the rhythm pounding and driving and can belt out the climactic tones." *Newsweek*, in the first of many brutal critiques of Liza, declared: "Liza Minnelli is engaging, but far from accomplished; and it is unpleasant to see her rushed into a big Broadway show at nineteen, as though she were another Barbra Streisand. But Miss Minnelli lacks Miss Streisand's equipment. Her voice is thin, her movements stiff, her presence wobbly and uncertain."

In contrast, *Variety* wrote, "Audiences who expect just to ogle 'Judy Garland's daughter' should leave applauding an excellent on-her-own performance by the girl. Miss Minnelli has intriguing stage presence, a good voice and a captivating manner." *Time* said, "At 19, Liza Minnelli is a star-to-be, a performer of arresting presence who does not merely occupy the stage, but fills it."

And finally, Walter Kerr wrote in the *Herald Tribune:* "Liza Minnelli, who no longer needs to be identified as Judy Garland's daughter and I apologize for just having done so, has many a fetching way about her. Her smile, for instance, is marvelously unsteady, always eager to shoot for the moon, always on the verge of wrinkling down to half-mast....she acts lyrics extremely well."

Looking back on *Flora, the Red Menace*, Ebb and Prince assessed where it went wrong. Ebb said, "To say the least, *Flora* was a disaster. It just did not work. The book was sort of strange and the score sounded like a series of revue numbers because it wasn't connected by the strength of the libretto."

Prince felt the reviews killed *Flora*. "By the time we previewed in New York, I began to believe we had a hit. But the reviews on Broadway were awful and they needn't have been. Liza's voice reminded you of her mother and best of all for me, she moved wonderfully."

Yet *Flora* won Liza reasonably good reviews and a Tony—quite an achievement for a nineteen-year-old. More important, it positioned her to pitch for the lead in a show she desired even more, *Cabaret*. Hal Prince and Fred Ebb were deeply involved in *Cabaret*'s production, but that didn't help Liza. Even though she wanted the part and had connections with the production people,

Prince was adamant the lead role of Sally Bowles be played by a British actress. This didn't faze Liza. She was determined to get the part.

Liza mounted her campaign with stories to the press about how much she wanted the role, how right she was for it, and how she had auditioned fourteen times (a considerable exaggeration since she only auditioned once). Her strategy didn't work, and the stage role went to Jill Hayworth, who opened with the play on Broadway in 1966.

Meanwhile, Liza was working so frequently with Fred Ebb that Peter became jealous. "I'm sure Peter misunderstood my devotion to Fred just as I distrusted his coterie of acquaintances," she said. Even so, when they were both in New York at the same time, she and Peter were the golden couple, doing discos and clubs nightly and reveling in the charmed circle of the young, the rich, and the wanton that was so popular in Manhattan in the late 1960s. Still, Liza wasn't happy about the people Peter saw when he was away from home and, sometimes, when he was at home.

Since Judy wasn't touring, the Brothers were relieved of being her nervous opening act and free to develop their American career with help from some savvy agents. They quickly found a niche for themselves in the Playboy club circuit which, at the time, was very hot. Hugh Hefner was opening Playboy clubs in various resort locations and launching *Playboy* magazine, which further popularized the clubs.

A *Variety* reviewer characterized the Allen Brothers: "Both men have good voices, but it's the high degree of enthusiasm which they project that really puts them across. Their show's pace is fast and jovial with up-tempo selections such as a rocking 'You Can Have Her' that engenders the strongest response, although the pair makes a solid impression with a tender 'Try to Remember' from *The Fantasticks* and a mellow treatment of 'It's Feeling Good.' Chris does a nice job of providing guitar backing for several songs and brother Peter handles dance routines with vigor."

While the Brothers were performing on the Playboy circuit,

Fred Ebb was working with John Kander on the idea of a new musical as a vehicle for Liza, and at the same time, creating a hot nightclub act for her. The first didn't happen, but the second did. Fred took over the multiple roles of being Liza's mentor, friend, confidant, partner, and collaborator.

Of Ebb, Liza said, "Sometimes I think I'm just a figment of Fred Ebb's imagination." She gives him credit for her success, "I've had fabulous guidance from Fred Ebb, who has been my Svengali since I was seventeen. He's really guided my career brilliantly."

Indeed, from the moment they met, Ebb was instrumental in every step of Liza's career. Fred put together her first nightclub act at the Shoreham Hotel in Washington, D.C., and has been involved in almost every act since.

About her first club act, Liza remembered: "I asked Freddie to help me, even though he'd never really done anything like it before. We didn't have money or experience, but we did have faith in each other's talent and judgment. We hired a choreographer because we liked the lining of his jacket and we put together an act in three acts like a Broadway show. When I performed, I was performing hoping it would please Freddie."

Ebb steered Liza away from material inviting comparisons with her mother, and with the exception of "New York, New York," he was fairly successful. He especially advised her against doing Judy's material, until Liza was a star in her own right.

About their personal relationship, Ebb said, "Liza has a deep need for complete trust from anyone who doesn't need her for anything. Liza, like her mother, can't be alone easily and she knows it. In every situation, Liza always looks for a person, usually masculine, to depend on, to be close to."

Often, Fred Ebb has been that person, the one to give her the final words of encouragement before she opened a new show.

For her first nightclub act, Liza worked with two dancers, Neil Schwartz and Robert Fitch, and an orchestra. Her show was highlighted by a chic and sexy wardrobe that allowed her the freedom of movement her dancing required while showing off her trim figure and the incredible legs she would feature so often. The act consisted of eighteen numbers, including "Everybody Loves My Baby," "Too Marvelous," and "Gypsy in My Soul" plus a special new song Ebb wrote for Liza, "Songs I Taught My Mother."

They opened September 14, 1965, in the Blue Room of the gigantic Shoreham Hotel overlooking Rock Creek Park in northwest Washington, D.C. It was the beginning of a national tour taking them to the Sahara in Las Vegas, the Coconut Grove in Los Angeles, the Persian Room in New York's Plaza, and the Deauville in Miami Beach. Liza borrowed money from her agent and friends of Kander and Ebb to launch the tour and a lot rode on the reception at the Blue Room.

With so much at stake, the opening was almost jinxed when Judy called Liza fearful Liza would ridicule her mother in her act. It was one of those phone calls nobody needs when they are on the edge of an important event. Fortunately, Liza handled it and her cabaret debut came off.

The electricity Ebb and Liza wove on opening night stood the audience on its collective ear. One critic declared, "Her songs, dances and patter are magnificent and they are written to make the most out of her remarkable talent and personality."

Variety reported, "She put the full-house opening-night audience on its feet, which is very unusual in the huge, sophisticated Blue Room. She is one of only two or three performers who have received a standing ovation on opening night in the last fifteen years."

Her gig at the Shoreham Hotel broke all existing attendance records.

After the *Flora* fiasco, this success was sweet wine for Liza and Fred Ebb. This was especially a great breakthrough for Liza because she was doing a smashing sophisticated cabaret show on her own with no help from Mama or Daddy. She was Liza—not Judy's daughter. Yet she acknowledged the legacy of her mother. "I'm not a star yet, but I'm on my way," she said. "It's kind of an advantage my mother is Judy Garland. I know why people come and see me. I hear them talking in the lobby. They expect a carbon copy—or they expect me to be no good. Originality is one thing they don't expect."

During this period Judy was experiencing new failure. She married Mark Herron November 14, 1965, soon after Liza's Blue Room opening. The marriage quickly collapsed a few months later. Friends deserted her, and Judy made more pathetic suicide tries. But nobody paid attention to her suicide tries anymore. Everyone was resigned to the fact someday Judy would succeed in killing herself, ending her misery and theirs.

On a happier note, the Blue Room opening was also a triumph for Fred Ebb and bonded him and Liza professionally.

Ebb, who bears a resemblance to the late actor Richard Burton, said: "She (Liza) is the constant woman in my life and I am the constant man in hers. There is no reason at all why Liza and I shouldn't have been lovers. I guess we just knew too much about each other. Plus there were just too many other guys in her life. But the essential thing about Liza is she's an assertion of life. She went through crazy, sordid things with her mother I *still* find hard to believe. One push either way would have made [Liza] crazy, but somehow—between her father's calming influence, her mother's love of life and marvelous sense of humor, and Liza's own talent— she came out of it.

"It still amazes me sometimes," he continued. "You know, feature by feature, Liza's not beautiful. But the whole is greater than the sum of her parts and when she shines, she's devastating. But the real secret of Liza's appeal? She flatters an audience. She really cares for them. She makes people want to look after her. She's everyone's kid sister; every guy's dependent girl."

Charged up by her triumph in the Blue Room, Liza was filled with determination to show what she could do before an all-important New York audience. Her next stop was the Persian Room of the Plaza Hotel on February 9, 1966. Her appearance instantly sold out. The audience loved her and so did the critics, except the *Newsweek* writer who earlier panned Liza in *Flora*.

In both instances—*Flora* and the Persian Room—the *News-*

week critic seemed outraged Liza was young: "Nineteen-year-old Liza Minnelli's song-and-dance act at New York's Persian Room is, on the surface, flawless: smooth, quick-paced and high-stepping. She has a pleasant voice, in spite of a need to take refuge from high notes in shouts. But all the slick Las Vegas arrangements couldn't get her to sing "He's My Guy" or "They Wouldn't Believe Me" as if she meant it. A girl has to have lived a little to sing about the seamy sides of life and love."

"Flawless" wasn't good enough for *Newsweek*.

Leonard Harris of the *New York World Telegram and Sun* reflected what the audience demonstrated. "Liza Minnelli proved she could sock the stuffings out of a song, dance beautifully for a singer—and even pretty well for a dancer—and turn on the built-in spotlight that is the *sine qua non* of the cabaret performer."

Liza was hot in Manhattan. And soon after, in December 1966, her Capitol album *There Is a Time* came out and did well. It didn't turn into a huge seller, but it did earn her the Grammy award for Album of the Year.

Liza's cabaret career, at least, was blossoming. Next came stints at London's Talk of the Town in May 1966, a command performance for Prince Rainier and Princess Grace of Monaco, and the Coconut Grove in Los Angeles's Ambassador Hotel. French star Charles Aznavour heard her at the Coconut Grove and arranged to book her into the Olympia Music Hall in Paris, where they appeared on a double bill. Liza began what would become a lifelong love affair with French audiences, who think of her as an American Edith Piaf—coincidental since Aznavour had a long professional connection with Piaf.

It would also become a lifelong relationship at various levels with Aznavour, a romantic idol to many women with his French singing presence and curious background. He is a small man— about five-foot-three, 112 pounds, wiry, and quite Americanized in his food tastes. His favorite foods include ice cream and hot dogs, and his favorite pastime is driving hot sports cars very fast.

Aznavour came from Armenian immigrant parents who fled

the infamous Turkish massacre early this century in which his grandparents, uncles, and aunts were slaughtered. His mother Knar and father Misha Miagmignon Aznavorian made their way to Paris, where Charles was born May 22, 1924. Both parents were on the stage, with Misha playing various instruments and Knar acting. They were saving to start a restaurant while the family lived on the edge of poverty. Growing up in a theatrical family, Charles attended the Ecole du Spectacle, a school for the performing arts in Paris.

By the time Charles was nine, he was getting modest stage roles, and soon he and older sister Aida were performing anywhere they could. Charles shortened his name to Aznavour so it would fit on theater marquees. At the end of the war, Charles developed a nightclub act with Pierre Roche, another singer and composer. He had a lot of acting experience by this time—eleven years of it—but not much singing experience and he approached the new act with some trepidation. But he was encouraged by another singer for whom he occasionally worked as a chauffeur. Her name was Edith Piaf.

One day Piaf looked over some music Charles and Pierre had written and summoned Charles alone to her bedroom. She suggested he and Roche might be able to open her act. But when Charles asked how much they would make, Piaf exploded: "For crying out loud, you miserable little penny pincher. You have the opportunity to appear in the same show as Piaf and you dare to ask how much you will be paid? All Paris, all Paris—do you hear—is falling at my feet trying to get on my program. Everyone in Paris would consider it a chance of a lifetime."

Piaf was known for her temper tantrums, her ambition, her drinking and, of course, for her singing talent, so Charles wasn't put off by her blowup and they began an eight-year association. "Charles," she said, "I'm taking you along. You can take care of my lighting and little details like that. You can make yourself useful, and it will teach you your trade."

It sounds denigrating, but Piaf was simply establishing the power relationship. She helped Aznavour develop his singing and the idiosyncratic throaty quality that would become his signature sound. Piaf also got involved in Charles's love affairs, which were tumultuous and involved very young women. Charles got married for the first time in 1947, when Liza was three, to a woman named Micheline by whom he had a baby girl, Patricia Seida Aznavour. The marriage was strained from the beginning because Charles traveled so much and was totally absorbed with his career.

In 1965 Aznavour opened at the Ambassador Theater on Broadway in a one-man show, *The World of Charles Aznavour*. Liza saw one of these shows while appearing at the Persian Room. She said, "I thought it was the greatest thing I'd ever seen! That somebody could sing a song and it was like a little movie, that each piece had a life of its own, that it was acted. It's miraculous!"

Success as a nightclub singer wasn't enough for Liza, she wanted more. She wanted to be a stage and screen star and couldn't wait to get back on the stage, which she did in a summer stock production of *The Pajama Game*. Film roles eluded her until her mother meddled once again and got her cast in a British movie, *Charlie Bubbles*. Liza didn't know Judy had promoted her for the role and for a lot of other jobs since their appearance at the Palladium.

Although it was shocking for Judy to discover she had given birth to her own greatest competitor, she soon after reverted to her role as mother. She kept looking out for parts Liza could play and trying to help her daughter's career sub rosa. She wanted Liza to succeed but didn't want to hurt her pride by having Mama obtain jobs for her.

Judy was a close friend of Michael Medwin, the producer of *Charlie Bubbles* and suggested Liza for one of the supporting roles. The film starred Albert Finney with Billie Whitelaw as his wife. Liza was cast in the role of Finney's adoring secretary and mistress, which required Liza to strip down to panties and bra for a brief seduction scene.

It was Liza's first grown-up movie role, and she learned a lot by working with Finney and following the advice of her father who told her to throttle back her natural intensity. He cautioned her such intensity was good on the stage, but overwhelmed the camera.

"Don't press," Vincente wrote her. "Remember you register so strongly and so easily you can project any emotion from ecstasy to anger and still be in control. I am delighted you are doing this picture and I think it's a marvelous break for you. I feel absolutely sure you'll be fresh and great and appealing and something completely new."

Unfortunately, when *Charlie Bubbles* was released in the United States in early 1968, it was only a tiny bubble on the American screen before it disappeared completely.

The movie received good reviews, including a surprisingly good one from Liza's old nemesis *Newsweek*, whose Joseph Morgenstern wrote, "Every single performance in the film has a life of its own and several leave you drunk with delight and desperate for just one more scene with Liza Minnelli." It was a movie and Liza enjoyed her part in it, but it was not the starring role in a big American movie Liza wanted.

Liza was shuttling back and forth searching for what would be best for her career while still engaged to Peter Allen on the theory he was best for her private life. Actually, they were living separate lives by this time with Peter and Chris performing at gay clubs and hanging out with Peter's crowd and Liza seeing her friends.

Her father was against the marriage, because he thought they were too young. Her stepmother Denise echoed Vincente's view and underscored it by saying she wouldn't attend any such wedding. Besides, Judy changed her mind about the young man and didn't approve of Peter's lifestyle and their relative youth.

Liza's father said: "She was just twenty years old. They were both quite young and I thought she should wait. They were both also on the brink of professional careers and I knew the survival rate of such marriages was infinitesimally small. And yet, marriage to Peter was, I knew, something Liza wanted very much. My eventual consent was one more request of Liza's I could not refuse."

Liza and Peter had been engaged over two years and most

people were saying it was time something happened—namely, marriage.

Peter, who had a traditional English aristocratic look with the slight hawk nose and protruding chin, did something smart and mature when he learned of Vincente's objections, as Vincente himself later described: "Peter wrote me a respectful letter in which he tried to dispel my reservations about his marriage to Liza. I was impressed he was so tradition-bound he felt he had to ask for Liza's hand."

Daddy reluctantly approved and so did Judy. Liza was delighted because she loved Peter and he made her laugh. On February 21, 1967, the couple obtained a license at the New York City Hall where Liza joked with newsmen, "Peter and I have been engaged for two years and it's taken us that long to get down here."

On March 3, 1967, they were married at the apartment of Liza's agent and friend, Stephanie Phillips, or at the apartment of Mr. and Mrs. Richard Friedberg, depending on which newspaper account you read the next day. The reception followed in the Central Park West apartment of Liza's business manager, Marty Bregman.

While it was a festive wedding performed by Judge Joseph A. Macchia, with Pam Reinhardt as maid of honor and Paul Jasmon as best man, the star of the wedding was not the bride as it was supposed to be—it was the mother of the bride. Once again Judy and Liza were in competition. But the wedding was also a brief reconciliation between the two after many fights and arguments over money Judy demanded from Liza, which Liza sometimes sent and sometimes didn't.

An international note was added by the attendance of Peter's mother Marion and sister Lynne from Australia. Liza gave them a quick tour of Manhattan and bonded with her new sister-in-law instantly. They hauled Marion out to buy a dress for the wedding, but she balked when she saw the prices. It offended her lifelong frugality to spend as much on one dress as she would normally spend on food for two or three months. Liza arranged with the store clerks to present various dresses without price tags and one was finally selected. Everyone was happy.

The high point for Marion and Lynne was meeting Lillian Roxon. Roxon was an Australian journalist operating out of New York with regular columns in Australian magazines. She was adored by Aussie women. Peter described what happened: "My mother and sister flew over from their new hometown of Bondi for the wedding a few days before and were still spinning from meeting Liza and my mother was naturally shy around Judy who was no ordinary mother-of-the-bride. However, as the reception went on, Mum relaxed and when I brought Lillian over to introduce her, we found Mum with two of our other guests, Van Johnson on one side and Yul Brynner on the other, chatting amiably away.

" 'Mum, this is Lillian Roxon.'

"My mother's jaw fell. After all those years of reading 'Letter from Lillian' in *Woman's Day*, here was a *real* celebrity!"

Judy came to the affair escorted by her second ex-husband, Vincente, but quickly focused her flirtatious attention on her third ex-husband, Sid Luft, to the amusement of some and the discomfort of others. Discomfort could not begin to cover what Liza must have felt when it turned out she was also in competition with her new husband's gay lover. Peter spent their wedding night with him, not Liza.

This was at a particularly tough time in Judy's professional career as she was appearing before packed houses some nights and sparse audiences on others. It was the beginning of another of many unpleasant times in the relationship between Liza and Judy. During this time, Liza was forced to look after her half siblings Lorna and Joey. Their mother was doing Ethel's old routine but with a refinement. Instead of simply locking them in or out of her hotel suite, Judy banished them to a separate section of the hotel under the care of sitters while she indulged her emotions and drug habit in seclusion. Judy refused to see her children by Luft except by appointment, which added absurdity to the bizarre arrangement.

Interestingly, twenty-one-year-old Liza did not fall into this pattern of behavior exhibited by her mother and grandmother. She said her fifteen-year-old sister and twelve-year-old brother could stay with her and Peter. At the same time, Liza began to hide from Judy because she couldn't stand some of their emotional confrontations. Peter assumed the role of dominant adult in the family, trying to hold his life with Liza together while providing a haven for Lorna and Joey and shielding Liza as much as possible from contact with her mother.

As Liza told a reporter for *Good Housekeeping* in 1968, "Our house is a haven for them [Lorna and Joey] when Mama is in a bad mood and they need help and peace." Mama wasn't in "a bad mood." Mama was zonked out on drugs and booze and feeling frightened and sorry for herself. The miraculous thing about Judy at this point in her life was her ability to go from the depths of drug despair to the stage, where she mesmerized thousands of people with her vitality and the intimacy of her performance.

January 1968 was an important month for both daughter and mother. Liza opened at the Empire Room of the Waldorf, dazzling an opening night audience that was itself brilliant with stars. Judy, having lived through a disastrous December during which she bombed at Madison Square Garden, lost the lead in the Broadway production of *Mame* and was evicted from her hotel suite for lack of payment.

The very night she lost the *Mame* role, Judy reluctantly attended Liza's show at the Empire Room, and Liza invited her onstage for a duet of "When the Saints Go Marching In." They brought the audience to its feet cheering. Liza insisted afterward that Judy, Lorna, and Joey take Liza's Waldorf suite while Liza stayed with her husband in their East Fifty-seventh Street apartment. That night proved Judy's magic was still there, but she was destroying it with her chemical addictions.

Meanwhile, Peter and Chris were being helped by the British musical invasion of America. The Allen Brothers were Australian, actually, but most American audiences couldn't tell the difference. Their clean-cut image and sweet singing was a strong contrast with the Rolling Stones. Their engagement book was filled with appearances around Manhattan, in some of the top clubs in the country, and on various TV shows.

In Manhattan, Peter and Liza were latter-day incarnations of F. Scott Fitzgerald and Zelda, showing up together at such night spots as Il Mio, Ondine, Le Club, Arthur, and Aux Puces. But even though they were together, they were drifting apart because neither liked the other's friends. Throughout the turbulent 1960s, Liza was not a to-the-barricades protester against the Establishment, its wars, and its policies. Rather, she was an integral part of the Establishment, running with the society "in" crowd that was reported on in the trendy publications and observed by the stargazing society reporters.

Peter likened this crowd to a soup bowl: wide and shallow. He thought them boring, mean-spirited, spoiled hypocrites and preferred people he felt had artistic talent, substance, depth, and no money. He and Liza still partied all night but at different ends of Manhattan—she on the upper East Side and he on the lower West Side in Greenwich Village. Physically and intellectually they were living at opposite ends of the spectrum.

9

Pookie Adams's Time

N ot satisfied with her nightclub success, Liza sought another stage production or movie. The movie possibilities didn't seem promising since Hollywood wasn't doing musicals in the mid-1960s. One role she focused on for several years was Pookie Adams in *The Sterile Cuckoo,* the story of adolescent first love with all its excitement, awkwardness, dreams, and disappointments. Liza didn't care if she did it onstage or on the silver screen. Liza originally heard about the story from a friend in 1965 and got a copy of John Nichols's novel.

"I read it straight through that night," Liza said, "It was a strange feeling, but I felt a deep understanding and sympathy for Pookie Adams. It was like the same things happened to her happened to me not very long ago. I knew if a film was made of *The Sterile Cuckoo,* I would play it."

When Liza first read the story, she tracked down the publisher and the people who had purchased the movie rights, Alan Pakula and Robert Mulligan. "I went to their office and told them when they decided to make the film, I was the one who should play Pookie. I did the same things to them I did to Fred Ebb and George Abbott for *Flora, the Red Menace.*"

Pakula and Mulligan were startled by this direct assault from an actress in search of a role, but Pakula was sold on the idea. "I couldn't separate Liza from Pookie. She had such a passion for the character, a kind of wild, passionate enthusiasm."

When Pakula found financial backing at National General, he told them Liza would play Pookie. It took some time for the laughter to subside, but when it did, the executives at National General studios said no way. They had their own ideas for Pookie, including such actresses as Patty Duke, Elizabeth Hartman, or Tuesday Weld. Pakula said without Liza there would be no movie. So there was no movie.

Liza was depressed the project was killed, but flattered that Pakula, who produced *To Kill a Mockingbird* and *Love With the Proper Stranger,* thought enough of her as an actress he would scuttle the movie rather than do it without her.

In March 1968 when the project was revived, Liza tested for the Pookie role again. She wanted the role so much she committed only to short engagements so she would be available if offered the part.

When July came and there was no word on *Cuckoo,* Liza was tempted to accept the female lead in a Broadway show based on *The Apartment,* a successful comedy movie starring Shirley MacLaine and Jack Lemmon. The play entitled *Promises, Promises,* had an equally distinguished parentage as a David Merrick production with music by Burt Bacharach and Hal David. Virtually everyone thought Liza should take the role in what was sure to be a hit show. It was, but she didn't appear in it.

In the minds of her mother and friends, Liza waiting for *The Sterile Cuckoo* was foolish for at least five reasons: It might never be made. Liza was not yet a big enough star to get temperamental and artistic in her choice of roles. It was a crazy dramatic assignment involving a weird, unsympathetic character and not the musical part that was her natural genre. Most people in the business thought the role was far beyond Liza's acting range. Paramount, which was then the only studio considering the movie, didn't want her.

Nonetheless, Liza was determined to play the role of Pookie

Adams, and events would prove her right. The only other people enthusiastic about casting her were Vincente and director Pakula, who said, "Liza was the only person I seriously considered for the role despite pressure from the studio for a more established figure."

The picture was finally made with Liza as Pookie. Pakula arranged a financing deal with Paramount and called Liza in Las Vegas where she was appearing and asked her to come to Los Angeles. Shooting began in September 1968 at Hamilton College in upstate New York.

Pakula praised the way Liza handled the difficult role: "I've never seen anybody get more joy out of working and it's contagious. I'd tell her the story just as I'd tell it to a child. I remember one scene where we had difficulty and I was trying to explain what I wanted, and I talked a lot, possibly more than I should have. After a while she got up and said, 'OK, let's try it.' She did and it was right."

The Sterile Cuckoo is the story of bewildered young lovers trying to make a connection with the real world. Pookie is a lonely girl who becomes the aggressor in the affair and forces herself onto freshman student Jerry, played by Wendell Burton. It culminates in a charmingly clumsy seduction scene filmed in a modest room at a Lake Oneida beach hotel. In time, Jerry realizes that, though he enjoys the sex and likes Pookie, he doesn't want a serious relationship. He tells her on the telephone their great love affair is over as Pookie, jammed into the phone booth in her dormitory, listens in pain.

This phone booth scene brought Liza raves from audiences and critics and was said to be the one sequence that guaranteed she would get an Academy Award nomination. The scene, which is the climax of the film, was shot on the first day because bad weather kept the crew inside. It was done in one take, which was so remarkable the crew applauded Liza when she finished—an amazing response from a blasé film crew.

Pakula felt his stubborn insistence on Liza for the role was justified. "I couldn't believe it would happen, but it did," he said.

"They were absolutely stunned. They didn't know from Liza Minnelli. They knew from Judy Garland, but they didn't know Liza."

"We yakked it out in rehearsal, but I didn't know how to work it," Liza said. "I was scared to death—but right before I stepped in front of a camera, it hit me like a rock and I just did it."

That approach would become common for Liza, who would come to a scene not sure how to play it, then suddenly have a revelation to fit the film's demands. Often, she was right. Occasionally, she was wrong. Part of her success, of course, came from guidance both her mother and father had given her over the years.

In the phone booth scene, she remembered her father taught her to read scripts and eliminate all but the important words so she could get the image to be conveyed. "You're as thin as a *toothpick*," Liza explained. "You take the word that is the point of the sentence. Then, raise your eyes on it. You're as *thin* as a toothpick. In *The Sterile Cuckoo*...in the telephone scene, there's a line where I have to say, 'I didn't have a sandwich with my father' and I used the lesson Daddy taught me and made the most important word 'sandwich.' 'I didn't have a———with my father.' It was very, very, very important."

The movie everyone believed would prove a disaster received great reviews after its release in October 1969. Liza earned an Academy Award nomination for Best Actress—as great an achievement at twenty-three as her Tony was at nineteen.

The toughest film reviewer in New York, Pauline Kael of the *New Yorker,* raved, "Liza's just about perfect! Her sad quizzical persona—the gangling body and the features that look too big for the little face—are ideal equipment for the role. She's very funny and is probably going to be acclaimed as a great actress." *Los Angeles Times* film critic Charles Champlin characterized Liza's performance as "warm, sad-looking, serious-funny, touching and beguiling."

Liza didn't win the Oscar, but she did win this accolade from critic Rex Reed: "Liza is wonderful as Pookie Adams. She plays her to the hilt with awkward horn-rimmed glasses, eyes like chocolate jawbreakers, a twitching nose like a bunny with hay fever and a funny heehaw laugh that crashes through your heart like a flash of sun on a foggy day. It's the kind of performance that breaks hearts and wins Oscars."

And Christopher Isherwood, on whose writing part of *Cabaret* is based, said Liza was a lot like his character Sally Bowles.

10

1969—A Very Bad Year

Nineteen sixty-nine may have been the most emotionally tumultuous year of Liza's life.

During the first two months of the year, she was busy traveling and planning for the next movie she wanted to do, *Cabaret*. She shuttled between Los Angeles, Paris, Miami, New York, and Puerto Rico, playing a club date, appearing in a TV special, and talking with Fred Ebb about getting the Sally Bowles role when *Cabaret* went to film.

Along the way she bonded with a poor, starving, maimed dog she found in Puerto Rico. The dog seemed both vicious and pathetic at the same time. Before long Liza rescued "Ocho"—named after the nightclub near where she found him—and he graduated from the gutter to the lap of luxury. He caused some trouble when he bit wardrobe mistress Rita Standler, forcing Liza to pay $7,500 in damages and Ocho to be defanged. But finally Ocho settled in with Peter and Liza.

While Ocho became part of Liza's life, her mother was absent much of this time. Judy married her fifth husband, Mickey Deans, in a March 1969 ceremony attended mostly by the press. They then moved to London. Mickey was managing New York disco Arthur when he met Judy in August 1967, and after their marriage he tried to find Judy work. He almost settled on filming a day in the life of

Judy Garland with a Swedish film company but balked when he discovered the crew had shot nude footage of Judy. Then he tried to sell backers on a chain of Judy Garland theaters, but there were no takers. Meanwhile, Lorna and Joey were in California and Liza was making movies. Judy was going through another difficult, depressing time and was as remote and removed from her children as she had ever been.

While waiting for something to develop with *Cabaret,* Liza, who was getting more savvy about the business, agreed to make a movie with Otto Preminger after long negotiations over money and options. Preminger saw a working print of *The Sterile Cuckoo,* which had not yet been released, and was struck by her talent. He said, "Liza had a strange Chaplinesque humor that came through her eyes and body. She had the qualities of a star."

The script was *Tell Me That You Love Me, Junie Moon*—a comedy-drama adapted from Marjorie Kellogg's novel. The story was about three handicapped people: an epileptic (Ken Howard), a wheelchair-bound gay man (Robert Moore), and a girl with a badly scarred face (Liza). These three are released from a hospital and try to make it living together. The film also featured James Coco, old friend Kay Thompson, Fred Williamson, Nancy Marchand, and Anne Revere. Critic Leonard Maltin described it as "moments of comedy, melodrama, [and] compassion expertly blended by Preminger in one of his best films."

Director Preminger wasn't at his best with the cast and particularly not with Liza, who regarded him as an impossible tyrant. The role would have been tough for any actress since it involved one of a woman's worst nightmares: losing her physical beauty. In *Junie Moon* the audience sees Liza with her lover in an outdoor scene where he convinces her to strip naked while her boyfriend unleashes a stream of obscenities to get sexually aroused. Junie Moon finds this routine ridiculous and mocks him. He turns on her, beats her, and finally pours acid over her face and arm and leaves her writhing naked on the ground.

Liza did a scheduled nightclub appearance at the Sahara Hotel in Las Vegas, and by June 10 was getting ready for *Junie Moon* by talking with author Kellogg, disfigured women, and the doctors who treat them.

"For the duration of the film, Junie Moon and I were the same person," Liza said. "I felt what she felt; but I felt it as Junie Moon, not as Liza Minnelli, the actress."

For disfigured women, initial treatment is usually a surgical attempt to restore the woman's appearance. Then comes the long and hard part, the psychological rehabilitation. If a woman is disfigured and cannot afford plastic surgery to restore her looks or such surgery isn't medically possible, she can become frightened, despondent, and filled with dread. This was the kind of woman Liza was to portray in *Junie Moon*. While researching her role, Liza studied how the disfigured women she met handled contact with strangers. Some seemed ashamed and tried to hide their disfigurement; others defiantly flaunted their scars and dared strangers to stare.

For Liza, shooting the film was arduous because it began with several hours in the makeup chair under the hands of Charles Schramm, who created her horribly scarred face. Liza said, "I got too used to how it looked. So before the scene where I see my face for the first time and cry with shock, I went into a room by myself and told myself every ghost story I could think of. I scared the bejesus out of me!"

Early in 1969 both Liza's parents made new tries at romantic liaisons. Judy had married Mickey Deans in a Roman Catholic ceremony in London. He would later write a biography of Judy entitled *Weep No More My Lady*. At the same time Vincente was estranged from Denise, who had fallen in love with Prentiss Cobb Hale, a department store tycoon from San Francisco. According to society columnist Doris Lilly, Vincente was brokenhearted but found British publicist Lee Anderson good therapy. Soon they were living together and would later marry.

Judy's marriage came at the worst time in her life. Despite occasional moments of excellence, her concert performances were getting generally worse as her career soured and her use of drugs and liquor increased. She desperately needed a strong figure like Vincente, Sid, or Liza in her daily life to set her straight. Mickey Deans couldn't do it. He was dazzled by Judy and her lifestyle and ignored the warnings of friends who said he was buying into a very bad scene.

When Judy and Mickey visited New York, her friends tried to get her into a hospital, but she refused to go. Instead she called Peter one night when Mickey was away and insisted Peter take her to Aux Puces, a club where he was well-known and popular. Peter did what Judy wanted and they had a wonderful evening reminiscent of the nights in Hong Kong and Tokyo when the two first met. Judy dressed like she did in her younger days, with a white embroidered sweater over a black dress and a straw hat with flowers. Everybody was drinking heavily, with Judy downing straight triple vodkas and getting drunk to the point she left her sweater and hat behind when they went home. It was a bittersweet night, as Peter would later remember.

On the weekend of June 20, 1969, Liza and Peter retreated to Southampton on Long Island to unwind and so Liza could think about *Junie Moon,* which would begin shooting soon. During the serene Sunday morning of the 22nd, the phone rang with the message Liza knew would someday come. Peter took the call. It was Liza's secretary Deanna Wenble with a message from London. Peter went to wake up Liza wishing he never had to tell her the news he carried that morning.

"Darling," he said sorrowfully, "you better wake up. I have something to tell you." Liza sat up instantly with terror in her eyes. "Is it Mama? Is Mama sick?" Peter said later, "I shook my head and told her Judy died."

Judy was dead. And so was a part of Liza.

Just six years before, in the summer of 1963, the then forty-one-year-old Judy and seventeen-year-old Liza bonded closer than ever before. Judy's star was fading and Liza had just come off the success of her first professional off-Broadway engagement in *Best*

Foot Forward. The two were probably never as close as they were that summer, with Liza probing into Judy's love affairs and Judy recognizing her little girl was on the verge of becoming both an adult and a professional performer. Judy tried to teach her everything she should know personally and professionally about their shared craft. Judy felt strongly about concentrating on the meaning of the lyric when delivering a song. "You never lose the thought behind the word," she said. "You are not just singing a note. Just because you're holding a note, don't think the emotion of the word is over."

Liza learned a lot from Mama that summer six years before. Now Mama was gone. Peter said after he broke the news to her, Liza went outside, sat down on the grass, and cried uncontrollably for five minutes.

Judy's husband Mickey had gotten up in the middle of the night in their Cadgogan Lane cottage in London. When he awoke, Judy wasn't beside him. He checked the bathroom. The door was locked and no one answered his call. Reluctant to break the door down, Mickey went outside, found a part of the roof he could climb, and looked in the bathroom window. To his horror, he saw a naked Judy sitting on the toilet motionless, with her head on her hands. He forced the window open and reached for Judy. She was cold and stiff. When he got into the bathroom, he was shocked at how she looked. "I noticed her skin was discolored with a red and bluish tinge and Judy's face was dreadfully distorted. Blood came from her nose and mouth and the air escaping from her mouth sounded like a low moan."

The coroner ruled, with typical British reserve, that Judy died of "accidental death by an incautious dose of barbiturates." She had just turned forty-seven.

The same day the medical examiner's verdict was announced, a private physician who treated Judy held a press conference in which he told the world: "She had been living on borrowed time. When I examined her about eight years ago, she had cirrhosis of the liver. I thought if she lasted five more years she would have done very well.

She lived three years longer than I thought she would. She was always a fighter. She was under great stress, but for her it was always, 'The show must go on.'"

Another revelation came later from Sonia Roy, the wife of a British musician, who said she and her husband Harry were with Judy the night she died. She said Judy told them she was very depressed and all in her life was lost—she was $4 million in debt at the time—and she had decided to take her own life. Mrs. Roy said they talked with her for a long time and believed in the end they had convinced her not to do anything so drastic and final.

In some ways, it was a predictable ending for a fabled star whose body and spirit deteriorated even while her voice remained capable of brilliance.

One of Liza's first calls was to her father in Hollywood, where he was working to complete *On a Clear Day You Can See Forever* with Barbra Streisand for Paramount. It was the highest-budget musical Vincente had ever made and he was apprehensive lest anything go wrong. His marriage to Denise was on the rocks and they were just waiting to work out a settlement.

Vincente described Liza's call in his autobiography: "On Sunday, June 22, I was organizing the shooting for the coming week, when the telephone rang. It was Liza from New York.

" 'Daddy...'

" 'Darling!'

"There was a pause on the other end of the line. 'Mama died today.'

" 'Oh, darling...I'm so sorry.'"

Vincente wrote Liza seemed in total control, almost philosophical. But she was also concerned about the job that had to be done.

" 'I have to make sure she didn't kill herself,' Liza said. 'Mama couldn't have done that. She was in such a great mood during the last few days.'

"I comforted Liza as best I could. More long silences. 'I'd better go, Daddy.'

" 'Keep me informed, darling.'

" 'Okay.'"

Ray Bolger was beside himself when he heard his *Wizard of Oz* costar had died. "The last time I played the Waldorf, last spring, Judy came in to see me," he said. "It was a very warm, sentimental night for me. Someone in the audience called out, 'Come on, Judy, sing "Over the Rainbow."' I was afraid she would be embarrassed, so I said Judy had already sung herself into their hearts and she needn't sing if she didn't feel in the mood. That pleased her. Her face lit up and she became beautiful. She looked absolutely marvelous. But then I don't have to tell you about that expression. You've seen it in the movies."

Critic Rex Reed summed up his feelings about Judy: "We loved her when she was happy and we loved her when she was blue and most of the time she was both. Nobody who ever saw her or listened to her records ever thought she needed a last name. It was always *Judy*."

E. Y. Harburg is a name not known to many people. He was the lyricist for "Over the Rainbow" and some of Judy's other well-known songs. He knew her and her life and, perhaps, her soul. "There was never a real world for Judy Garland," he said. "It was a phony world right from the word 'go,' when her parents got her into vaudeville at the age of four to sing 'Jingle Bells.' From there on, this little kid was exploited because she had a personality, a little voice and a talent for the stage. She had no childhood. And then, at the age of fourteen she had a bang-up voice. Her voice, I think, was one of the greatest in the first part of our century. She went right through bone and flesh into the heart."

Liza learned Kay Thompson was back in New York from Rome and called her immediately. Thompson, one of Judy's closest friends, had seen her through many hard times while they both were at MGM and helped protect Judy during her occasional lesbian episodes, including one with Kay. Kay and Liza had not seen each other for eight years, and the timing of their reconnection was fortuitous even if motivated by the tragedy of Judy's death.

The first thing Kay said to Liza was: "I'm going to throw on a pair of slacks. I'll be right over. Let me tell you something before I hang up. She had one of the most wonderful lives anybody ever could ask for. She had everything she wanted. There was nothing, if she wanted it, she couldn't go after, no matter what her complaints and tragedies and all that."

Kay was Liza's godmother and now became her mentor, mother figure, and companion—a major force in Liza's life. Most agree Liza was depressed and bewildered about the death of her mother. She loved Judy and worried about her when she was alive, yet was also disgusted by her and competed with her for the attention of audiences. But she was determined to be as strong as she needed to be in this crisis. "I wasn't going to panic or run away from the truth," Liza said. "Instead, I just pulled myself together for the funeral."

In some way, Liza may have felt a deeply sublimated relief over her mother's death. Now, perhaps, Liza could be judged as Liza and not a pale imitation of the towering talent of Judy Garland. Perhaps there would be some peace in Liza's life without the irritating responsibility of caring for Judy. In a sad, perverse way, Judy's death set Liza free whether she wanted to admit it or not. Liza would never again be locked out of a home by her mother nor would she have to deal with a suicidal drug addict.

Kay's guidance was a blessing during this trauma because of the cruel criticism made about Liza's behavior at the time. It may be the death of Judy so troubled many of her fans they had to strike out at someone, and it didn't seem fair Judy should be gone and Liza still there. In any case, Liza's every statement and move were scrutinized and put in the worst light by some grieving Judy fans. There were those who saw evidence of Liza's glee in her mother's death, saw proof Liza was on drugs, believed Liza wasn't as classy a lady as Judy had been, and on and on.

In truth, Judy secretly was fed up with some of her doting fans' fantasies, which were more reflective of their own unfulfilled dreams than those of Judy. Making *The Wizard of Oz* had been a painful experience for Judy for many reasons. Judy would rather have forgotten it as just another movie, but the magic of the film captured the imagination and longing of America and enshrined—Judy might say imprisoned—her in the Land of Oz forever. Even today when some people hear Judy singing "Over the Rainbow," they are moved to tears. Judy's private assessment: "I've had rainbows up my ass."

Liza called Mickey in London and discovered he was such a wreck that she assured him she would take care of all the arrangements. Kay helped Liza with the funeral plans. They began by deciding the funeral should be at Frank Campbell's funeral home on the corner of Madison Avenue and Eighty-first Street because it was dignified and quiet. They talked with Judy's ex-husband Sid, who thought the services should be held in California, but Liza said no because Judy hated California and loved New York.

Just before one A.M., Kay and Liza were in deep, quiet mourning at Kennedy Airport as they met the TWA Star Stream carrying the still stunned Mickey Deans and Judy's plain brown coffin. Accompanying them was Rev. Peter Delaney, the priest who had married Mickey and Judy just months before. This same minister would officiate at Liza's third wedding ten years later.

Kay and Liza tried to make all the arrangements as much in keeping with Judy's wishes as they could. Judy told everyone she wanted to be cremated because she feared being buried in a box in the ground. Liza thought about it and even considered for a moment carrying Judy's ashes with her so she could throw them in the air wherever she traveled all over the world.

However, Mickey refused to let Judy be cremated and he was supported by ex-husband Sid Luft, who, when Liza told him that was her mother's wish, screamed, "God! No, you mustn't, no, you can't." Besides being horrified at the prospect, Sid insisted Lorna, sixteen, and Joey, fourteen, would be devastated.

Liza and Kay decided the solution was to place Judy's body in a white coffin, because the standard mahogany was too depressing, and put it in an above-ground mausoleum in Hartsdale, New York. For the public viewing, Liza had her makeup man Charles Schramm prepare the ninety-five-pound Judy. She was dressed in a high-necked, gray chiffon wedding dress and placed in a glass-top coffin. Liza insisted on the glass top to protect her mother's body from overzealous fans. The viewing room was draped with floral arrangements, and Liza asked that no one wear black but rather make the occasion a happy good-bye to a loved one.

Before the public showing, Liza went in to see her mother alone. As she looked at this legendary woman who had given her life, the tears welled and her throat tightened. She thought how tranquil and beautiful her mother looked. Little Dorothy from the Land of Oz was finally at peace.

Twenty thousand people showed up to pay their respects and 350 people attended the service presided over by Father Delaney. Mickey Dean was the only one of Judy's husbands to attend. Vincente was shooting *On a Clear Day You Can See Forever*, and no one was sure where the mysterious Sid Luft was. The stars present included Mickey Rooney, Lauren Bacall, Jack Benny, Sammy Davis Jr., New York Mayor John Lindsay, Otto Preminger, Burt Lancaster, Lana Turner, Freddie Bartholomew, Spyros Skouras, Pat Lawford, and Dean Martin.

James Mason, her costar in *A Star Is Born*, gave the eulogy: "I traveled in her orbit only for a little while, but it was an exciting while and one during which it seemed the joys in her life outbalanced the miseries. The little girl whom I knew had a little curl right in the middle of her forehead and, when she was good, she was not only very, very good, she was the most sympathetic, the funniest, the sharpest and the most stimulating woman I ever knew.

"She was a lady who gave so much and richly both to the vast audience whom she entertained and to the friends around her whom she loved that there was no currency in which to repay her. And she needed to be repaid, she needed devotion and love beyond the resources of any of us.

"The person who probably of all the world knew Judy best is her older daughter, Liza Minnelli. I am going to quote, with her permission, some words attributed to her in the English newspaper

I was reading three days ago. Her tribute to Judy was personal and moving."

Mason then read Liza's farewell to her mother: "'I wish you would mention the joy she had for life. That's what she gave me. If she was the tragic figure they say she was, I would be a wreck, wouldn't I? It was her love that carried her through everything. The middle of the road was never for her. It bored her. She wanted the pinnacle of excitement. If she was happy, she wasn't just happy. She was ecstatic. And, when she was sad, she was sadder than anyone. She lived eighty lives in one. And yet, I thought she would outlive us all. She was a great talent and for the rest of my life, I will be proud to be Judy Garland's daughter.'"

At the end of the eulogy everyone rose to sing. Kay and Liza insisted Judy's final good-bye be festive. Printed sheets of "The Battle Hymn of the Republic" were placed at each pew. Judy loved the song and sang it on her TV program when President Kennedy died. Liza and Kay thought Judy should be serenaded the same way.

Peter Allen remembered, "When it came to the chorus, 'Glory, Glory, Hallelujah!' Liza, Joey and Lorna who were standing in a row holding hands, started to crumble. In a second, there was Kay Thompson behind them, with her long thin arms around all three. She started stomping her feet in time to the music and said, 'Sing! God damn it!' and they sang. We all sang at the top of our voices."

The odd thing about both Mason's eulogy and Liza's statement to the press was there were no fond recollections of Judy as a spiritual person, a mother, or a friend. Liza said, "I wouldn't change a thing except maybe asking God to let me have my mother a little longer than He did. But, I have enough warm and wonderful memories of love and kindness and feeling from both my parents to keep me going the rest of my life."

Kay's calming cohesiveness continued after the close family members retired to Peter and Liza's Fifty-seventh Street apartment. As Peter recalled: "Kay Thompson was still holding everything together. She was just incredible. I mean later that night at the apartment she had everyone, Joey, Lorna, Liza, all around our piano teaching the Williams Brothers's parts to 'How Deep Is the Ocean.' She understood music was the only thing that would keep the family from falling apart."

Peter's own memory of Judy was poignant, and in its own way, unlike the more complex feelings many others had for her. "Judy was one of the first Americans I'd ever gotten to know," he remembered, "and she colored forever my view of American people. To me she was the epitome of everything good about this country. Warm, frank and funny, she possessed the spirit to win. Judy didn't win all the time, but she never stopped trying. I'll always remember our years together."

Afterward, a doctor gave Liza Valium to calm her nerves. Looking back, Liza believed that's when her own drug dependency started. Mickey Deans remembered how the day of the funeral ended: "Sleep deserted the rest of us (except for Joey)....We seemed isolated in our numbness....The tension was growing. The telephone rang. It was a friend of mine from New Jersey. 'Why don't you all come out here?' he suggested. 'May do you some good.' We went to a car-rental agency and hired a convertible. I drove, with Lorna in front with me and Peter and Bob in the back seat with Liza. We started up the East Side Highway and, all I can say is, despite the traffic, it seemed to all of us there was total silence and no world outside of ourselves. The sky was unbelievably high, brightened by a solitary shining star. Nobody spoke. In desperation I switched on the radio. All of a sudden, there was the sound of Judy's voice. I jumped, nearly losing control of the car, reacting with horror for Liza and Lorna.

"Judy was singing, 'The Man That Got Away.'

"It was as though she were here in the car with us. As though she was saying she'd always be with us. We were in another dimension. We seemed to be coming back to life. And we were finding unbelievable comfort....And then suddenly Liza, with her marvelous instinct for knowing, for being able to turn to something, cried out, 'Go, Mama, go!'"

Judy Garland was dead and it broke the world's heart.

11

Going on With Life

Yet another of those incredible incidents that dogged Liza whenever her mother was involved followed Judy into death: They couldn't bury her.

The crypt in which she was to be placed cost $3,000 and no one wanted to pay for it. Liza said Mickey Deans ought to pay, and Mickey said Liza ought to pay. None of the other ex-husbands or children or friends or studios wanted to get involved. So Judy lay in her white coffin in the basement of the mausoleum administration building for more than a year until November 4, 1970, when somebody—it was rumored to be Frank Sinatra—paid the $3,000 and Judy was put in her crypt.

As noted earlier, in one important area, Liza was not a clone of Judy. Liza realized she didn't know how to manage her money, so she hired a professional to do it. Judy neither recognized her financial inabilities nor did anything to correct them. It was not clear how deeply in debt Judy was when she died. She said just before she died she owed $4 million; others estimated the debt at a couple of hundred thousand.

In any case, some of her creditors assumed they would not be paid. But unknown to most people, after all the other estate matters were settled, Liza spent a good part of 1973 working the nightclubs of London with her cabaret act to settle her mother's debts. She understood the importance of paybacks whether they involved money, performances, or favors.

However, on the day after the funeral, Liza flew back to Boston to shoot *Tell Me That You Love Me, Junie Moon*. It was unpleasant because she was still coping with Judy's death and hated working for Otto Preminger, who proved to be a self-indulgent, arrogant boor even though he was a directing genius. Liza said the only thing she learned from the great director was never to make another movie with him. He offered her time off to mourn her mother, but Liza decided burying herself in work was the best therapy.

There were problems on the film with labor unions demanding more featherbedding and local authorities objecting to women getting naked in their cemetery. In one instance, a woman tried to sue Liza and the production company for dancing naked on her late husband's grave.

Liza responded heatedly, "I was not nude. I had the front part of a bathing suit pasted on top and bottom and they only shot my back, which is about as sexy as a dog. It was night and the shot was beautifully lit. Besides, if she only looked back on my life those past few months, she would have known I could not do anything like that."

To cap off the problems, after the film crew shifted location to Naples, Florida, in September, Liza was felled by another kidney stone attack and was rushed to the hospital. Kay Thompson remained with Liza as combination guardian, confidante, and advisor just as she did for Judy during the MGM years. To make it easier, she was given a supporting role in the film, that of the odd Miss Gregory. Liza was willing to talk to the press about her professional work, but not about herself and her personal life.

About working with Preminger, she said, "Otto's theory is the actor is hired to act and he must be ready at all times. He wants the work done immediately and perfectly. You get the impression with Otto you don't have time to ask questions and you come in and don't ask and, if you do it wrong, you get yelled at."

Judy's death forced Liza and Peter to think seriously about their lives singly and collectively. Liza was anxious to become Sally Bowles in the movie version of *Cabaret* because she knew it would be her signature role—just as Judy knew the same about the role of Dorothy in *The Wizard of Oz*. The two characters were totally different yet it was as if Liza and Judy were each fated to find a single role that would color their personas permanently. For Liza, Sally Bowles would be just as author Isherwood created her—wanton, wild, and sadly bohemian. Moreover, Liza knew she needed to make a musical and get past the comparison with her mother.

"I think," she said, "there had to come a time when I did a musical, so the public could make a *final* comparison and say, 'There she is in a musical movie and that's what her mom did. And she's holding her own!'"

At the same time, Judy's death made Peter turn more inward. He started to write what he regarded as songs of substance drawn from his life experiences and observations. The first was called "Six Thirty Sunday Morning," which he composed walking through Central Park on his way home after being out all night without Liza. The divergence of their two lives was obvious to those around them and to Liza and Peter themselves.

By December 1969, everybody—especially Liza and Peter— knew their marriage was over, but they didn't do anything about it immediately. For one thing, Liza's success fed the relationship's failure. Peter and Chris were growing more successful but still struggling to gain celebrity status, while Liza was acclaimed a star— particularly in cabarets and concert halls. She commanded $250,000 a film at a time when such a salary was considered a lot of money.

They separated during the holiday season though they didn't make a formal announcement of the split for several more months. Finally, in March or April 1970, Peter officially dissolved the two most important relationships in his life: his marriage to Liza and his professional partnership with Chris. Another important relationship had ended with Judy's death eight months earlier.

Liza didn't want to get a divorce immediately because it would mean Peter might be deported to Australia. Besides, Liza claimed the separation was temporary. "It was just due to the pressures of trying to be a Super-everything."

Peter agreed. "We separated so we will have something to put back together again—not to get a divorce. I love Liza and Liza and I are the only two people who have to know it or believe it."

Privately, Liza said: "I hated Peter's friends and he disliked mine. Marriage to Peter was miserable—horrible! When we got married we were equal in terms of career success. Then we started playing [the plot of] *A Star Is Born*. I went up and he went down. Peter almost broke up when I started making it big. As a matter of fact, the competition nearly killed us both. That's when I said, after Peter, I would never marry another entertainer. Ever, ever."

Peter, who eventually did become a successful entertainer, later said to talk about his marriage with Liza was boring and that he didn't care to do it. He never called her and she never called him. And they both liked it that way.

"I began to take my career really seriously the day Liza and I split," he declared. "Liza and I knew the marriage wasn't working— she was going off in one direction and I was going off in another. The day Liza left me, it was like a weight being lifted off my shoulders."

As it happened, the day Peter separated from Liza and Chris, he met comedian David Steinberg at one of Manhattan's clubs, Hippopotamus. Steinberg was impressed by Peter's music and asked him to open his comedy act a few weeks later at the Bitter End. Delighted with the opportunity, Peter began writing more songs for his new solo act. By June 24, 1970, when he opened for Steinberg at the small, intimate cafe, he had an appealing act that played well with the audience and club owner Paul Colby, who later booked Steinberg and Peter as a duo.

Chris and Liza sent encouraging telegrams. Chris said, "I know you'll be great tonight. Thinking of you, Love, Chris." Liza's read, "Dear Peter, All of my thoughts will be with you tonight. Be marvelous as always. Love, Liza."

Peter moved out of the Fifty-seventh Street apartment he

shared with Liza to a smaller, more appropriate place on Bedford Street in the Village. In moving, he left behind the chic, shallow crowd to which Liza belonged and began making new friends more in tune with his thinking and sexual inclinations. He was plumbing a more intimate self than he had for the Playboy clubs or the Miami–Las Vegas circuit. To put groceries on the table while he found his inner self, Peter worked for Metromedia Records writing songs for Bobby Sherman. Liza was also getting on with her career. She finished *Junie Moon* and returned to the Manhattan cabarets and nightclubs where she made audiences cheer.

Meanwhile, twenty-four-year-old Liza lapsed into the kind of romantic marathons for which she would soon become famous—or infamous—with a variety of lovers picked up in a variety of places. There was French heartthrob Charles Aznavour, playboy Baron Alexis de Redé, French film romantics, Jean-Pierre Cassel and Jean-Claude Brialy, and Rex Kramer, an Arkansas native she met in Houston in November 1969, six months before she and Peter officially separated. Kramer was part of the musical group Bojangles.

Rex seemed willing to hang around and would bring Liza to visit his family in rural Smackover, Arkansas. She signed a deal to have Bojangles play as her backup and they appeared together at the Empire Room of the Waldorf in early 1970.

Reviewer John Wilson for the *New York Times* considered them a hard act in a tough venue: "The audiences she is facing twice a night have been trying to eat or drink in a setting that catches the essence of the Times Square subway station at 5 P.M.—tables sardine-packed, a yammer of high-pitched voices ricocheting off the walls....When Miss Minnelli comes on, the subway ambiance changes to Fillmore East....[At the end of her act] suddenly she dashes offstage to return riding a mobile platform with a four-piece rock group, the Bojangles, in full cry. She belts, she prances, she postures, leaps in and out of the arms of the four Bojangles in a lavish display of exuberant energy."

Clearly, during those days Liza was having a good time. She

and Rex were in love and very physical about it in public, to the amazement of those around them. The only catch: Rex was married.

Of course, Liza was also married, although it might have been hard to detect given the different lives she and Peter were living at this point. Peter was writing a rock opera called *Soon* that opened on Broadway in December 1970. *Soon* was Richard Gere's acting debut, and Peter took credit for advising Gere to get out of hippie clothes and into tight jeans and T-shirts.

Soon turned out to be a flop, but Peter made friends with Joe and Leslie Butler, who owned a small bar and restaurant called the Talkhouse, and Peter agreed to appear there. After he started performing again, Peter came to realize his relationships with Judy and Liza distracted him from finding his own musical roots. The Talkhouse was a perfect place for him to perform because he felt good with an intimate crowd of fewer than one hundred people instead of the huge cabaret circuit crowd.

After playing at the Talkhouse for a time, Peter took a break and went on vacation to Australia with his mother and sister. The trip home revitalized him and he returned to America energized with renewed confidence. He also realized he would have to do something about his estranged wife and their strained and strange marriage. He turned to his music and wrote "Harbour," which was his way of saying good-bye to Liza.

In addition to her love affair with Rex Kramer, the early months of 1970 were filled with exciting career opportunities for Liza. She got movie offers, television proposals, and, best of all, the nomination for Best Actress of 1969 by the Academy of Motion Picture Arts and Sciences for her work in *The Sterile Cuckoo*. But the biggest emotional rush came in May 1970, at the Cannes Film Festival. There she learned *Cabaret* would be shot in Germany later in the year and the part of Sally was hers. She would be paid $250,000.

The other person who was ecstatic about making the film was director Bob Fosse, one of the premiere choreographers of his day, who would play an important role in Liza's professional and personal life. Just as *Cabaret* would become a signature role for Liza and a landmark in her career, the film would be responsible for Fosse's professional resurrection. He and Liza both had a lot riding on *Cabaret*.

Fosse was stagestruck at a very early age. Born in Chicago June 23, 1927, to Cyril and Sarah Stanton Fosse, he was drawn to two things all his life—theater and women. Both would be cruel, demanding, yet satisfying mistresses. He took dance classes at a young age. He loved ballet, tap, and acrobatic dance, and at age thirteen he joined Charles Grass as one of the Riff Brothers appearing at vaudeville shows, strip joints, and movie houses.

In 1945 Fosse joined the navy and toured the Pacific for two years doing shows for GIs before his discharge and moved to New York in 1947. There his exceptional dancing talent brought him a number of jobs in choruses, reviews, plays, TV, and stage shows. Starting in 1953 MGM gave him a contract to appear in musicals such as *Affairs of Dobie Gillis, Kiss Me Kate,* and *Give a Girl a Break,* and he began what would become a lifelong shuttle between Hollywood and Broadway. He didn't really like Hollywood, but he knew he would be seen by millions of people in the movies while Broadway was limited to audiences of a few thousand.

In 1954 at age twenty-seven he won his first Tony Award for choreographing the Broadway show *The Pajama Game.* Noted critic Walter Kerr wrote, "The dances by Bob Fosse...are fast, funny when they ought to be and neatly dovetailed into a hard-driving book."

Still, in Bob's mind, the big money and big fame were in Hollywood. Fortunately, women were in both places. His early marriage to Joan McCracken failed, but his second marriage on April 3, 1960, was to the woman who would remain in his life to the end, actress Gwen Verdon. He had countless affairs, but painful as it must have been for Gwen, it didn't change her devotion to him. Even after they separated, she was content to remain legally married to Fosse for years. He created many dances and productions just for Gwen, including *Redhead*, which became the hit of the 1959 Broadway season.

He played the lead in the play *Pal Joey* in 1961 and took charge of *How to Succeed in Business Without Really Trying*, which ran for 1,417 Broadway performances and won more Tonys than any musical in the history of the Broadway stage. Then he returned to movies to create a vehicle for Verdon that looked good in concept, but turned out to be a disaster, the film version of the Broadway hit *Sweet Charity*. Universal Studios forced Fosse to substitute Shirley MacLaine for Gwen in the title role, and it was all downhill from there.

"When I finished it," Fosse said later, "I thought it was very, very good. I guess I put too many cinematic tricks in it. I was trying to be kind of flashy. That's a pitfall on your first film. I don't know what went wrong. The trade papers predicted it would be the biggest moneymaker of all time. Suddenly, *Time* magazine whacked it, *Newsweek* whacked it. It just didn't do well and Universal undersold it."

At the time, there was a lot of turmoil at MCA/Universal which distracted attention from promoting and distributing the film. David Begelman, Fosse's agent at CMA, said, "The failure of *Sweet Charity* caused a rift at the highest echelons of MCA. There was a group of people who thought the company just didn't know how to make movies. They were making a lot of money in television, but they had gone for seven or eight years without any big success in feature films."

MCA had lost $80 million by producing a string of flops: *Thoroughly Modern Millie, The Loves of Isadora,* and now, *Sweet Charity*.

Fosse was in trouble in Hollywood. As he quickly learned, "I got so cold. No one called me. No one wanted anything to do with me." He was getting calls from Broadway, where they respected his ability to create and direct winning and profitable musicals, but those calls were not what Fosse wanted. Begelman understood Fosse thought himself a failure in the business in which he wanted to succeed. Fosse didn't want people to think he had to return to Broadway because he was a failure in Hollywood.

"It's a real comment on show business," Fosse said, reflecting on what happened to him because *Sweet Charity* flopped financially. "I was offered about 43 movies after the smash reviews in *Variety* and the *Hollywood Reporter,* but after business went down, nobody would talk to me. You've heard the story before, but I can testify to it."

Two pictures saved MCA/Universal and Bob Fosse. The movie everyone seemed to agree kept Universal in the movie business was *Airport,* which recouped the losses from the previous musical disasters.

The movie that saved Fosse's Hollywood career came to him by accident when he went to Neil and Joan Simon's Manhattan townhouse for dinner. Gwen stayed home because their marriage was crumbling, so it was a party of five with Hal Prince and his wife Judy as the other couple. Prince had just returned from Germany to Broadway and a Stephen Sondheim project that appealed to him more than his alternative—directing the movie version of Prince's stage production, *Cabaret.*

The idea the director's slot might be open for *Cabaret* excited Fosse. Prince told Fosse the producer was Cy Feuer, and Fosse arranged to lunch with his friend Feuer the next day. Feuer was a great admirer of Fosse's work, but he was faced with a serious problem. Filming *Cabaret* involved a lot of money and he needed to convince the Hollywood money people his personnel choices were right. He had already run into another problem because he was sold on Liza playing the lead. One reason Prince declined to direct the film, which he didn't tell Fosse, was he didn't want Liza as Sally Bowles. Prince thought Liza was too American and the Sally Bowles role must be acted, as it was onstage, by a British actress. But after Feuer saw Liza's act at the Olympia Theater in Paris, he was convinced Liza not only could play Sally Bowles, but she actually was Sally Bowles.

So Feuer told Fosse he had to tread softly so as not to scare away skittish financiers at Allied Artists and ABC Pictures. Neither spoke about the box-office failure of *Sweet Charity*. This concern was exacerbated by the fact that *Sweet Charity* was budgeted for $7 million and cost $10 million while the entire budget for *Cabaret* was only $3 million. The Hollywood people wanted an experienced director such as Joseph Mankiewicz, and Cy had to interview every reasonable choice. Nevertheless, Feuer convinced his backers Fosse should direct *Cabaret* because Feuer would keep tight financial control and Fosse was the best man for the musical numbers critical to the movie.

Much of the movie would be shot in Bavaria to save money and the composer and lyricist would be Liza's old buddies John Kander and Fred Ebb. The script was changed from the stage version but was still loosely based on Christopher Isherwood's work *Berlin Stories* and John van Druten's *I Am a Camera*.

So Fosse and Liza were thrown together to make *Cabaret*, the story of Sally Bowles, a British singer floating in the midst of the debauched Berlin nightclub scene of the 1930s as Hitler moved to power on the ruins of the collapsing Weimar Republic.

12

The Cabaret Life

T he news about *Cabaret* excited twenty-five-year-old Liza, but the exultation of May in Cannes was offset by the disappointment of her first American TV special in June 1970. The special seemed unfocused and failed to make the most of her talents as a concert performer. However, Vincente Minnelli, though not well, managed to see his daughter give a smashing performance at the Ambassador Hotel in Los Angeles. Her performance buoyed his spirits considerably. It was the second time that year he saw his daughter receive public accolades. The first occurred in April at the Academy Awards.

This happy event was followed by the July 1970 release of *Junie Moon,* then considered a critical question mark. Some critics praised the movie, Preminger, Liza, and others in the cast. *Newsweek* continued its attack. "How many times will the public want to see Pookie Adams?" asked the magazine's Paul Zimmerman. Ann Guardino in the *New York Daily News* praised her performance, "Liza rates an Oscar in this Four Star drama." *Newsday's* Joseph Gelmis assessed her work, "Liza Minnelli's struggle gives this film a perverse appeal both grotesque and very touching." Some observers worried the *Sterile Cuckoo* and *Junie Moon* roles were too dramatic and too arty for a supposedly upbeat and funny nightclub per-

119

former. They saw a typecasting in the two movies that put Liza in the wrong kind of role.

Even so, *Cabaret* overshadowed any other minor distress. Liza immersed herself not only in learning the Sally Bowles role, but in *becoming* Sally Bowles. She focused on the music and art of the era such as the compositions of Kurt Weill, the art of George Grosz, and the films of Elisabeth Berner. She studied Berlin in the 1930s, an era of wanton indulgence, despair over losing World War I, and anger at the inept Weimar Republic government that ruled Germany in the 1920s and early 1930s. The immoral excess of pre-World War II Berliners is the theme of *Cabaret*.

Cabaret juxtaposes the decadence of Berlin during this time and Sally Bowles, an oddball English girl in search of nirvana who comes to Berlin to be an actress. She quickly descends into the debauchery of the time, supporting herself by singing in a blue-lit subterranean cabaret and giving herself to easy sex. In one affair she becomes pregnant by a bisexual lover who volunteers to marry her, but she chooses abortion instead.

"It was so glamorous in Berlin then," Liza said. "The writers were in Paris, but the fun seekers were in Berlin and there was this insatiable quest for joy." Liza got into the mood of the part by wearing thrift shop clothes reflective of the period and feeling like Sally.

Her assessment of the character she played: "Sally is a girl who improvises her whole life and her fantasy of tomorrow is so strong she really can't take a good look at now." Some thought that was a pretty good description of Liza Minnelli at the time.

As usual, Liza's father helped her research the role and prepare for her transformation. For example, Liza was trying to get a picture in her head of exactly what Sally looked like because author Christopher Isherwood only provided a sketchy description. "When I told Daddy I was doing *Cabaret*," she said, "Daddy told me I should look special, but also like me."

Liza originally conceived of Sally having a Marlene Dietrich look, but her talk with her father and her review of the material he

Cabaret revisited: Liza in her signature *Cabaret* costume in her stage special, *Liza With a Z,* 1972. (Globe Photos)

(Above) Dancing in love: Desi Arnaz, Jr. with Liza in his arms on the dance floor, 1972. (Globe Photos)

(Left) Son of Tinman with daughter of Dorothy: Husband Jack Haley Jr. out with Liza, 1974. (Globe Photos)

(Opposite) Surprise! Surprise! A surprise birthday party for Liza in 1991 on her forty-fifth birthday. (Photo by Adam Scull, Globe Photos)

(Above) The sisters: Lorna Luft and Liza Minnelli together and smiling. (Photo by Ralph Dominguez, Globe Photos)

(Right) In the Studio 54 days: The late designer Halston with soulmate Liza in the days when Studio 54 was the main chic Manhattan hangout. (Globe Photos)

(Opposite) London AIDS Benefit: Liza singing at the Mercury AIDS concert tribute. (Alpha/Globe Photos)

Fun at a library benefit: Ben Vereen accompanies Liza to a benefit for the New York Public Library for the Performing Arts, 1993. (Photo by Stephen Trupp, Globe Photos)

White House dinner: Liza with boyfriend Billy Stritch attend 1995 state dinner in honor of the president of South Korea. (Photo by James M. Kelly, Globe Photos)

Singers helping singers: Liza attends preview performance of *Victor Victoria* for a Society of Singers benefit in 1995. (Photo by Henry McGee, Globe Photos)

dug out convinced her to create instead the pixie look with hat, halter top, bow tie, garters, and black net stockings that would become her *Cabaret* trademark. "The concept of having a definite look started when I told Daddy I was going to do *Cabaret*," she said. "He asked, 'What are you going to look like?' and I got a blank expression on my face and said, 'I don't know. What should I look like?' He answered, 'I don't know.' End of conversation. Then three days later I walked into his room and on his bed were books and pictures and things to help me."

Vincente also advised her to pay attention to how Fosse reacted and how she appeared in the dailies or rushes, showings of the film as it is shot every day. Vincente said she should decide if she was seeing herself or somebody else. If she was seeing somebody else, she was doing it right.

Fosse reacted to Liza well and they strove to make the film as accurate a reflection of the times as possible, including a small but meaningful touch described by Liza. "We wanted to show the decadence and decay and perverse atmosphere of Berlin," she said. "We even used real drag queens! And the women extras hated us because they had to grow hair under their arms. When we finished shooting, we gave a party and everyone presented them with razors and soap and they celebrated by shaving."

The shooting in Germany proved exciting if somewhat uncomfortable for Liza. She liked the crew, and Rex, who had left his wife back in March, joined her. But there was a lot of tension in Germany then. World War II had ended twenty-five years before, but the Germans around the film location didn't like the depiction of the Nazi era they wanted to forget or even deny.

Beyond that, Liza said, "In Hamburg we went to the dens of sin on the Reepersbahn where they still had semblances of cabarets going. There were lesbian fights in mud puddles on stage and pornographic shows in which the audiences were invited to participate. No wonder I was a bit uncomfortable the whole time we were there."

Soon Liza's attention was pleasurably captured by Desi Arnaz

Jr. They met at a party in June that the seventeen-year-old son of Lucille Ball and Desi Sr. attended as the date of Liza's friend, Gayle Martin, Dean's daughter. Desi was mentally added to Liza's list of possibles. Meanwhile, she occasionally slept with Peter—they were technically still married—and with Rex, who was also technically married to Margaret "Peggy" Louise Kulbeth.

It was all great fun until Peggy lost her sense of humor and talked with Texas lawyer Donald R. Royall. Royall said he thought Liza used her money, influence, and charisma to mesmerize that naive country boy and steal him away from patient, loyal, and loving Peggy. So on Peggy's behalf, Royall sued Liza for alienation of affection.

The press, of course, loved it. The *New York Post* called her a homewrecker, and Liza said some uncomplimentary things about her detractors. The lawyers in 1970 sought $556,352 in damages, and Liza, to avoid a messy, unpleasant public lawsuit, settled out of court in May 1972. Even after Peggy got the money, Rex wouldn't leave Liza.

"I knew Rex was only using me, but I worried about him," Liza declared. "I was afraid he might do something silly. He said he would only leave me if I was desperately in love with someone else."

Given Liza's track record, a new love affair would have been easy to arrange. In any case, Liza soon left Rex. Besides, Desi Arnaz Jr. was on her list.

13

1971—A Better Year

T he year 1971 looked better for Liza than the previous two years in a number of ways. First, her father's health was getting better after some heart problems. Second, she would play Sally in *Cabaret*. She continued concert and club dates and personal dates with men such as Baron Alexis de Redé, who was in her life once more in 1971. As the Oscar ceremony of April 7, 1971, approached, she asked her father to escort her. The delicious anticipation of this major event excited the twenty-five-year-old Liza.

Shortly before the Oscars, a moment of terror occurred when Liza impetuously hopped on a motorcycle with her dinner date, actor Tony Bill, and zipped down Sunset Boulevard. She ended up in an ambulance speeding to a hospital with a broken shoulder and tooth, kidney damage, and a messed up face requiring twenty-nine stitches and the real-life services of Charles Schramm, her makeup artist on *Junie Moon*.

A few weeks later, Schramm performed his sorcery on her face just before the Academy Awards and made her look grand on the outside even though she was a wreck on the inside. Onstage they announced the nominees for Best Actress: Genevieve Bujold for *Anne of the Thousand Days*, Jane Fonda for *They Shoot Horses, Don't They?*, Jean Simmons for *The Happy Ending*, Maggie Smith for *The Prime of Miss Jean Brodie,* and, Liza for *The Sterile Cuckoo*.

After the envelope was ripped open, the winner was announced as Maggie Smith for *The Prime of Miss Jean Brodie.* It was a disappointment in the barnlike Dorothy Chandler Pavilion in the Los Angeles Music Center, but Liza took the decision in good grace—perhaps because she was on prescribed tranquilizers just as she was during her mother's funeral. She was still flattered to be nominated and her father was understandably proud. The tranquilizers would become a problem in time because Liza is sensitive to drugs and small doses have a greater effect on her than on the average person.

On the day following the Oscar ceremony, Liza formally announced to the press her marriage to Peter Allen was over. Around the same time a similar announcement occurred regarding her father's marriage to Denise while he was away from Hollywood directing *On a Clear Day You Can See Forever*. Budgeted for $20 million by Paramount; as previously noted, it was the most expensive musical he ever directed.

Vincente had begun hearing rumors about Denise seeing other men. A gossip columnist published the rumors, which so troubled Vincente he called Denise and asked her point-blank about it. She dismissed the rumors out of hand saying, "Don't worry about it. It's nothing."

As Vincente would relate later: "When I returned to California, I learned otherwise. Denise informed me she didn't know if she wanted to stay married to me. It was a great shock. We'd grown apart and I wasn't even aware of it. Until that time, she'd been a marvelous wife who'd made a very happy life for me. But if this was what she wanted, I wouldn't stand in her way. It took her some time to make up her mind, but Denise eventually decided we would divorce and she would marry another man. The divorce was granted [in] August 1971, and I was now a three-time loser and not sure I'd ever marry again."

He began seeing Lee Anderson, a British publicist who had previously been married to a French millionaire and an American cattle trader. He said, "Her warmth and companionship have meant a great deal to me." In time, she would become the fourth Mrs. Minnelli.

In September 1971, fifteen months after she saw Desi Arnaz Jr. at the party, twenty-six-year-old Liza ran into him again when he came backstage after her concert at the Greek Theater in Griffith Park, Los Angeles. Immediately, nineteen-year-old Arnaz began pursuing Liza as she played club dates in Las Vegas and Lake Tahoe. He was considered the hottest stud in Hollywood, having chased all sorts of women and sired Patty Duke's son while she was twenty-five and married to someone else. At the time, Desi was seventeen and single. He began proposing to Liza from the start and they even exchanged rings—but she was still technically married to Peter.

Then she raced off to Paris for repeat hit performances at the Olympia and in Baron de Redé's bed. Liza was a one-woman sexual revolution. The ever vigilant press discovered the Minnelli–Arnaz romance and followed them everywhere, publishing story after story about the golden children of movie stars in a wonderful romance that placed them in trysts at the Arnaz family beach house in Del Mar, California.

Liza was having fun confusing the press by describing Desi as her fiancé one minute and too young for her the next. She would sometimes dismiss their seven-year age difference as immaterial. "Desi is really much older than his age. He understands my need for calmness. He knows I hate abrupt changes of emotion."

And she felt the same way about her rendezvous with de Redé when she ran off to Paris. "When I was with him," Liza would say of the Baron, "I was in the most relaxed atmosphere I had ever been in. But my God! Our relationship was not as serious as all those people made it sound."

When she returned from Paris and the Baron, Desi was waiting and saying such things to the press as: "I just want everyone to know Liza and I are deeply in love. We feel we've been married all our lives and it would be wonderful if she had my baby. I want her to have my baby—I want her to have *all* my children—and I don't care if we're married or not! Just the picture of Liza pregnant with my child gives me goose pimples."

Getting married at that moment in 1972 wouldn't work because Liza was still married to Peter.

And there was the Lucy problem. Lucy was crazy about Liza. But what Lucy didn't love was the idea of Liza and Desi running around acting married and going into the baby business before actual nuptials. Desi would say: "Liza and I don't see any need for marriage. We don't need that jazz. We're not going to be bound by that trap—if we fall out of love, we're going to go our own ways. Plain and simple, no bickering, no ugly proceedings. Marriage is unrealistic. They expect you to devote a whole life unselfishly to one person."

Desi's statement must have reassured the woman he wanted to bear all his children that if things got difficult he'd be gone, no bickering and no ugly proceedings.

Then Desi bumped into Mama and that spawned another juvenile statement. "Mother doesn't want Liza and me living out of wedlock and she cringes at the idea of our having a child out of wedlock. It's a struggle between what we want and what Mother wants. We don't know what to do—please ourselves or please Mother."

Rarely has a child been so anticipated as Desiderio Alberto Arnaz IV. His parents were the first family of television and the most beloved couple in America, Lucille Ball and Desi Arnaz III, more commonly known as Lucy and Ricky Ricardo on the popular *I Love Lucy* series. When Lucy became pregnant with Desi Jr. during the show's second season, it sent Desilu Productions (Lucy and Desi's company) and the entire CBS network into an uproar. They were faced with the choice of canceling one of the most popular shows of all time or becoming the first network to admit there was such a thing as sex by airing a show featuring a pregnant woman—a major taboo at the time. Under pressure from Lucy, the decision was made that Lucy and Ricky would have a baby in their show.

Great pains were taken to avoid offending anyone, with various clergymen being consulted, none of whom found the idea of a married woman getting pregnant on TV offensive. The censors cringed, but all they could do was ban the actual word *pregnant.* So Lucy was never "pregnant" on the show—she was just "expecting."

The whole season was planned around the pregnancy, culminating with Lucy giving birth during the January 19, 1953, show. Care was taken to air this episode as close as possible to the time of the actual birth. The promotion experts at Desilu and CBS were aided by the fact Lucy had already given birth to one child, Lucie Arnaz, three years earlier by cesarean section. That meant she would have to have cesarean delivery of this new child as well, which gave the network executives better control on scheduling the climactic episode.

A media blitz and huge promotion campaign took place with contests for viewers to guess the exact time and date of the birth and the sex of the child—even though the show's writers decided four months before Desi Jr.'s birth the Ricardos were going to have a boy. Every precaution was taken to ensure no one outside those involved with the production—not even President-elect Dwight D. Eisenhower—would find out the child's sex before the program was broadcast. On January 19, 1953, at eight P.M., more than 117 million people—71.7 percent of all the possible viewers in America—were glued to their sets to witness the birth of "Little Ricky."

That episode remains the most-watched television program in history. To put it into perspective, the next day's telecast of President Eisenhower's inauguration, only the second inauguration to be televised, scored four full rating points lower with 67.7 percent of viewers.

The timing of Desi Jr.'s birth and the television birth of Little Ricky were only ten hours apart, with the actual birth occurring first. When Desi Sr. heard it was a boy, he said, "That's Lucy for you. Always does her best to cooperate." Head writer Jess Oppenheimer, when he heard Lucy followed the script, wrote, "Terrific. That makes me the greatest writer in the world. Tell Lucy she can take the rest of the day off." If Desi Sr. and Oppenheimer were pleased, the public was ecstatic. The Arnazes were flooded with so much mail—27,863 cards and letters, 3,154 telegrams, and 638 packages—they hired four extra secretaries to handle it.

Naturally, all the hype sold millions of dollars' worth of merchandise. Desi Sr.'s song, "There's a Brand New Baby at Our House," zoomed to the top of the *Billboard* record charts. The song was originally written eighteen months earlier in honor of Lucie Arnaz, but no one seemed to care because it was making money.

Desi Jr. became America's youngest celebrity. He was a television star without having appeared on television—the infant Little Ricky was played by James Ganzer. And Desi Jr. appeared on the cover of the premier issue of the magazine that would become the most popular in the world, *TV Guide*.

This was the climate in which Desi Jr. would grow up. As a child, he was closely associated with the Little Ricky character, and in real life, Desi became close friends with Richard Keith, actually Keith Thibodeaux of Lafayette, Louisiana, who played Little Ricky on the show.

In a bizarre psychological situation, Desi wanted to become just like the boy who became him. When Little Ricky learned to play drums on the show, Desi wanted to play drums, and when Desi Jr. was three, his father bought him his first drum set. In 1957, when he was four, Desi and his sister made their acting debut on the final half-hour episode of *I Love Lucy*.

Since they were old enough to talk, they had been pestering their parents to have them on the show. When Desi Sr. developed diverticulitis and was forced to give up the strenuous pace of the weekly program, they got their chance as extras in a crowd scene. Lucy and Desi Sr. encouraged their children's early performing attempts.

Lucy would say: "The children used to study everything we did on the program. They'd look at the clock and say, 'They're on again' and rush to the TV. After it was over, they'd get up and do the whole thing, word for word. They did the songs, the dances and we loved it and encouraged it not just to prepare them for show business, but to teach them to express themselves. We built a little theater for them out in the garage where they put on shows with their friends."

Lucy was always the disciplinarian. She also acted as the main protector of her children. She hovered, worried, and as her daughter Lucie would say, was a complete control freak who needed to be in charge all the time.

Desi Jr. wasn't quite as tough on Mom. "My sister and I came along pretty late in my mother's life, so when we arrived it was like a miracle to her. I think this increased her normal protective instinct about a thousand percent to the point where it was almost like a living thing within her."

This insightful assessment of his mother was certainly a lot more rational than anything he would say about his relationship with Liza. Lucy and Desi Sr. divorced for the second and final time—the first was in 1944 before either child was born—in 1960 when Desi Jr. was seven and Lucie nine. It wasn't a happy time. In the divorce, Lucy cited Desi's "propensity for irrational urges" and his propensity for natural urges that turned into frequent philandering. Lucy got the divorce and custody of the children and was determined to continue their strict upbringing.

Lucie remembered: "Mom was very strict about everything. She drilled manners into us, insisted we show respect to our elders and taught us words can hurt. When we did something she didn't approve of, we were grounded and sent to our rooms. My mother must be the all-time champion grounder. You could say I spent two years of my childhood in solitary!"

Desi Jr. had a rough time living with his mother and sister because, said one observer, Lucy would take out her frustrations with her ex-husband on him. She labeled him a bad boy early on, just as she labeled his father. Lucy blamed him for things that went wrong in the household or in her life, and he soon reacted by playing the role into which she cast him.

Lucie joined with her mother to pick on her younger brother, and even though she claims to have been taught by her mother words hurt—or perhaps because she was taught they hurt—Lucie used a lot of hurtful words against her brother. She ridiculed his baby chubbiness, calling him "Blubberbags," and did destructive things like breaking his drums. In 1961 the anxiety lessened when Lucy married comedian Gary Morton, who became a buffer among the feuding parties.

Aside from the show business childhoods they shared, Desi Jr. and Liza also shared musical backgrounds.

At twelve, Desi joined two guitar-playing friends, thirteen-year-old Dino Martin (Dean Martin's son) and fourteen-year-old Bill Hinsche to form Dino, Desi, and Billy, a group that originally played for its own amusement. Then Frank Sinatra heard the trio and signed them to his Reprise Records label and the group took off. They had a huge hit with "I'm a Fool" and appeared on *The Dean Martin Show, The Ed Sullivan Show,* and *Hollywood Palace* for $4,000 an appearance. They went on to form their own music publishing company and began touring, with mobs of adoring teen girls in their wake everywhere they went.

In 1968, by the time Desi was fifteen and a half, his rock career had ended, but he and his sister continued to pal around with some very unsavory types. Their schoolwork deteriorated, they seemed headed for trouble, and Lucy decided they needed closer supervision. She hired them to play her children Kim and Craig on her new TV series, *Here's Lucy.*

Ever the professional, she paid them scale and, as Lucie recalled, "Mom told us straight out if we weren't good enough, we wouldn't be on a second season. She said she'd find a way to write us out of the show and she really meant it."

The two were allowed to drop out of school—taking them away from some of the kids Lucy didn't want them to be with—and were given a private tutor. The show didn't do well, critics called the kids "totally talentless," and things got worse at home because now mom was both the tough boss at work and the rigid disciplinarian at home.

Desi remembered: "Lucie and I had two different relationships with my mother: parent-child at home and employer-employee at the studio. Mom would treat us—rightfully so—as cast members at work, but we would still take things personally that probably weren't intended that way. When most people are hassled at work, they can blow off steam when they get home. But it didn't work for us."

So the two children lived for the weekend when they could escape their mother and stay with Desi Sr. and his wife Edie on their ranch. This caused even more friction in their relationship with Lucy, who resented having to be the bad guy while Desi Sr. got to have all the fun.

In July 1969, the month after Liza lost her mother, Lucie turned eighteen and left home, leaving Desi Jr. alone to deal with their mother. To escape, he turned to liquor and drugs. Soon he was suffering headaches and depression as well as experiencing sharp fluctuations in his weight. Beyond that, he had serious coordination problems affecting his work to the point he finally appealed to his mother for help.

Lucy immediately checked him into a detoxification clinic, which helped only while long as he was there. When he got out, he was drinking again, playing the big man around town, and establishing himself as a ladies' man like his father. He had numerous affairs facilitated by his status as the son of two big stars and as an erstwhile rock star and short-term TV actor. Then in early 1970, Patty Duke, the former child star and Oscar winner for *The Miracle Worker,* gave birth to his son.

Though Desi Sr., Edie, Lucie, and Gary Morton all visited Patty and the baby in the hospital, Lucy remained conspicuously absent. Although she did finally consent to see the child and even changed its diapers, she never acknowledged he might be her grandson.

Two years later, in late 1971, Desi's relationship with Patty ended and he began seeing another Hollywood legend, Liza Minnelli.

Cabaret was edited and due for release a year after filming was begun. The premiere date was February 13, 1972, at the Ziegfeld Theater in New York, but the excitement had already begun to circulate throughout media and show biz channels. *Cabaret* was proclaimed a film to see, and Liza was sensational beyond belief. *Cabaret* was the first mass audience performance by Liza since her mother's death freed her to be herself. Moreover, *Cabaret* was a vehicle that was strictly Liza. Judy could not have played Sally Bowles because she was etched in the public mind as lovable, innocent Dorothy from Kansas with her dog Toto. She could never have portrayed the sexual explorer and nightclub singer in black garter belt, net stockings, and heels.

There were a few detractors, but Roger Ebert of the *Chicago Sun-Times* reflected the main reaction to Liza in *Cabaret*: "Sally is brought magnificently to the screen by Liza Minnelli, who plays her as a girl who bought what the cabaret is selling. To her, the point is to laugh and sing and live forever in the moment. To refuse to take things seriously—even Nazism—and to relate with people only up to a certain point. She is capable of warmth and emotion, but a lot of it is theatrical, and when the chips are down she's as decadent as the 'daringly decadent!' dark fingernail polish she flaunts. Liza Minnelli plays Sally Bowles so well and full it doesn't matter how well she sings and dances, if you see what I mean."

Rex Reed was ecstatic and wrote in the *New York Daily News*, "*Cabaret* is dazzling! Sound the trumpets! *Cabaret* strikes gold! It's a cause for rejoicing. Liza Minnelli defines the word 'star'! She has her own inner radiance and the built-in charisma of her mother's own heart-rending magic and that's good enough for me!"

Some critics complained Liza's performance was beyond the story and the movie and too good for either of them. Ironically, Joseph Gelmis, the *Newsweek* reviewer, said what probably pleased Liza most, given her constant struggle to become Liza. "You will not have to make any allowances for her overpowering ways. She is what she is and you either like her or you don't." She made the covers of both *Newsweek* and *Time*.

The movie also returned about $4 for every dollar spent and that's what matters most in Hollywood. It cost $4.25 million to produce *Cabaret* and the movie initially returned more than $18 million, with more due from video rentals in years to come. *Cabaret* was also a financial success for Liza because her standard fee of $250,000 a picture went significantly higher—although Liza was not as concerned with money as with finding an acceptable vehicle for her talents. She had rejected sure financial successes in the past and opted for what instinct told her was the best role at the time.

The success of *Cabaret* made it possible for Liza to be more selective in what she would do. Liza rejected several lucrative offers that came as a result of *Cabaret*. At this point in her career—and more important, in her life—she wanted to do the thing she had dreamed of for twenty years since she first rode the camera boom at MGM watching her father direct movies.

Zsa Zsa Gabor remembered those days when she was acting on the MGM lot. "We would film at MGM and I would look up at the boom and see this tiny little girl with enormous brown eyes staring down at me. That was Liza."

She wanted to make a movie with her father, a sentimental desire given his recent heart problems and his age. For the rest of 1972, they both looked for the right movie.

Vincente had made *On a Clear Day You Can See Forever* the year before and the movie hadn't done well even though it starred Barbra Streisand. Critics said it should have been called *On A Clear Day You Shouldn't See This—Ever.* Unfortunately, Vincente's stock with the Hollywood gurus was slipping.

In the 1960s there was a considerable change in the mood of the country with demonstrations and the rise of the irreverent youth culture. The classic MGM-style musical wasn't as popular as it had been and films needed to have meaning to the counterculture. The male lead in *Clear Day* was offered to Richard Harris, Frank Sinatra, and Gregory Peck, and all turned it down. There was a three-year break between the play becoming a hit on Broadway and Paramount bringing it to the screen. Vincente hadn't been on a sound stage in five years or made a musical in a decade. After filming began January 6, 1969, he endured the breakup of his third marriage when he discovered Denise was having an affair. In addition, his ex-wife Judy died during the making of the film.

In the end, *On a Clear Day* was, as Vincente himself assessed it, "not my greatest musical success, but neither was it Paramount's greatest musical failure." It made respectable money at the box office but not enough to excite the bean counters. Ironically, the movie became an important picture because it promoted the career of an actor one professional observer characterized as "an obscure and suitable unconventional actor, then a second-billed biker, acid-tripper, and general purpose maniac in Roger Corman drive-in movies." His name was Jack Nicholson and his next movie was *Easy Rider*.

In spite of all the downsides to *On a Clear Day*, Arthur Knight, writing in the *Saturday Review*, spoke highly of Vincente's direction. "What Minnelli does so well is to search out the essential qualities of his star performers, to frame them in ways that heighten the intimacy between them and the audiences and to surround them with an aura of glamour that makes them at once larger than life and very real."

So with that film behind him, father and daughter began to actively search for a suitable vehicle for their joint production. There were many things that would make this early 1970s project difficult to bring to fruition. For one, *On a Clear Day*'s weak showing hurt Vincente's bankability as a director. And he was sixty-six and, some thought, out of date. While he looked for the suitable film project, he collaborated with ghostwriter Hector Arce in writing his autobiography, *I Remember It Well*, published in 1974 by Angus and Robertson of London.

If Liza and Vincente had trouble settling on the right film to make together, Liza did find the right television special to do. It was two years since her first, disappointing TV special, which suffered from lack of focus. This time the program would focus on twenty-seven-year-old Liza and be made the way she wanted when it was taped for NBC at the Lyceum Theater in New York City on May 31, 1972. She was helped by two of her professional mentors, the ever-present Fred Ebb and Bob Fosse. They titled the show *Liza With a*

Z and taped it in front of a live audience. The result was electric compared with the special two years before. *Liza With a Z* aired soon after the hit run of *Cabaret* and certified her as a star.

The one-woman show was well-received and she won an Emmy for Most Outstanding Single Program in the Variety and Popular Music category. After the broadcast on September 10, *Variety* proclaimed: "Miss Minnelli has shown in the past she has great instincts for live performance and responds well to that form of entertainment.…Fosse and Ebb turned her more toward what seems to be her 'own way'…and her response was that of a great trouper on the brink of establishing her own distinctive mark in the show-biz world." To be recognized for being Liza and not Judy's daughter made Liza feel good.

Between the time the TV special was taped and aired, Liza was romantically involved with Desi Arnaz Jr. At the beginning of the summer of 1972, Liza traipsed after Desi to Japan where he was involved in a movie about Marco Polo. The media feeding frenzy began. Earlier, in May, Liza and Desi exchanged gold rings and made an official but ambiguous declaration of their engagement. Liza put it this way, "We won't get married for a while, but surely within the next few months."

Lucy was delighted since she knew and loved Liza and thought she would make a more suitable wife than Patty Duke. Lucy made her feelings clear as to what she wanted in a wife for her spoiled son. "Long before Judy died, Liza took the responsibility of raising her half sister and brother, so she tends to fuss over Desi like a mother hen. They're very good for each other, and I couldn't be happier."

Everyone was happy including Desi Sr., who announced on September 6, 1972, the two would marry in his Las Cruces, New Mexico, home. It would never happen. By the time of Desi's twentieth birthday on January 19, 1973, the wedding plans were over.

Unthwarted, ten days later twenty-seven-year-old Liza connected with the son of another star from the previous generation, Eddie Albert. She met twenty-year-old Edward Albert at the

Golden Globe ceremony where both received awards—she for *Cabaret* and he for Most Promising Male Newcomer in *Butterflies Are Free*.

It was quite a time for Liza. In 1973 she swept up the Golden Globe for Best Actress in a Musical and the Academy Award for Best Actress—both for *Cabaret*. Later in the year, she took home an Emmy for *Liza With a Z*. And she finished the year with Edward Albert, her new boyfriend du jour. It was a triumphant year by any standard and one even Judy could not have matched. Edward said he liked "older women" like Liza. "I believe, as a woman matures, she becomes more female." However, romance with Edward was over almost before it got started.

Soon after walking off the stage with an Oscar for *Cabaret*, Liza was walking onto the stage of the London Palladium to an adoring audience. It was a special place in her heart and in her life. Then on May 11, 1973, one year after becoming engaged to Desi, another man came into her life. He was mature, sophisticated, and world famous. He was forty-seven years old.

His name was Peter Sellers.

14

The Sellers Romance

It was quite simple and straightforward: Peter Sellers saw Liza and wanted her. Unlike some of the younger, more fragile lovers in Liza's life, Sellers knew women and what a man must do to take their breath away. That's what he did with Liza. For one, he attended her performances and was with her constantly. Sellers, an inveterate womanizer, was smitten. He said, "It was like an express train bearing down on me and I simply could not resist her."

Admittedly, Liza's past romantic record would hardly qualify her as a tough sell, but she swooned in the first few days Sellers came into her world. She felt the need to officially announce the end of one romance before launching a new one and did so May 22 in a short press conference at London's Savoy the day after she and Sellers were seen publicly cuddling at the Trattoo Restaurant.

"It's all very simple," she said. "My engagement—Desi's and my relationship—has been deteriorating for some time; pleasantly, luckily. We are no longer engaged. It's all called off."

It was exactly one year since Desi announced their engagement to the world. Liza's statement came as a shock to Desi, who heard about it on a Los Angeles television news show. "It all happened so fast. Liza and Peter dated two or three times," Desi said, "then she told me she loved him. I wish we hadn't broken up. I loved Liza. I still do."

Desi found immediate happiness in the arms of his new flame, actress Victoria Principal.

Hollywood reporter James Bacon, friends with almost everyone involved in this complicated affair, described a scene in Lucy's dressing room: "On the table before us was a newspaper with a front-page story announcing Liza and Desi Jr. had broken their torrid engagement. From every side Lucy was assailed to find out what happened. Officially, all she could say was she was surprised. But as an unofficial godfather of Desi Jr., I could be more blunt, 'It's the best thing that could have happened to him. I love Liza, but she wasn't right for Desi.' Lucy gave me a knowing look and said, 'From your ears to God's ears.' Her silence was eloquent; my impression was she agreed.

"Lucy was very fond of Liza and still is. She never once interfered with her son's tempestuous romance, even though Liza was seven years older than Desi. 'How could I interfere?' asked Lucy. 'When men are young, they like older women, when they are old they like young girls.'"

Meanwhile, Desi's film *Marco* was such a huge turkey it barely got released. In fact, some people claimed it wasn't released—it accidentally escaped. His next film, *Billy Two Hats* in 1974, didn't do much better. He turned his attention from films and Liza and toward Victoria and television.

"I fell in love with this man and I am pleased to say he fell in love with me," Liza announced about Peter Sellers. "We both believe in humor and in having good times." "We haven't found anything we disagree on," he echoed.

Liza made a whirlwind return to the States. Assisted by Kay Thompson, who always seemed to be there when she was needed, Liza quickly loaded her most important belongings into trunks and flew back to London. At the airport, Sellers was in disguise—something he did well and for a living—and met Liza and Kay. With that, Liza moved in with Sellers at 11 Eaton Mews North. Kay, who was now part of the traveling group that went everywhere Liza went, also moved in—something Sellers didn't like.

To prove he was vigorous and virile enough to keep up with his young love, Sellers would work all day on the set of his film *Soft Beds, Hard Battles*, then he and Liza would dance all night. He said, "At last I've found the sort of woman who'll take care of me." In actuality, he found the sort of woman who would exhaust him.

Roy Boulting, the director of *Soft Beds, Hard Battles*, said: "By this time the film studio was under daily siege [by the press trying to get stories about this hot new romance between Peter and Liza]. Moreover, the nightly courtship was showing up in Peter's work. Action needed to be taken. I went to Liza and said, 'Look, Peter has a heavy makeup call every day at 6:30 A.M. He can't go to Tramps every night with you, cover the disco scene before he goes to bed and snatch only an hour or two of sleep before reporting to the studio. He just can't cope, Liza. Nor can we.'"

"'Roy,' she said, 'it's not my fault. I do a pretty good spaghetti. I'd just love to stay home and feed Peter. It's him who wants to hit the town every night.'

"In desperation," Roy went on, "I said to John [one of his colleagues on the film production staff], 'Can we change the shooting schedule so as to give Peter a week or ten days to get this thing in perspective?'"

A new schedule was arranged and the couple went off, claiming they were madly in love. "We're as good as married," Liza said. But it simply was just too much for Sellers. The additional time he took with Liza proved to be the beginning of the end. One day Sellers confided to Boulting, "Liza and me. It's all over. We've split up."

The Sellers romance may have been the most inexplicably torrid affair of her life, a life filled with more romances than almost anyone can count. The official announcement came from Liza on June 19, 1973. "Yes, it is over. No, I have no regrets. How can I regret anything that was so happy?"

The affair lasted five weeks.

Liza shifted quarters back to her usual eighth-floor suite at the Savoy Hotel. The press first learned of the split when they saw Liza's piano being moved out of Sellers's apartment and returned to the Savoy.

The Minnelli–Sellers liaison was just too juicy for British newspaper editors to exercise tasteful restraint. The age difference undoubtedly caused friction, as suggested by Liza's comment at the time that she had become tired of Sellers's name, wealth, and fame.

Frederic Davies, the well-known British psychic, predicted the breakup before he ever met Liza and it immediately sent her to the phone to talk with him. Davies later reported Liza visited him. "She came to my home in mid-June," he said. "We talked a little and then I read the Tarot cards for her. I told Liza the romance was ill-fated. She became slightly emotional, dabbed at her eyes and confessed she was thinking of breaking off the romance. All I could tell her was it seemed to be the right course for her. And, three days later, on June 20, Liza publicly announced her romance with Peter Sellers was over."

Liza's explanation: "It's over, but Peter is marvelous and we had a lovely, lovely time. You sing another song and you find someone else. It's just like a marvelous circle. I think of people like—Oh, my God, there's so many people in the world to meet and to know and to ask."

Sellers kept another woman's personal belongings in his closet in a box labeled "Titi." It stood for Countess Christina "Titi" of Wachmeister—a twenty-five-year-old model and daughter of Sweden's ambassador to the United States. Sue Evans, his secretary, was in charge of hiding it whenever Liza was around. She was also responsible for making sure Liza's box was hidden whenever Titi visited.

Not exactly a match made in heaven.

15

The Winter Garden Show

I t was the end of summer and beginning of autumn in 1973 and twenty-seven-year-old Liza seemed to be traveling everywhere and was seen with everyone. She went to Italy to talk about doing a movie for Franco Zeffirelli. There, a little more than two weeks after splitting up with Peter Sellers, she became involved with actor Dyson Lovell. Then she was off to Paris to be in a fashion show and New York to plan more concerts, including one at the Winter Garden in Manhattan that would build on the successful format she used in her one-woman show at the London Palladium.

The concept was an expanded version of her nightclub act. She picked the Winter Garden to introduce the new and improved Liza because in show business circles it had the reputation of being the house of hits and mega-star performances. She got together with Fred Ebb, John Kander, Deanna Wenble (her secretary), and Art Azenzer (her accompanist) at Ebb's Central Park West apartment at the beginning of January 1974 to work out details and run through the concert. There would be no other stars and the only other performers would be her backup musicians and dancers. It was going to be Liza alone for an hour and a half.

It was a gutsy call on Liza's part because she would have to carry it off with ninety minutes of singing, dancing, and patter. She wanted this to be the way she did her first one-woman show on

Broadway. The production was appropriately named *Liza, Starring Liza Minnelli*. The printer didn't get it right and ran off the tickets with Minnelli misspelled "Minelli." What caused an even bigger stir in 1974 was the price of the tickets—a previously unheard of $15 each. Scalpers were getting ten times as much for them and even more.

Misspelling and high price aside, weeks before her landmark Winter Garden appearance, tickets went on sale for Liza's three-week stand at the 1,442-seat amphitheater. The entire run sold out in thirty-six hours.

Tom Buckley of the *New York Times* explained why: "The show is generating the kind of electricity in this energy-starved theater season that can't be provided by all the oil of Araby. For one thing, it will be Miss Minnelli's first appearance here since her Academy Award for *Cabaret* and her Emmy for her 1972 television special made her an international star. For another, she returns as a hometown girl who made good. Ever since she decided in her mid-teens to seek a career in the theater, the city has been her home. Most of her oldest and closest friends and advisors live here."

Liza confirmed Buckley's assessment when she responded, "It's a *terrific* city. It's still the Big Apple. I like it better every time I come back." She noted this time she could relax for two weeks after finishing her thirty-city national tour plus a week in Vegas and a TV special in England. She spent her time resting, shopping, and enjoying unhurried meals and visits to the theater. The major business she engaged in was to talk with director Zeffirelli about a movie he had in mind, but Liza was more likely, most people thought, to join another Italian director, Vincente Minnelli, in the father-daughter movie project they had wanted to make for such a long time.

On opening night at the Winter Garden, January 6, 1974, twenty-seven-year-old Liza and Fred Ebb went through the same pep talk they had had from the beginning of their association with Liza's first cabaret show at the Shoreham Hotel in 1965.

Ebb said, "What I always tell her is you can't presume on

audiences. You can't let yourself think success is your due; you've got to earn it; your energy level and your desire to please must always remain high."

Opening night ticketholders were rewarded with a Liza show that overwhelmed them. The curtains opened with a twenty-eight-piece orchestra under the direction of Jack French. Liza blasted the audience with her opening high-octane "Say Yes" number followed by a singing and dancing experience that delighted everyone.

The Winter Garden performance was a breathless display of Liza's versatility and revealed several aspects of her talent. For one, like her late mother she was obsessed with choreographing every movement, song, setting, step, and element of the performance. This attention to detail is critical in producing a quality performance that is consistent show after show. She also insisted on the best production people she could get and only those who understood her. At the Winter Garden she employed French as conductor and Marvin Hamlisch as musical coordinator. The show was written by Ebb, with lighting handled by Deanna Wenble and costuming by Nancy Barr. Most important, the show was directed by Bob Fosse, her director in *Cabaret*. She was dating Fosse at the time.

Generally, the reviewers loved Liza—the show and the performer—with Clive Barnes writing in the *New York Times*: "Liza makes it seem like summer again and in every respect, *Liza* is a winner. It is probably her nervousness, those stretched-out moments of the spirit, that makes Liza's performance so exciting. Her vitality is unusual. It is not the sheer powerhouse drive of some singers, but rather the result of some exciting internal tension. It is compulsive and, for all its ease, a little agonized. She has a voice that can purr, whisper, snarl and roar. Her ability to act in singing was suddenly once again made luminous. She reminded us this was not just a girl who could belt out 'Cabaret' to make juke-box bonanza, but also acted the closest thing to Isherwood's Sally Bowles seen on stage or screen. But why only three weeks, Miss Minnelli? Stay longer next time."

Douglas Watts, the reviewer for the *New York Daily News*,

mentioned a similarity to her mother's work, a comparison Liza hated: "Liza proves to be an engaging, but far from magnetic, entertainer. And, for whether or not she and her groomers care to admit it, the image of the plucky Judy Garland is never far off, particularly when, in a velvet suit with knee breeches and patent-leather pumps, Liza slams home with 'Mammy.' She unavoidably calls to mind Judy's 'Rock-a-bye Your Baby With a Dixie Melody.' Liza, even with all her tremendous energy and appeal, is not yet a Sinatra or Streisand."

In time Liza would regularly appear in concert with Sinatra and the late Sammy Davis Jr., and comparisons with Streisand didn't matter since Streisand was terrified of making public concert appearances such as Liza and Judy routinely made.

New York Post critic Anthony Mancini said, "Liza has a clarion voice and her songs urge us—against the odds—to drink long drafts of life. She carries it off because of her ability to create a bond of instant intimacy. She dances like a colt and most of the time is just Liza With a Z and alchemy."

While Liza was like her mother in performance, she was unlike her mother in that she avoided close personal contact with her fans. She did not want to touch or connect with fans crowding around the stage after a performance. Both mother and daughter were very private and introspective people, but Judy's fans would not know it and Liza's fans would. At the end of each Winter Garden show, Liza pulled back from any physical contact with the audience.

In one illustrative instance, Alan W. Petrucelli, a chronicler of Liza, described his meeting with her: "It was Christmastime 1970, and we were having dinner together at the Empire Room of Manhattan's Waldorf Astoria Hotel. Rather my parents and I [Petrucelli was thirteen at the time] were having dinner. Liza was performing. My mind never digested what we ate for dinner (I believe it was chicken divan). But I have never forgotten the dessert: two hours of sweat and silk, drama and dance, sequins and song. Liza live! Saturday, December 19, 1970, marked the first time I saw Liza in person. It would not be the last.

"After the show, I approached Liza for an autograph. A towel was wrapped around her neck to absorb the excess perspiration from her face. She was exhausted. She took one look at my outstretched hand, pen and paper and cried, *verbatim,* 'No, no, please! I can't!' It was the best turndown I ever received."

Clearly, Liza understands she must be onstage to be a star and must make certain public appearances and talk to some reporters— all part of the dues that have to be paid for the celebrity status and material rewards she enjoys. But personal contact with fans is not something she relishes.

As Liza said: "I'm a private person and I don't give a damn what people write about me. Don't get me wrong—I love gossip about other people's pasts. I just don't like talking about my own. People are always asking me, 'How was it?' What they can't get through their heads is the past is finished for me. I've lived it. So I cannot think why it should be so interesting."

Contrast that with the audience interplay of Judy Garland's tour of twelve cities that ended in Carnegie Hall April 23, 1961, with a sold-out house. Critic Judith Crist was awed by the experience: "I remember Leonard Bernstein, the tears running down his face, screaming [and] Hank Fonda 'Bravoing.' No one intended leaving the theater. It was absolute pandemonium. It ended and the *entire* audience…ran to the footlights with their arms in the air screaming 'Judy! Judy!' and she touched all the hands she could."

The audience was caught up in a shared emotion of adoration for this extraordinary talent whose genes, gratefully, were transmitted to Liza, then sixteen years old and in the front row with Lorna and baby Joey. Shana Alexander also described Judy's performance: "Judy Garland is not only the most electrifying entertainer to watch onstage since Al Jolson, she has moved beyond talent and beyond fame to become the rarest phenomenon in all show business. Part bluebird, part Phoenix, she is a legend in her own time."

That's what destiny also held for Liza. When she performed in the Winter Garden years later, the show was a smash, judging by the response of the public and the standing-room status of every performance. *Variety* called Liza: "Not just a song and dance girl but also an actress getting a lot of her effects facially and through body English, she has a piquant mixture of confidence and diffidence, of wham and subtlety. Everything hung together. The faithful were not disappointed. The squares gave in. The engineered hot-rod pace never slackened. It was show business at its professional best."

That judgment was echoed at the box office where an astonishing $413,815 gross was collected for the run of the show. In late January 1974 the show ended, and Liza's nightclub tour and romance with new lover Ben Vereen began.

16

1974—THE YEAR
OF BEN AND JACK

L iza and Ben Vereen first met May 30, 1972, in New York while Ben was playing the role of Judas in the hit Broadway musical *Jesus Christ Superstar*. Liza was in town to tape her TV special, *Liza With a Z*, for NBC. Ben said of their meeting, "Liza had just done *Cabaret* and I was doing *Jesus Christ* when I met her. She would drop by with Bob Fosse and she'd help me in my performance by giving me some great advice."

A year and a half later Liza was giving him advice about other things, too, and their romance started in earnest, although they initially kept it quiet. This may have been due to Ben being black and married, even though both would later say neither fact mattered.

By February it obviously didn't matter because they made *Newsweek* with a stunning photo by Francesco Scavullo. It showed a topless Liza being held from behind by a topless Ben with his arms around her breasts. The picture certainly let the world know about their quiet little romance.

"It was a great, fantastic photo," Ben said. "Liza was in front and I was embracing her. It was in the Robert Redford issue, but it was our inside picture that made the big, big sales. As a matter of fact, I still have the original photograph."

147

Ben Vereen began his career as a minister in training. Born in Miami, he grew up in the tough Bedford-Stuyvesant district of Brooklyn where his father worked in a paint factory and his mother was a theater wardrobe mistress. He attended the Pentecostal Theological Seminary in Manhattan, but his stay there didn't last long.

"The ministry was the only alternative for me to the ghetto," he said. "But, I was always being saved, getting on my knees and ridding myself of the demon." Later Ben would say he came to show business because it had things in common with preaching; it enabled him to reach out and move people.

Soon after the *Newsweek* photo appeared, Ben and Liza traveled to San Juan, Las Vegas, and Rio for Liza's scheduled shows. The two carried on in public, touching and kissing. They had a wonderful time in Rio, but that didn't keep Liza from trolling for other men and catching playboy Pedrinho Aquinaga, acclaimed the best-looking male in Brazil. There followed four blazing hot days of love culminating in the public announcement that they would marry and Liza would become a Brazilian housewife.

When Liza returned to the United States, she and her mentors were concerned that while she did well in nightclubs and concerts she hadn't made any movies for several years. Her explanation was forthright. "I wanted a certain kind of thing to do next; I didn't want to settle for less. So, I decided I'd just wait. I won't do films just for the sake of being in the movies. I'd rather perform in front of a live audience."

But she and her advisors were also concerned about the demographics of her live audiences—thirties and up. They thought they needed to tap into the youth market because young people spend more money on concerts and records, particularly singles, and Liza didn't have many successful singles. The trick was to attract the youth market without losing the audience Liza already had.

Consistent with catering to her existing audience, she made the usual appearances in 1974. In April she performed at the Academy Awards and in *Love From A to Z,* a Charles Aznavour TV special shot earlier in Great Britain. That month she also picked up a Tony Award for her Winter Garden show. The *New York Times* praised her appearance in the Aznavour special because she had toned down her act, become less strident, and "even shed that lurid Theda Bara eye soot."

Liza also appeared in several of the benefit shows that are a staple in every performer's schedule. In March she did a charity gig for actor Jim Stacy, a friend who tragically lost his arm and leg when the motorcycle he was riding was hit by a drunk driver. And she appeared with Carol Channing and Tony Bennett in *Jule's Friends at the Palace,* a salute to Jule Styne.

Continuing to think about the youth audience, as female performers have done since 1951, she accepted the Woman of the Year award from Harvard's Hasty Pudding Society. She delighted in the attention, riding in the parade in a 1940 Lincoln with the top down, cheered by fans and revelers.

Thinking more about tapping into the youth culture, Liza decided she needed a man with a woman's name, Alice Cooper. Cooper—whose real name is Vincent Damon Furnier—was the hottest stage star in the youth market, and Liza wanted to work with him on joint appearances and records for their mutual benefit. Liza tried adding appearances by Alice Cooper to her concerts, but the audience response was disappointing. Later she performed on one of Cooper's records, *Muscle of Love.* Unfortunately for Liza, the younger audiences didn't materialize.

Another project that did not end well for Liza, and a lot of other notable people, was an alleged investment scam known as Home-Stake. This was an oil-drilling tax shelter that collected about $100 million from celebrities such as Liza, Candice Bergen, Buddy Hackett, Oleg Cassini, and Senators Jacob Javitz and Ernest Hollings. It ended in bankruptcy.

What did lift Liza's spirits was a new lover. Another son of an older movie star, forty-one-year-old Jack Haley Jr. had the reputation of being a relentless ladies' man. But he and Liza had much in common. They were both children of Hollywood, New York, and the entertainment world and shared many of the same experiences. They were also both children of Oz.

Jack Jr. was born in Los Angeles October 25, 1933, and was surrounded by show business from the beginning. His father, Jack Haley Sr., was a distinguished stage and film actor even before his best-remembered role as the Tin Man in *The Wizard of Oz*. His mother, Florence McFadden Haley, was once a Ziegfeld girl and an Earl Carroll beauty. Jack's godparents were Fred and Portland Allen, while Mr. and Mrs. Ed Sullivan were his sister Gloria's. Jack Jr. first met Judy, the future mother of his unborn bride-to-be, when he was only six years old and a regular visitor to the *Oz* set at MGM.

According to Raymond Strait, author of *Hollywood's Children*, Jack Haley Jr. was different from a lot of tinseltown kids. "Unlike many of Hollywood's children," Strait wrote, "Jack Haley Jr. is secure about himself, his work and his place in the world. As a youngster growing up in the streets and hills of Beverly, he appears to have retained only the positive aspects of the celebrity carnival. Candid about himself, as well as his family, I seriously doubt there is a Haley 'closet.' Jack Haley Jr. is the contemporary filmmaker, not a neurotic misfit trying to escape the shadow of a father beside whom he stands quite tall and proud."

In 1973 Jack became director of creative affairs at MGM, where he tried to convince studio head Jim "the Smiling Cobra" Aubry to make a movie highlighting all the former MGM musicals for which the studio was famous. Aubry allowed him to do some preliminary work that Aubry showed MGM executives. They were wild about it and encouraged him to finish it. He did, but only by leaving his executive post at MGM to devote full time to the movie he entitled *That's Entertainment*. The result was the most dazzling, thoroughly enjoyable documentary on Hollywood musicals ever made. It earned Jack the nickname "The Wizard of Was."

Liza and Jack met in 1959 when Jack, then an officer in the air force commissioned to produce training films, was on leave and attended a birthday party for his friend George Hamilton. Liza, then fourteen, struck twenty-seven-year-old Jack as an interesting youngster. They spent most of the party talking.

While doing *That's Entertainment,* Jack renewed his acquaintance with Liza, who he had also seen at the 1974 Golden Globe Awards. The nice kid he met at George Hamilton's party had grown up! Liza, now a star in her own right, was narrating a segment of *That's Entertainment* devoted to her mother, the centerpiece of many important MGM musicals, including the studio's biggest money-makers. Jack and Liza were soon constant companions and a few weeks later announced their engagement. As entertainment reporter Hank Grant noted, "I believe every girl should be engaged to marry Jack Haley Jr. at least once in her lifetime."

Immediately after announcing the engagement, Liza said they would get married—unless they decided not to. Before the marriage could take place she had to divorce Peter Allen. Amidst the confusion, Liza and Jack sped to Europe for a vacation, which delighted fan magazines, tabloids, and gossip columnists. The daughter of America's sweetheart from the Land of Oz marrying the son of America's favorite Tin Man.

It didn't matter that Liza was twenty-eight and Jack forty. In Liza's view: "Jack was so full of life, he left all those youngsters around Hollywood at a standstill. I just knew marrying an older man would be the best thing I could do. Older men are more experienced in life and I felt Jack could give me security to start with. And his eyes—those wonderful blue eyes! I fell in love with those first! I could always tell he had something going on behind them."

Meanwhile, husband Peter Allen decided to file for divorce after a property settlement arrangement was worked out. Peter wasn't happy about getting the divorce or about being married but separated. Still, as he said later, "When you've been separated longer than you were married, it's time to get a divorce."

Liza decided it would be fun to live in Jack's Devlin Drive house in the Hollywood Hills, but she didn't count on the number of Hollywood ladies this would irritate, including some of her friends.

She quickly found out Jack's reputation was justified. "I had some very jealous ladies to deal with," she said. "I think they came out of the woodwork and they were all mad at me!"

As Liza put it, she and Jack were just having fun. "I'm married to my career. I have no time for marriage. Jack is merely a friend. Anyway, I'm still married to Peter Allen and that's where the matter rests."

During the interim while he and Liza were still married, Peter was building his new career. In 1973 he was invited to perform at Reno Sweeny, "the" nightclub in Manhattan with a loose dress code that permitted guests to show up in jeans, black tie, or anything in between. It was the sort of club Liza and her friends enjoyed and she showed up one night during Peter's engagement with Lorna and Ben Vereen. Peter and Liza were barely civil.

The following year Allen wrote the song, "I Honestly Love You," which became a hit for Olivia Newton-John. He also recorded his first album for A&M Records, *Continental American.* Ironically, another of Liza's lovers, Bob Fosse, used music from this album in his film *All That Jazz.* Peter was doing well professionally, but there was still someone he missed—the woman who turned his life around and opened up the future for him as no one else ever did. Her name was Judy. She was the object of his musical tribute when he wrote the song, "Quiet Please, There's a Lady on Stage."

Meanwhile, Liza and Jack were in New York where they saw Sammy Davis's new Broadway show. Afterward they attended a round of parties in Nice and Monaco, where they were guests of Prince Rainier and Princess Grace. Then Liza launched a tour starting with two weeks in Vegas at the Riviera Hotel. It was the same show she did at the Winter Garden and it sold out before she opened on July 10. *Variety* again praised the performance. "She has become the total mesmerizer, her performances moving to near perfection."

At the midnight show opening day, Liza announced she and Jack were engaged to be married. A New York court granted Peter a divorce the next day, July 24, 1974, on the grounds the couple had not lived together for the last four years of their seven-year marriage.

Liza recalled: "We were driving along Hollywood's Sunset Boulevard and he just said, 'Let's get married!' I said 'Okay.' It was as simple as that, but it wasn't impulsive. Both of us had been thinking about it. Both of us knew this was it."

Everyone seemed to approve except Jack's jilted lovers, women like Nancy Sinatra, Jill St. John, and Sue Lyon. Nancy was probably most disappointed since she and Jack were engaged in 1969 but never married. Vincente Minnelli approved enthusiastically, in contrast to his apprehension over the Peter Allen marriage.

Liza shared her desires with reporters: "I want a man who is gentle and kind and has a good sense of humor, is intelligent, fun to be with—somebody you'd like to spend your time with. If somebody loves you, they give you their name. It's about all they've got in the long run. I believe in tradition. I was born in tradition. My parents were very romantic. I got married [to Peter] as a girl and I never really understood the consequences of my actions. We were like two kids playing at life. I never once thought about children because I was one myself. Around the time I began to feel I was ready, it was too late."

Then Liza left to fulfill another demanding set of bookings: concerts in widely separated places such as Pennsylvania, Spain, Canada, Minnesota, Iowa, Indiana, and Ohio. After Liza's appearance on *The Tonight Show*—a month after they officially got engaged—Liza and Jack were married on September 15, 1974, in Montecito, a wealthy suburb of Santa Barbara. The ceremony was performed by Beverly Hills judge John Griffith. Their parents did not attend although Jack Sr. and Vincente were at an intimate reception at the elder Haley's home immediately after the ceremony.

Everyone was worried when Liza was an hour late for the ceremony, but she eventually arrived. Sammy Davis Jr. and his wife

Altovise served as best man and matron of honor. Liza's longtime musical mentor, Fred Ebb, gave the bride away. Sammy's reaction to his role: "I really feel like an uncle to that girl. I was best man because, after all, Jack and Liza are two of my best buddies."

Jack's wedding gift to his bride was a gold and diamond bracelet inscribed: "I offer you all my worldly goods, my name and my heart."

Liza wore a cheery yellow Halston pantsuit and yellow accessories, including a gold and diamond bracelet. Probably the most dramatic accessories were her Beth Levine shoes coated in thousands of red sequins, which reminded people of the magical ruby slippers from *The Wizard of Oz*.

The following evening, the newlyweds were feted at an exclusive guest party hosted by Sammy Davis Jr. and Vincente Minnelli at Ciro's nightclub on the Sunset Strip. The couple reveled in their celebrity friends and the posh club with its view of the city spread out below. The guest list included Elizabeth Taylor, Shirley MacLaine, Zsa Zsa Gabor, Johnny Carson, Rita Hayworth, rockers Alice Cooper and David Bowie, Fred Astaire, George Hamilton, and the Edgar Bergens. It was a night Hollywood would remember for a long time.

Liza's designer guru, Halston, attended under unusual circumstances. As he described his quick six-thousand-mile journey to make an appearance: "I just had enough time to get from the airport to the hotel, shower, shave, and put on my tuxedo. I left for New York on a 1 A.M. flight, but it was worth it. Liza's just like my kid sister."

A London honeymoon was the start of a marriage Jack, Liza, and all their friends hoped would last. Jack got a special wedding present a few hours before the ceremony when he learned he had been appointed president of 20th Century Fox's television division. He held the position until he resigned in 1976 to become an independent producer. But his new job would restrict his ability to travel with his wife, whose work took her all over the world.

And there were other early warning signs all might not be well. Rumors abounded that Jack and Liza's marriage was not what it seemed. According to reporter Barbara Grizutti Harrison of *Mc-Call's,* Liza saw Jack as a father figure. Harrison may have drawn that inference because Liza referred to Jack as "Daddy" and "Vincente." In any case, it is clear Liza perceived Jack as loving, protective, and calm, which may have been a relief after Peter Allen and his crowd.

17

Hell in Mexico, Heaven in Chicago

Liza's success in films was demonstrated by the four hundred or more scripts showered on her in the hope she would pick one and make it a hit movie. Finally, at the beginning of 1975, she chose *Lucky Lady*, which turned out to be another of those misnamed affairs. It was the story of Claire, a gin-runner's moll caught up in a dream of money that goes wrong. Once again, many people wondered whether Liza made the right choice even though the film costarred Burt Reynolds and Gene Hackman with Stanley Donen directing.

Liza's explanation: "I chose to do it because it was the first script since *Cabaret* I really liked and I must have read 400 scripts by then! It was also the first movie that featured two biggies with a woman in the middle. I would have done it for anything in the world!"

She was given top billing in a movie with two seasoned stars. It was planned as a comedy about Claire Dobie (Liza), a brassy-haired—actually the color was described as tangerine—singer down on her luck who falls in with two bootleggers during Prohibition. They make a fortune running whiskey from Mexico along the Baja California coast to the United States. The film was to be shot in Guaymas, a Mexican coastal town on the Gulf of

California. Comic stories, plays, and movies often thrive on confusion among the characters, and *Lucky Lady* had that right from the start of shooting in February 1975—except most of the confusion developed among the real-life players.

Fan magazines and tabloids have always fueled the assumption that when a film crew goes on location to some tropical or exotic clime everyone in the cast is in everyone else's bed and the costars are madly in love. Naturally, the press followed this pattern and instantly linked Burt Reynolds with Liza because Burt had just broken up with his longtime squeeze Dinah Shore. In fact, it was Liza's sister Lorna who was bedding Burt, but Liza didn't want the world to know so she simply denied the rumors. "I haven't slept with anyone but my husband since I got married," she said. She regularly phoned Haley in Hollywood, where Jack was reading the gossip and was not happy about it.

The producers were unhappy about *Lucky Lady* because shooting had taken twice as long as the three months originally scheduled. Part of this delay was due to rough winds and water which made it impossible to shoot the sailing footage they needed. Many people connected with *Lucky Lady* viewed the production as a mess and a rash of finger-pointing seized them. Liza said, "Guaymas is not 'sort of dreadful.' It was *truly* dreadful!" To ease her boredom, Jack flew down every weekend and showed movies with a small projector, using a suspended sheet as a screen.

The Mexicans preferred free-spending "yanquis" to the mostly British crew Stanley Donen hired. Later both Liza and Burt would severely criticize director Donen for miscasting and mismanaging the film. They were unaware the director was also getting calls from the studio people in Hollywood who saw the daily rushes and dictated changes, including changing the ending, which originally had Reynolds and Hackman killed by G-men.

The ending dictated by the studio was a tired shot of happy, rich, married Liza thinking back about the good old days. The studio executives, lead by production boss Alan Ladd Jr., son of the famous movie actor, tailored the final scene to please Midwest audiences who didn't want Hackman or Reynolds to die. It was, apparently, the *Smokey and the Bandit* syndrome in which Reynolds defies the law, gravity, policemen, reality, and good taste to survive for another day and another movie.

In keeping with the Hollywood mode, director Donen foolishly tried to please everyone. For example, Liza left the set before the final revised scenes could be shot and flew to Italy to make another film, *A Matter of Time.* To accommodate her, Donen and crew—Reynolds and Hackman included—flew to Italy to shoot the new ending. Liza did it, but she didn't like the new ending or the rest of the film.

"I was shocked and stunned by what Stanley did to the picture," she said. "It was not the same film I set out to make. The ending changed the whole tone of the picture—it was too light, without any real meaning. They cut out all the tender, meaningful scenes—all the film's guts—and now it's just as silly as an old *Road* picture with Crosby, Hope, and Lamour."

Reynolds echoed Liza's comments. "Stanley Donen ruined the picture—it's an abomination! *Lucky Lady* could have been a classic and meant another Oscar for Liza. I'll never work with Donen again."

A more mature, experienced actor's opinion was more consistent with the realities of making films. "I saw both Liza and Burt's points of view," Hackman commented, "but when it comes down to the final crunch, it's up to the director."

As for Donen, he was a bit more direct, probably more direct than he was in making the film. "Liza is an emotional child and I told them if they didn't like it, they could lump it. I made *Lucky Lady* for the millions of people who paid to see it. Not just to please a couple of actors."

In a sidebar to the summer of 1975, Sid Luft, who angered Liza when he sold some of her late mother's personal belongings, was found in contempt of court for harassing Barnett Glassman for trying to sell twenty-eight tapes of old Judy Garland shows. The court referred to Sid as "an unemployed ex-spouse of Judy Garland fallen on hard times." Apparently, Sid was calling prospective buyers of the videotapes, describing Glassman as a pirate, a racketeer, and a crook—none of which Mr. Glassman appreciated. The judge gave Sid a suspended five-day sentence and fined him $500.

Meanwhile, Liza was in New York. John Kander and Fred Ebb had a musical on Broadway, *Chicago*, about a notorious killing that occurred in the Windy City in 1924. The star was Gwen Verdon, who would become famous for her role in another musical, *Damn Yankees*.

The show opened July 1, 1975, but Verdon became sick with a throat infection a few weeks later, leaving Kander and Ebb without a star. "We just mentioned to Liza we were in a spot and she was the first one to come up with a suggestion," John said. She offered to take Gwen's place, which she did starting August 8. She played the lead of Roxie Hart for the next five weeks until Gwen could return.

Everyone was pleased Liza would temporarily appear in Gwen's place, but Liza knew she had only six days to prepare for the part. She asked that her substitution for Gwen not be officially noted on the billing or in the advertising. She was afraid she might fail or might steal some of the spotlight from Gwen. Still, when a simple announcement was made to the press about the substitution, tickets for Liza's five weeks sold out in less than half a day.

Critic Stanley Lebowsky cast Liza's appearance in the light of returning past favors for those involved in the production. "Liza did the show out of respect for Kander and Ebb," he said. "She's never forgotten what these men have done for her career. But she also did it for Bob Fosse, the show's director. He was her dear friend and it was her payback."

New York Times reviewer Clive Barnes told his readers about the temporary substitution, saying the producers wanted to make as little as possible of Gwen's replacement. While all Liza's performances quickly sold out, there were lines to get tickets for the Verdon performances as well. Besides, Barnes thought the way the producers handled the short-term change of leads was silly. "It would be comparing white wine with red wine—Miss Verdon is a dancer who sings and Miss Minnelli is a singer who dances and both are separately and distinctively adorable."

Barnes had long been a fan of both, particularly Liza. He wrote: "One would hesitate to designate Miss Minnelli as beautifully decadent, but her wide-eyed innocence, belting voice, and knowing manner all help to give her portrayal of the doe-eyed, baby-face killer, Roxie Hart, lovable reverberations and schmaltzy bitterness. As a performer, Miss Minnelli is larger than life and twice as beautiful. She has a monumental show-business personality, but a certain gamin quality that suggests the soul and the heart of a Piaf.... But it is fundamentally her vulnerability that makes her so appealing."

Liza's paranoia about getting physically close to fans surfaced again during the five weeks she played Roxie Hart. As the offstage announcer intoned each night at the Forty-sixth Street Theater that Liza would substitute for Gwen Verdon, the audience demonstrated they had come to see Liza. In one case, a member of the audience jumped onstage during the performance and started running after Liza. This bizarre behavior by her fans forced her to devise different disguises and ways of sneaking in and out of the theater. On one occasion when doing that failed, she had no alternative but to sprint for her waiting limo as if she were a gazelle pursued by a pack of jackals.

Another cast member, Chita Rivera, described what it was like. "When Liza came into the show," she said, "everything went *crazy!* Fans would try like hell to grab her onstage, to try and sneak backstage—anything to see her. It was phenomenal! I remember one night, as we were taking our final curtain calls, this girl jumped onstage. The curtain came down and she was still there. Liza screamed, 'Run, Chita!' I didn't know what was going on and, before I knew it, Liza was out of the damn theater! Then, this girl grabs *me!* I figured she wanted Liza's autograph, but no, she was holding scrapbooks of *my* career! What a hoot! I later told Liza and we laughed for days. Who would think someone wanted *me?* In those days, honey, *everyone* wanted Liza."

When her substitution was over, Liza underwrote a big party at the St. Regis Hotel for everyone connected with the show. It was a nice touch on her part since it should have been the other way around, but she wanted to be seen as the classy lady she was. Fred Ebb showed some class, too, when he gave her a gold charm shaped like a Lifesaver candy to thank her for rescuing the show at the last minute.

Another professional accolade came from Chita as she recalled the time she and Liza spent together on the stage. "I've been in musical theater a long time and I figured I knew how to bow [to the audience]. Wrong! When Liza came into *Chicago,* she showed me how to *really* bow. You see, there are bows; then, there are Liza bows."

Chicago brought Liza back to New York in the mid-1970s during the disco craze when sex, with or without cocaine, was more available than lemon meringue pie at the one remaining Automat in Manhattan. The phenomenon was symbolized by the transformation of an old broadcasting facility into the mecca of cool, the disco club Studio 54, or simply "Studio," as the "in" group called it. Halston quickly became the high priest of this new temple of hedonism and Liza his high priestess.

18

Father and Daughter Film

Father and daughter continued to dream of making a movie together. "I had been waiting to do a film with Daddy ever since I was five years old," Liza said. "It was a matter of finding the right subject." Something by F. Scott Fitzgerald appealed to father and daughter because, as Vincente Minnelli envisioned: "The crazy hedonism of the twenties became a stereotype with the great elegance of the decade forgotten. It wasn't just a period of the Charleston, flappers and hot-cha-cha. The twenties were also dominated by the likes of Otto Kahn, the Metropolitan Opera, and the expatriates in France. Liza and I agreed our approach would be one of style and taste."

Unfortunately, none of Fitzgerald's works seemed workable, and other possibilities didn't materialize. They kept looking, and Vincente returned again and again to *Film of Memory,* based on Maurice Druon's 1954 novel *La Volupte d'être* about the final days of the Marchesa Luisa Casati.

The marchesa had been an international beauty in 1910 and toast of the elite and rich men of her time, but now, remembering her glory years, she was faded and living in a seedy Roman hotel. The novel tells how a simple chambermaid, inspired by her tales, relives her life. The plot was used in *La Contessa,* a 1963 English play starring Vivien Leigh.

163

After the publication of his memoirs in 1974, Vincente was eager to make a dramatic movie again, this time with daughter Liza. In early 1973 Vincente had found out *Film of Memory* could finally be optioned and became very excited about the prospect.

He said: "When I first read the English translation of the Maurice Druon book, I felt it would make a marvelous picture. The book was optioned by several film producers over the past years and whenever I put my offer in on it, it was either too little or too late. I gave up hope I'd ever be involved with that lovely story."

When Vincente heard he might have an opportunity to make *Film of Memory,* he decided Liza would do well in the lead role even though he had not visualized her in the part when he previously bid on the story.

Unfortunately, Hollywood had changed a lot in the way it did business by this time. It was no longer the era in which studios decided what movies would be made. Independent producers now did all the things studios used to do, and Vincente was not accustomed to that role. He was making the last picture of his life and, in a way, the most important because it was a valentine to his fans and his family. But he was burdened by a multitude of new responsibilities. For assistance, Vincente unwisely sought the guidance of a pair of old-timers, producers Edmund Grainger and Jack H. Skirball, who also were strangers to the new way of making motion pictures. They offered the project to every bank and studio in Hollywood without success.

Nobody wanted to finance and distribute the project. Neither the story, the star, nor the production company excited investors. As Sam Goldwyn used to say, everyone wanted to be "included out." In desperation, they made a deal with Samuel Z. Arkoff of American International Pictures, who made films for drive-in customers uninterested in the cinematic art. Arkoff was regarded by many filmmakers as a rich, successful embarrassment to the industry.

Arkoff bought into the project not because he loved the script, but because he loved the idea of Vincente Minnelli making a picture for him, thus elevating his stature in the film industry. So in the fall of 1975, Vincente began the film working out of Sam Arkoff's American International Studios. Things improved when Vincente's prestige attracted two Hollywood legends to play significant roles in the film. Ingrid Bergman would play the aging countess with Charles Boyer as her husband. Vincente added more cachet to the cast with a sprinkling of European actors that added glamour without costing too much. These included Amedeo Nazzari, an older Italian matinee idol; Fernando Rey, who was beloved by Spanish audiences; and Ingrid's daughter, the young Isabella Rossellini.

Vincente had not directed a film in six years and was determined to make this movie his monument film. Vincente, Grainger, Skirball, and Arkoff decided they hated the title *A Film of Memory* and changed it to *Carmella*. They then decided they hated *Carmella* and changed it to *Nina*. Next they decided they hated *Nina* and changed it to *A Matter of Time*. They started shooting in late 1975 once Liza got away from *Lucky Lady*.

The film was jinxed from the start even though it had a talented cast and Geoffrey Unsworth as cinematographer. John Kander and Fred Ebb wrote a couple of original songs and John Gay did the script. For one thing, it was scheduled to be shot in fourteen weeks, but that schedule ballooned to twenty weeks because of Italian labor strikes and Italian film labs with quirky hours and a penchant for destroying film. Predictably, the shooting schedule ran too long, the costs too high, and the final rough cut three hours too long. Arkoff, fearful his money was being wasted and the whole project would fail, relieved Vincente of final supervision of the film so he did not have control of how it was edited. Editing is a critical step in the filmmaking process and there are often several different versions of a picture depending on who supervised the editing.

Liza was also anxious about several things. This would be the only film she would make with her dad and she wanted it to be perfect. "I always wanted to work with Daddy and why not?" she said. "He's a genius at what he does. He's a perfectionist and it shows in his work. From watching Daddy on the set, I learned not only about film, but about life."

Lucky Lady had opened Christmas Day, 1975, to poor reviews, including Liza's own. Beyond that, there was a sharp increase in the number of kidnap threats against her, but she didn't want to worry her father or other members of the cast. "I was afraid of kidnap threats so I had more security than anyone else. I arranged it with the studio, but Daddy never knew it."

When they finished shooting, Vincente had a clear idea how the final movie should look. Sam Arkoff also had a clear idea how the profit-and-loss statement should look. The two ideas were totally out of sync. As critic Stephen Harvey later assessed the result: "Arkoff…hacked away at the story, throwing out much of the flashback material and eliminating one character entirely.…To compensate, he tossed in some travelogue snaps of Rome Minnelli hadn't even shot; most damaging of all, Arkoff disfigured the movie's structure by enclosing the story within those shots of Nina-as-diva, which turned the whole mess into a kind of fourth-rate *A Star Is Born*."

Arkoff's editing briefly ignited a crusade for many Hollywood purists and devotees of good film. Martin Scorsese got almost every director in town to sign a protest petition. But Hollywood being Hollywood, the bottom line prevailed as it usually did.

In the end, Vincente was disgusted with the final cut and disavowed any association with it. So did Ingrid Bergman, who was upset because even if she took her name off the film everyone would still see her in the movie. And Liza wasn't happy either because this was the movie she long wanted to make with her father and it became her second film disaster in a row.

New York Times film critic Vincent Canby didn't like the movie, which opened October 7, 1976, at Radio City Music Hall. He wrote: "The film is full of glittery costumes and spectacular props. Its principal star is Liza Minnelli, whose appearance recalls her father and whose voice and mannerisms recall her mother. She has talent of her own, but it comes to us through the presence of others. Liza's eyes seem to have been widened surgically to play this part. *A Matter of Time* has moments of real visual beauty, but because what the characters say to each other is mostly dumb, it may be a film to attend while wearing your earplugs."

Probably the most hurtful review came from David Sterritt in the *Christian Science Monitor:* "*A Matter of Time* falls flat and it looks choppy. Even Rome looks stale. The Minnelli team is a losing one."

Pauline Kael was outraged, not at the Minnellis but at Arkoff and how he mangled the film: "From what is being shown to the public, it is almost impossible to judge what the tone of [Minnelli's] film was, or whether it would have worked at any level. But even if his own version was less than a triumph, that was the film I wanted to see—not this chopped-up shambles."

In the end, as a sad kind of revenge against Arkoff, the film was an enormous financial disaster, too.

Critic Harvey assigned an additional role to *A Matter of Time* in the life of the Minnellis, which had less to do with the film than it did with father and daughter. "Despite so many blunders and miscalculations," Harvey said, "for those who care about Minnelli's movie legacy, *A Matter of Time* is a touching last farewell to the obsessions of three decades. It is in fact Minnelli's own film of memory, surveying his most treasured motifs as if its director knew there would never be another time to express them."

Regretfully, word around New York and Hollywood was that the Haley marriage team was also a losing one. Making two movies kept Liza apart from her husband and running a studio kept Jack away from Liza. Their all-consuming careers took each of them to different parts of the world for long stretches of time. As president of 20th Century Fox Television, Jack divided his time between Hollywood and New York. He went to Mexico most weekends to be with Liza when she was shooting *Lucky Lady* and talked on the phone with her when she was in Rome doing *A Matter of Time*, but it wasn't enough.

Liza contended: "Any woman who's in love with a man wants to have his children. Jack gave me the greatest gift a man can give a woman—his name. I want to carry it on. And, though this may sound old-fashioned, I'm happy being married to the most wonderful man in the world. Jack and I sit home a lot and watch TV. I also like to cook for him. I enjoy cooking because that's part of being a woman and a wife."

So much for the storybook dream that didn't actually reflect their life. Jack's protestations sounded more realistic with an edge that suggested some of his feelings were not being expressed. "When we were first married, we had to be apart while Liza made *Lucky Lady*," he said. "Then she went to Rome for *A Matter of Time*. I had to stay in Los Angeles and only saw her occasionally. It was a strain—a physical hurt—but we knew it had to be this way. We knew [the separations would] never be pleasant, but we never thought they'd be intolerable."

Of course, both Jack and Liza knew for a long time how to make their respective lives more tolerable and even fun. They both enjoyed reputations as industrial-strength party animals. The logical choice for Liza if she really wanted to have Jack's baby, watch TV, and cook, would be to stay home for a while. She had a show business career and was entitled to it, but she also could have chosen to devote as much time and effort to her marriage as she was willing to devote to her next movie, *New York, New York*. Even though the film would be made at her beloved MGM studios in Los Angeles, where she would have her mother's old dressing room, it would still keep her away from Jack and home. She would spend the next four and a half months working fourteen to sixteen hours a day making the movie.

While Liza and Jack's marriage had begun to disintegrate, Lorna was cementing a new relationship that started in the summer of 1976 with the lead guitar player of the Arrows, Jake Hooker. They settled together in a modest London apartment with some financial help from Liza. Lorna would never succeed in show business the way Liza did, even though she tried. Both Judy and Liza said Lorna had the best voice in the family. In the world of show business, however, Lorna was forever doomed to be known as Judy's other daughter. Eventually Lorna would become the daughter with the house, husband, and children.

19

A New Direction

Jack frequently visited Liza in Mexico, but it is not clear whether he knew Liza had another visitor from time to time—director Martin Scorsese. Liza and Marty talked for two years about Liza making a movie set in the immediate post–World War II period. It would be the romantic tale of big band singer, Francine Evans (Liza), in love with sax player Jimmy Doyle (Robert De Niro). It was, once again, a remake of Hollywood's favorite plot, *A Star Is Born*, wherein rising star marries falling star. The movie would be called *New York, New York*.

In the film, Jimmy and Francine first meet in 1945 in a crowded ballroom. Jimmy is obsessed with his music but success always eludes him while coming easily for Francine. Eventually, her success and his temperamental personality tear the couple apart. Scorsese said it was his valentine to Hollywood, and it was the first of his films to receive the financial backing he yearned to have.

By the time Martin began talking to Liza about taking the female lead, Liza was enough of a star to make demands. She loved the story and setting, but she didn't love the part. It was too small.

"Martin Scorsese mentioned *New York, New York* to me more than two years before we made it," she said. "At the time, it was a man's story, telling how he went from bandleader to record producer in the early years of rock 'n' roll. I told Marty I'd be interested in the film if the girl's role was beefed up. I wanted to see what went on *behind* the bandstand."

interested in the film if the girl's role was beefed up. I wanted to see what went on *behind* the bandstand."

Martin had the script rewritten to expand the role of Francine Evans. Even while shooting *Lucky Lady,* Liza was devouring fan magazines of the postwar era, talking with people, and meeting with Martin to develop the project.

"I borrowed Sammy Davis Jr.'s collection of albums from that era and listened to them for hours," she recalled. "I also studied film clips of big bands and talked to lots of knowledgeable people so I could get my brain completely immersed in the Forties."

She followed the same drill she used in preparing for *Cabaret:* immersion into the times in order to transform herself into her character. She also watched many of her father's and mother's films of the same period and talked on the phone to Kay Thompson, who gave her singing tips. The singers Liza listened to most were Lena Horne, Doris Day, and Helen O'Connell. She tried to learn their techniques without mimicking them. She also talked with the real-life people on whom *New York, New York* was based—Cleo Laine, an English jazz singer, and her husband, saxophone player John Dankworth.

Liza was enthused about *New York, New York* because she was playing a normal person: "For the first time in my life I didn't play a kook. Francine was just a nice, intelligent girl-woman, who also happened to be tough and ruthless. I understood her because I knew women like her in Hollywood. Yet Francine was never crazy. Bobby [costar De Niro] was the wacky one for a change."

De Niro, meanwhile, was learning to pantomime playing a saxophone under the guidance of musician George Auld. Finally, at the beginning of 1976, with Irwin Winkler as producer, Liza, Martin, and Robert got together at MGM Studios, on Soundstage 29, where Judy filmed *The Pirate,* and began filming *New York, New York.* Theoretically, the script had been rewritten to expand the Francine part and there was a lot of discussion about period details with each of the principals doing a lot of research. Yet when the film started, it was chaos because nobody seemed in sync with the script.

The actors soon began ad-libbing the movie as they went along, while keeping to the general concept.

Although she lost more than twenty pounds and was often on the set until dawn, Liza remembered it as an exciting experience: "The script wasn't right at first, so Marty asked us to improvise. We thought the story out as we went along, and for weeks, all we did was rehearse while Marty videotaped us. He then took the best moments from those tapes and gave us that dialogue. We were all under great duress, three people going bananas every day. It was exciting. It was also exhilarating. I can't even remember sitting down for the whole time. I always said, 'If I drop dead making this movie, it'll be a great way to go.'"

Liza's colleagues had other memories. Martin, as with his previous films, saw *New York, New York* through the prism of his personal life. "I wanted to make a different kind of film about a struggling band in the forties trying to make it—one that was totally personal," he said. "I thought there was really no difference between a struggling band in the forties and myself, trying to make it in this business with all the pressures. It's also about two creative people who are struggling. They don't know where their next meal is going to come from, and it's worse because they are on the road. The film deals with a relationship and how it grows and then gets destroyed and hopefully in the end is resolved."

In that way, it was not unlike the relationship between Martin, Liza, and Martin's wife Julia.

Producer Irwin Winkler was, as producers have been since the time of Greek drama and Euripides, worried about the cost of everything. "I was nervous!" he remembered. "We were going over budget. We didn't know from day to day what would happen. But, one incident stays with me. Marty and I were shooting very, very late one night. We were doing a scene with Bobby and Liza, by now it was eight-thirty, nine o'clock and we were on our 22nd take. Everyone was exhausted. The problems started multiplying. And, I said to Marty, 'Listen, you know at 22 takes how do you feel, don't you think we have it?' He said, 'You know Irwin, in the last take I think I saw a tear coming out of the corner of Liza's eye. I think if I go two more takes, maybe three, I can get the tear. Do you want me to go for the tear or do you want me to stop?' And, I said, 'Go for the tear.'"

Martin had a very different view: "There were a lot of people who would watch the set of *New York, New York,* for example, and they'd come back thinking they knew what we were doing; they knew exactly how we worked. And, there was no way, because all the actual directing was done in whispers and in the dressing rooms and nobody would see. We'd talk, or the actors would ask me, 'Please come here, I want to talk to you for a little while.' We'd talk and they'd ask me a lot of questions or they'd bring up a whole new point or we'd rework it. All that was done very, very privately and the show was done outside."

And a lot of the private whispering between Martin and Liza had nothing to do with the picture. Observers thought they detected more than just the film project developing between them, that there was a lot going on "behind the bandstand."

Liza's take on the making of the picture was based on what she said she saw in Martin's eyes, an intriguing concept. "I got my entire performance by looking at Marty's eyes," she said. "I think Marty understands the struggle between feelings and thought—that intellect and emotion are always at war in people. He seems to be able to bring that out and express it. Marty used to sit underneath the camera and kind of conduct my performances. I wasn't looking at him, but I could sense him, could feel him conducting me. I knew when he wanted me to speed up or to put a lid on it, to calm down. I think Marty knows and is able to get across to his actors without ever hitting them over the head with, 'it's not what you say, it's what you don't say on film that's important.' That's what's interesting."

As usual, there was as much talk about what was happening off the set as what was happening on the set—particularly with De Niro, a quasi-mysterious character in Hollywood because he is so withdrawn. Hollywood has always been intimidated by artistic talent that does not parade itself before the world. Actors such as De Niro,

Pacino, and Brando are enigmatic and therefore considered very deep—great artists whose every move must be heeded and from whom significance must be drawn, as if observers were reading tea leaves or runes. It was assumed that since De Niro was playing opposite Liza, they were having an affair. Liza pointed out De Niro was married to attractive black actress Diahnne Abbott, who was pregnant at the time.

Somehow they finished the movie, and its songs were a great showcase for Liza, particularly the title number which she would adopt as another signature song.

The movie opened on the eighth anniversary of Judy's death, June 22, 1977, as a benefit for Lincoln Center. The opening was followed by a big party at Rockefeller Center's Rainbow Grill high above the twinkling lights of the city so beloved by both Judy and Liza. For Liza, New York was an exciting place that stimulated her and allowed her freedom from fawning crowds.

"It's the only place where I can be totally anonymous," she said. "It's full of new people, new ideas, new brainwaves. There's the onslaught of glamour, all the great parties and, of course, that New York sense of humor." The night of the premiere, Liza, in a transparent red gown and hanging on to husband Jack's arm, savored the new people, the glamour, and the great party until dawn broke across the East River, Then everyone adjourned to a special breakfast hosted by Halston at trendy Studio 54.

Critics of *New York, New York* obviously didn't have as much fun viewing the movie as Liza had making it or celebrating the premiere. *Saturday Review*—in that day an important literary magazine—thought the movie was too long, but that Liza did well: "At two hours, thirty-five minutes—an hour too much—*New York, New York* doesn't come off. But it does offer Liza Minnelli at her most charismatic [with moments as a reincarnation of her mother, Judy Garland] and enough niceness to provide passable entertainment."

Penelope Gilliatt, writing in the *New Yorker*, was vicious: "Martin Scorsese has made some very fine pictures, but this is not one of them. There is the initial plagiarism of a title and an era, the fatuousness of the dialogue and the ersatz nourishment the story offers filmgoers homesick for the movies of thirty years ago. Liza Minnelli does a shameless copy of her mother. *New York, New York* is Ho Hum, Ho Hum."

Stanley Kauffmann's comments in the *New Republic* were particularly hurtful to Liza: "*New York, New York* is one more of the current avalanche of disappointing U.S. films. They tried to make a tough sentimental show biz story with lots of period songs...but the sentiment doesn't take and what's left isn't tough, it's occasionally repellent, but mostly tedious and trite. The picture, faults and all, might have been pleasant if it had some charm. Liza Minnelli has none, ever."

But *Newsweek*, which in Liza's earlier years savaged her repeatedly, took a much different view of *New York, New York*. Jack Kroll wrote, "Minnelli is overpowering in a scene in which she's recording 'But the World Goes Around.' Here the double focus is perfect: the dynamic singer is both Liza Minnelli and Judy Garland. It's not pastiche, but a moving synthesis of old and new."

Martin was less than kind when he described Liza's performance as an imitation. "You put a wig on Liza and she looks like her mother," he said. "What can I tell you?"

Later he admitted some of the picture's shortcomings were his own: "Eventually, I understood the picture. Jean-Luc Godard came over for lunch one day and he was talking about how much he liked *New York, New York*. He said it was basically about the impossibility of two creative people in a relationship—the jealousies, the envy, the temperament. I began to realize it was so close to home I wasn't able to articulate it while I was making the film."

While making the film, Martin was deeply involved in an affair with Liza, his marriage was coming apart, and his wife was on the set much of the time because she was the screenwriter. As was always the case with Martin Scorsese—his genius and his failing— he was personally involved with the picture and the story and the participants.

"I guess it's a good picture, though I think it's good only because it's truthful," he declared. "It's about two people in love with each other who are both creative [like Scorsese and his wife]. That was the idea: to see if the marriage would work....I was extremely disappointed when the movie was finished, because I had a really bad experience making it. Some people understand the ending and others just don't get it."

Yet Liza, who must have brooded about the comparisons between her and her dead mother, was enough of a trouper to accept the fact her recent run of movies hadn't set the world on fire. (Though she probably would have been happy to set some critics on fire.) She decided to return to the venue where she always succeeded—the stage. As she evaluated her career, "In 1975, I figured I could afford to do the movie. Then, suddenly, I started it and realized if *New York, New York* was a turkey, I would be in a lot of trouble because, Oh Mama!, in Hollywood, you're not allowed to have three bad pictures in a row."

While in the middle of *New York, New York*, Liza decided it was a good time to boost her career with a stage musical, at which she was unequaled. Unfortunately, she didn't have the same motivation to save her marriage. The stage musical turned into a giant chore for the same reason there were problems with *New York, New York:* Martin Scorsese. Martin was her film director, her lover, and director of her stage musical—something he had never done before.

Martin Scorsese is a son of Manhattan and a child of New York City where he was born November 17, 1942, to Luciano Charles and Catherine Scorsese, devoted Catholic parents whose life revolved around the garment district. Martin was a fragile youngster with asthma who felt like an outsider among the tough guys and street criminals in the Italian part of town. He was sick so often the other boys in the neighborhood called him "Marty Pill." His brother Frank watched over him when they went out or else Frank would leave Marty at home with their mother.

As Frank described the neighborhood: "It was very violent—

the gangs, the fights. It could break out instantly. In the middle of
the night, you could hear all kinds of fights and violence. You would
pull the shade down and go back to sleep, because it was none of
your business and, if you opened your mouth, you were in trouble.
You lived by the sword and died by the sword."

Martin became an altar boy, but had a hard time dealing with
the idea of sin, especially the sin of masturbation, for which he took
the prohibitions of the church literally. "I took it very seriously," he
said. "That's offensive to God and, well, maybe you should kill
yourself."

But when he finally confessed to his priest, the priest soothed
his concern saying, "No, no, it's nonsense. Don't worry about it.
You've just got to control certain urges and that [is] that."

Reassured, Martin decided he should become a priest and then
he would have the poise and confidence his priest had. He
reconsidered after he was transferred to Cardinal Hayes High
School in the Bronx and heard the priest there endorse the Vietnam
War as a holy crusade. That view went against everything Martin
believed. Even so, he tried to study for the priesthood but failed the
entrance exam for Fordham University's divinity program and
matriculated to New York University to study English. There his
interest veered to filmmaking. He began making films at school and
persisted until he was producing and directing commercially.

By 1976 Martin was in New York shooting *Taxi Driver*, a film
about loneliness turned into madness. The themes of his films up to
then presented a flawed character driven by some inner demon,
struggling to be heard or seen or to be in control of his life situation.
His films usually offered no relief, solution, or resolution—just
endless tension without release. Yet his heroes always tried to find
redemption no matter how twisted their path might be.

"Paul Schrader's script for *Taxi Driver*," said Martin, "was
about being angry at women and many other things. I felt very
strongly about it and part of that was not being able to communicate
or not being able to have that kind of relationship you thought you
would want to have with an 'idealized' woman. And, so the jealousy

and the anger were very, very real. It was crippling for many years. I think it had more to do with me than with them, that's for sure. A lot of feelings in *Taxi Driver* were about longing, the inability to be able to make contact. And, that was pretty devastating to make a movie about because you really felt it."

At the time Martin was making *Taxi Driver,* he was seeing Julia Cameron and was extremely jealous of her to the point of being paranoid.

After *New York, New York,* another project materialized for Liza. The idea for a stage musical originally titled *In Person* began with George Furth, who wrote several Broadway hits. Furth was intrigued by the story of Michelle Craig, a well-known and respected singer, and what happened in her real life. The format, which was popular in that era but is passé now, employed the use of flashbacks also found in *Lucky Lady.* The project began with Liza's old classmate Marvin Hamlisch writing the arrangements for the musical score. By the time Liza heard about the project, Hamlisch had been replaced by Liza's colleagues Kander and Ebb, which explains why she was given a chance to read the script. She loved it and wanted to do the role of Michelle, which she described as "the best Broadway part for a woman in years."

Naturally, Furth was delighted to get Liza as his star. She demanded Martin Scorsese direct the show, which should have alerted Furth to problems ahead. Martin was a movie director, not a stage director. But Liza wouldn't take the role unless he directed.

The costume designer, Theodora Van Runkle, also was in the wrong medium. She created clothes for movies, not the theater. When told to design costumes for the show's gypsies, Van Runkle designed clothes that would be found on the travelers in a Romany gypsy caravan. The only problem was "gypsies" was a stage nickname for chorus dancers and had nothing to do with a Bohemian ethnic group. Liza had to send an SOS to her pal Halston who redesigned her costumes at a cost of $100,000, paid by Liza herself.

On the Fourth of July, 1977, the curtain rose on a tryout in

Chicago. The original show had been rechristened *Shine It On* as a joint project of the Los Angeles and San Francisco light operas. Then renamed *The Act,* the musical moved on to San Francisco after some wicked reviews. One anonymous inside source summed it up after the San Francisco opening: "Liza's contract gave her the final say on *everything* including whether Scorsese was canned. At first, people wanted him off the show. Later those same people thought it might be a good idea if he stayed around because of their friendship. It was like Liza was out there working for Marty. The only problem was she was excessively loyal, and loved, perhaps, too blindly." A new version of the play appeared in Los Angeles. The reviews were pitiless. Dan Sullivan at the *Los Angeles Times* wrote, "*The Act* is the dumbest backstage musical ever, even to the point where you figure they've got to be kidding."

Meanwhile, three of the four people involved in the Scorsese–Minnelli love affair—Liza, Martin, and Jack—categorically denied any sexual activity between Liza and Martin. The fourth person, the pregnant Julia Cameron, Martin's wife, offered a more realistic view. She sued for divorce in August 1977, naming Liza and detailing the specifics of the adulterous affair, including times and places. Julia's fury was probably triggered when Martin gave Liza her gold locket.

Martin finally recognized he could not bring this stage production to New York without humiliating himself, his lover, and everyone connected with *The Act.* He came down with a suspicious asthma attack after a three-week run in Los Angeles and brought in musical doctor Gower Champion to sharpen up *The Act.* Liza put the best face on it to protect her lover: "He came in and told me, 'I know you're going to trust me. I will not let you open in New York as anything less than super. You've never worked with Gower, but we need help. Gower can add something terrific and I want only the best for you.' It's not like Marty stormed off somewhere to Italy. The show was always on his mind."

Later, Martin said, "I was doing a stage play—the only one I'll ever do, I think—called *The Act* with Liza Minnelli and I was having a very, very bad time. I realized I was out of my element, but I thought I'd stay with it until I discovered I really didn't like it. This was a very difficult and painful situation."

Liza was glad to see Martin step aside because of what it meant to their personal relationship. She said, "There's a wonderful line in *Cabaret*, 'Sex always screws up a friendship.' Marty is my closest friend in the world, my closest ally—besides my husband—and guiding force and I wouldn't want to destroy that."

Even without Champion's changes, *The Act*'s New York run had two things going for it. First, it was the source of so much controversy and press coverage that a lot of people were going to see it just to find out what all the fuss was about. Second, Liza was a bona fide star and people would pay money just to see her scratch her nose or jaywalk across Times Square.

So when it was announced *The Act,* starring Liza, would come to the Majestic Theater on October 29, 1977, the show sold out despite the fact the producers were charging three times as much a seat as for any other Broadway play at the time. The advance sales of the Broadway run of *The Act* were $2 million, more than any other advance sale in the history of the theater. From the viewpoint of *The Act*'s backers, the musical was a success before the first Broadway curtain went up. Predictably, opening night was a mob scene with major stars attending, police fighting to maintain some semblance of crowd control, fans with autograph books having a holiday, and the people connected with *The Act* delighted at the uproar because it meant profits.

Liza's mainstays were there, including her husband Jack and close buddies Halston and Sammy Davis Jr. Added to the mix were Elizabeth Taylor and Liza's ex and current lovers Bob Fosse, Desi Arnaz Jr., and Martin Scorsese. In addition, writer Pete Hamill, Martha Graham, Dick Cavett, and Andy Warhol were in attendance. The audience poured out its praise and acceptance of the performance, which was followed by an all-night party at Tavern on the Green for six hundred people who paid $35 a piece to attend. Liza sang and received more plaudits from the star-studded crowd.

Liza seemed able to galvanize her performance opening night. "I just put my mind in the right place. But seeing the funny side was important, too," she said later. "The week I opened, Donny and Marie Osmond were on the cover of *People*. Everywhere I went, I passed newsstands and smiling up at me were the Osmonds. So, on opening night, I got the usual crate of good luck telegrams, but my favorite read, 'Do it for Donny and Marie!'"

In some ways, *The Act* was less a musical than a concert, and for Liza that may have made the difference. She was onstage all but four minutes of the show and sang all but one of the songs. The critics approved of her effort. *New York Times* reviewer Richard Eder underscored the point when he wrote: "*The Act* is precisely what its name implies and it displays the breathtaking presence of Liza Minnelli. But George Furth's book is not just thin, it pretends to be there. It has little development or characterization of its own and, except for a stray line or two, it has only the most trite and synthetic dialogue. Still, Minnelli's voice comes tearing out exuberantly in the opening 'Shine It On,' it comes out in the tearing, bitter 'The Money Tree' and in the quiet 'There Where I Need Him.'"

In other words, what made *The Act* a success was leaving behind much of the original musical that failed in Chicago, San Francisco, and Los Angeles and turning the show essentially into a Liza concert. That's what her fans really wanted—and paid a previously unheard-of $25 a seat to hear—and why they would yell out requests that had nothing to do with the show.

Liza fan Rex Reed labeled it "an exhausting triumph," while Douglas Watts of the *New York Daily News* called Liza a second-rate Barbra Streisand, even though it is unlikely Streisand could have salvaged *The Act* the way Liza did. Watts wrote, "She is only a fair singer. She began as a flagrant imitator of Barbra Streisand and gradually leaned more and more to her mother's style so she's now an amalgam of the two. She's only a fair dancer and, let's face it, not exactly a knockout."

This was not a viewpoint shared by everyone, least of all a defected Russian ballet dancer regarded as the ballet megastar of the world, Mikhail "Misha" Baryshnikov. He seemed to see a lot of enticing things in Liza and she in him as the two danced their own secret bedroom ballet while *The Act* was in New York. To Liza he was a man with the most incredibly beautiful male form she had ever seen.

The fascination was mutual as they got caught up in a tornado of passion that pushed Liza's endurance to the edge because Misha was performing in Washington, D.C., while she was in New York. After each performance of *The Act*, Liza would hop a jet to Washington in the middle of the night, savor Misha's sinewy body, and fly back to Manhattan in the morning for a few hours' sleep before her next performance. Finally, an exhausted Misha ended their clandestine affair.

Despite *The Act's* initial success, trouble erupted. On December 8 a fire of uncertain origin broke out in Liza's apartment. She suffered smoke inhalation damaging her throat and had to cancel one performance. Four days before Christmas a 104-degree temperature sidelined her for a week, costing the producers almost $200,000 in losses. Three weeks later she was felled by another virus and the producers decided to shut down the show for the last two weeks in January 1978. Liza went into the hospital with a respiratory illness.

A flood of cards, letters, and flowers arrived to cheer her up, but no one but husband Jack and her press agent Lois Smith were permitted to see her. When the test results came back, the doctors decided she had a very severe virus. Jack described her condition: "Liza was so sick she didn't even know the days of the week." The treatment was a week of complete rest and recuperation at a Texas spa, the Greenhouse in Dallas.

She came back a new woman, she said, prepared to continue performances of *The Act,* but something was still not right. Her symptoms caused her to muff her cues and her lines and show up late for performances which, unlike her mother, she almost never did. On March 2 she didn't appear at all, complaining of stomach pain so bad "it left me too weak to stand."

Her illness was real enough according to her colleagues, including Barry Nelson, the actor who shared the lead with her in *The Act*. He said: "There were times when she was so sick we had to restrain her from going on. She always felt guilty if she missed a show. Liza's job was a lot harder than mine—she carried double the volume of work. Somebody once said a performer leaves bits of flesh on the stage after a show. I say Liza left some bones, too."

Still, she hung in there with the same dedication to audience her mother had, and the show went on as often as possible. *The Act* gave her two pleasures she relished. One was the Tony nomination for Best Actress in a Musical and the other was a connection with her next husband-to-be. It would be the third marriage for each. She won the award June 26. The husband would take a little longer. His name was Mark Gero.

It's with a Z—Not an s! Liza on her television special, June 1970, *Liza With a Z.* (Brown Brothers Photo)

Music in Manhattan: Liza with her backup group, The Bojangles, opening at New York City's Waldorf-Astoria Empire Room, 1970. (Globe Photos)

Hollywood kids at an opening: Caught in the crowd at the Hollywood 1972 premiere of Cabaret, Liza wades through the crowd with her then-boyfriend, Desi Arnaz Jr. (Globe Photos)

Five weeks in torrid paradise: With Peter Sellers during their steaming five-week affair in England, 1972.

The touring talent: Liza with the New Seekers during 1973 tour.

Big Hollywood and family occasion: Adoring father, movie director Vincente Minnelli, beams as daughter Liza receives an Oscar at the 1973 Academy Awards ceremony. (Photo by Doris Nieh, Globe Photos)

(Right) Sister act: Liza on stage singing a duet with her half sister, Lorna Luft. (Photo by Irv Steinberg, Globe Photos)

(Below) I remember it well—the book: Movie director Vincente Minnelli, at a book party for his autobiography, *I Remember It Well,* 1974. (Globe Photos)

I Remember
it Well VINCENTE MINNELLI
with Hector Arce

foreword by Alan Jay Lerner

(Right) Blond and brunette TV stars: Liza and Goldie Hawn together at the time of their television special, 1979. (Globe Photos)

(Opposite above) How about a cigar? Here Liza hams it up with *Lucky Lady* costars Gene Hackman and Burt Reynolds, 1975.

(Opposite below) Close friends forever: Liza with friends Sammy and Altovise Davis. Altovise was matron of honor and Sammy gave the bride away when Liza and Jack Haley married in Montecito, California, 1974. (Photo by Irv Steinberg, Globe Photos)

(Below) Give us Moore of Liza: Liza and Dudley Moore during filming of their first movie together, *Arthur,* 1981.

Those big brown eyes: Liza looks right at us with her famous big dark eyes.

20

Lifestyles of the Rich and Depraved

W hen one of America's premiere fashion designers flies across the country just to spend an hour at a wedding party, as Halston did after Liza's marriage to Jack Haley, it isn't because he is a casual acquaintance trying to sell a frock. To Liza, Halston was "Baby," and Halston responded with a glowing assessment of her: "Liza is everyone's pal. She's great fun, a great talent and a great lady to dress."

Halston's appearance at the Haley-Minnelli wedding signified a long and deep relationship between Halston and Liza that went back many years. It was more important than clothes, although Liza wore a Halston at her wedding and her attire was an important part of her stage persona and essential to her success. Liza met Halston in 1966 when he was at Bergdorf's and thought of her simply as Judy's daughter. When Liza went to Halston on her own in 1970, she had just been nominated for an Academy Award for *The Sterile Cuckoo*. She came into his salon looking for someone to help her shop.

Liza recalled the meeting: "Halston liked bosoms when bosoms weren't in. Everyone wanted to look like Twiggy and Halston looked at me and said, 'What are you doing? You've got a great bustline. You have to celebrate it.' And, I said, 'What?' Nobody ever talked to me as if I had any glamour or style or anything and he really did give it to me. That was before *Cabaret*. That was before anything."

According to biographer Steven Gaines in *Simply Halston: The Untold Story,* Halston understood who and what Liza was. He knew her weight fluctuated with her emotional state as it does with many people. Oprah Winfrey has made a career of focusing on her weight and discovering it was a reflection of how she felt emotionally.

Halston kept several mannequins of Liza that reflected her at various weights. During *The Act* in 1975 and later, Halston reportedly made several sizes for each costume because Liza's weight fluctuated so much. Her relationship with Halston solidified when she started seeing her various French lovers, Charles Aznavour, Baron Alexis de Redé, Jean-Pierre Cassel, and Jean-Claude Brialy and felt the need to be more glamorous and sexual to attract and hold their attention.

She suffered from a bad self-image and went to Halston for help. She thought she wanted to look like a "female Fred Astaire." Halston embraced the challenge, if not the vision, and immediately instructed her to order five pieces of Vuitton luggage. She did and he filled them with an entirely new wardrobe that created a dramatic new image for her. He told her to throw out everything else in her wardrobe. The next year, Liza was nominated for the International Best-Dressed Woman list.

Over the years, Liza and Halston grew very close. He always had time for her and she for him. Her stories never shocked him no matter how outrageous the stunt or affair. In fact, the more outrageous, the better for Halston. He was a positive force in her life, making her like herself better and improving her self-image. They frequently went out on the town and were seen in the "best" places that were "in" with the Manhattan jet set. Still, the times they enjoyed most were when they were alone together. He would cook for the two of them and they would drink wine and talk about life and death.

They endured their rough spots, too. In 1973, the year before Liza married Jack Haley, Halston's publicist Eleanor Lambert and

French designer Marc Bohan came up with an idea for a Franco-American gesture of goodwill. It called for five French designers to invite five American designers to join them in Paris for a fashion extravaganza. The French designers were Hubert de Givenchy, Christian Dior, Pierre Cardin, Emmanuel Ungaro, and Yves Saint Laurent. The Americans were Halston, Bill Blass, Steven Burrows, Anne Klein, and Oscar de la Renta. The Baroness de Rothschild was president of the gala committee and Princess Grace of Monaco was guest of honor.

The 520 seats available for the showing were priced at $235 each and sold out in less time than it takes to tell about the event. Income from tickets, plus some other contributions, raised more than $260,000 for the restoration of the 1769 building in which the showing was held. Halston put certain celebrity models in his show just to add a power edge to his presentation, and these included Liza. The overall show was run by the omnipresent, multitalented Kay Thompson, who directed and choreographed the affair.

A glitch developed during rehearsals as Halston waited for his models to go on. It seemed to the impatient Halston Kay was giving Anne Klein's segment of the rehearsal an inordinate amount of attention and care. He finally stormed out of the theater, taking his entourage of models and assistants with him, and proceeded to lock himself in his limo. He required some hand-wringing and groveling to satisfy his tweaked ego before he would return.

Liza came out, and as Eleanor Lambert recollected: "Liza banged on the door and stomped her foot, but Halston refused to get out of the car. So, Liza turned to the models and said, 'Listen, kids, we've got a show to do, so don't start this. You're in show business and the show must go on. Cut all this out and let's go rehearse.' They followed Liza back inside and left Halston in the car."

After a few minutes, Halston tiptoed out of the limo and back to his seat in the hall without saying a word. Liza and Halston would weave in and out of each other's lives this way throughout the 1970s and beyond.

Probably the only woman, among the scores in his life, who vied with Liza for top billing in Halston's affections—both professional and personal—was Bianca Jagger. Born Bianca Perez Morena de Macias, she married rocker Mick Jagger of the Rolling Stones in 1971 at the start of a sensational career as an international model. Jagger, whose crowd was also part of Liza's crowd, hung around with Halston, Andy Warhol, Truman Capote, and the like.

Jagger studied at the London School of Economics for three years before becoming the ultimate rock music outlaw by playing variations of American blues and soul songs. Liza got involved with Bianca in 1978 after Jagger switched his affections to Texas model Jerry Hall and dumped Bianca because of, among other things, her constant infidelities. After the separation, Bianca had an affair with Ryan O'Neal that lasted a relatively short time. She found solace and shelter at Halston's place at 101 East Sixty-third Street, known colloquially to New York jet setters simply as "101."

Halston took her in and appointed himself her chaperon and matchmaker determined to find her a rich man. She clung to Halston, because until she could pull herself together, she needed the comfort of a man without the problem of keeping him sexually happy. "Homosexuals make the best friends because they care about you as a woman and they are not jealous," Bianca explained to anyone who cared to listen. "They love you but don't try to screw up your head."

That wasn't exactly true of Halston and Liza. In the late 1970s when Liza was in a self-destructive period reflective of her mother—having an affair with Martin Scorsese while still married to Jack Haley—Halston provided a shoulder to lean on and some lines of coke to ease the pain and confusion. Liza exacerbated the pain and confusion after she and Scorsese finished *New York, New York* by going into *The Act* with him. Halston designed Liza's dresses for the musical using style and common sense that resulted in a lot of sequined gowns.

As Halston explained to Liza, "By this point in the show, you're hot and wet, so we'll put you in sequins so the sweat won't show. If you're going to be shiny, you might as well shine all over."

Through all this, Halston was Liza's father confessor, chaperon, and mentor. He introduced her to Dr. Robert Giller, who made a fortune giving celebrities massive shots of vitamins to help sustain and hype them up. His clientele reputedly included George Hamilton, Judy Collins, Carrie Fisher, Mikhail Baryshnikov, and Liza. Halston's most significant introduction was to Steve Rubell, who became his instant best friend for several years while Rubell ran Studio 54.

Author Steven Gaines described the relationship between Rubell and Halston this way: "They shared houses on Fire Island and boys in Manhattan, they vacationed together in Mustique and they flanked Liza Minnelli in her seat at the 1978 Tony awards."

Rubell's Studio 54 became the center of the chic universe of artistic Manhattan, and Halston was the Wizard of Oz who pulled the levers and dictated the dances. This was not the struggle for recognition and acceptance Peter Allen experienced. Instead, it was the chrome-plated, diamond-earring-studded ersatz bohemia of the famous and wealthy who arrived in limos and furs and consumed champagne, cocaine, scotch, and Quaaludes while talking about how difficult life was.

As Steven Gaines described it: "Every night there held some new, small titillation: a fat Elizabeth Taylor in a silly flowered hat with Halston in the disc-jockey's booth playing with the lights all night; Mick Jagger falling asleep on Baryshnikov's shoulder; Truman Capote giving a party for his own face-lift. There was the party for *People* magazine, and the Halloween party, and the Academy Awards party and the opening-night party for Liza when *The Act* opened on Broadway, and parties for Liza's birthday, Liz Taylor's birthday, Andy Warhol's birthday, and Steve Rubell's birthday."

The celebrity press gobbled up every tidbit dropped at Studio 54, particularly in the exclusive basement room whence gossip about sex and drugs (two obsessions of the Studio 54 crowd) emanated almost nightly. Rubell used to laugh at these gossip items. "The stuff that happened was much worse," he said. "You couldn't believe it."

Goings on at Studio 54 went well beyond the edge of propriety. Rubell and Halston loved to skate on the thin ice of what society would tolerate, and the possibility of being caught was a delicious prospect to them while the possibility of not being caught was even more delicious. For Halston and Rubell, the ultimate Russian roulette was unprotected sex and the attendant risks of sexual disease. Some things the two did would ultimately tempt fate just a smidgen too far, and they became victims of themselves.

However, it was not the drugs, booze, and sex in the basement that did in Rubell. It was not the ejaculation contest in which waiters and guests would see who could squirt sperm the farthest for the prize of a vacation with Rubell. It was not the drag party held at 101 on a hot July night where Halston wore an off-the-shoulder dress and heels and Rubell donned a side-slit, scarlet-sequined gown Liza had worn in *The Act*. (A newspaper columnist who swore never to breathe a word about the party at 101 lied, and told of orgies in the bedrooms and the place awash in cocaine and Quaaludes.)

What destroyed Rubell's reign was the same thing that ended the career of Al Capone, another strutting social tyrant who thought he was too powerful for society and the authorities. Rubell's nemesis was the bureaucratic banality of the Internal Revenue Service, epitomized by a middle-aged guy in a three-piece suit. Rubell couldn't resist appearing on a TV talk show and bragging about cheating the IRS on his income taxes.

By the summer of 1979 the FBI began questioning Rubell, Halston, and a lot of other people. Roy Cohn fought to keep Rubell out of jail, but lost. So on the eve of closing down Studio 54 and sending Rubell off to a white-collar prison, Halston did the only thing he could: He threw a going-away party for Rubell at Studio 54 at which Diana Ross sang. It may have been the requiem for that particular era and crowd, because people were beginning to sour on the juvenile antics and disrespect for the system that permitted them great comfort and wealth.

A cartoon in the May 29, 1978, *New Yorker* suggested Halston, and perhaps Liza, might be passé. The cartoon showed a wife talking to her husband at the morning breakfast table. She says, "I dreamt I was sitting in on a National Security Council meeting and, guess what, Liza Minnelli and Halston were there, too!"

Halston was hurt by the cartoon and what it implied. "You see and hear the craziest things about everyone—but I'm just a person like everyone else," he complained. "Well, not like everyone else. There is much more publicity, more picture taking. That's sort of the hardship part sometimes. Everyone knows who I am; but I don't know who *they* are."

In fact, there is serious doubt Halston really knew who *he* was.

21

Bye-Bye, Jack—Hello, Mark

During the last two weeks of January 1978, Liza was deathly ill with what doctors thought was pneumonia and spent her time in a New York hospital or at the Texas spa with Jack hovering and checking in daily to follow her condition. Some thought it was not pneumonia but too much late-night partying, cocaine, and Martin. She returned to *The Act* when it reopened January 30. By then the musical had lost $750,000. Three weeks later, on February 24, Jack and Liza officially announced their legal separation after four years of marriage. There were probably a number of reasons, including the Baryshnikov and Scorsese affairs and many others. Jack thought the separation would prove tempo-rary and he and Liza would soon be together again. Toward that end, he moved out of their apartment with the view of Central Park and into another in the same building, for convenient commuting.

Liza's approach was different. She viewed the separation as a preamble to divorce. She didn't want her future ex-husband to be a neighbor so she moved back to the apartment on East Fifty-seventh Street she once shared with Peter Allen. The divorce papers were filed in April. Jack was as gallant through the ending of the relationship as he had been during its beginning. He refused to talk publicly about Liza's conduct during their marriage and her infidelities. He preferred to say they had merely grown apart and divorce was best for both of them. Through the years that followed, Liza and Jack remained friends, unlike the postmarriage relationship between Liza and Peter Allen. Liza frequently called Jack for advice or moral support in the years immediately following their divorce. When Liza married again in December 1979, Jack wished her well and took the opportunity to make public his own relationship with actress Lindsay Wagner.

One relationship that collapsed toward the end of 1978 was between Liza and her former stepfather Sid Luft, who announced he would auction a lot of Judy's belongings on November 27 at the Beverly Wilshire Hotel. Predictably, Lorna and Joey stayed out of the controversy because Sid was, after all, their father. Liza's lawyers sought an injunction, but before the courts reached a decision, the auction took place. Sid collected about $310,000 including $60,000 for Judy's Rolls-Royce. Liza bought her mother's dressing table and a mother-and-child statue she particularly loved, which Sid would not give her. The episode left her angry, and while she and her stepfather later reconciled, their relationship was never the same.

Sid eventually became a pharmaceutical salesman.

Before their divorce, Jack left 20th Century Fox Television but continued to be a productive, well-liked, and respected independent producer of television documentaries. These included *Bob Hope's World of Comedy*, *Life Goes to War: Hollywood and the Homefront*, *Heroes of Rock and Roll*, the *Ripley's Believe It or Not* series, *Hollywood: The Gift of Laughter*, and *100 Years of the Hollywood Western*.

Professionally, Liza kept busy, but it was time for her to appear in another stage show or concert or go on a cabaret tour to keep up the momentum a star must maintain. For their next production Liza and Fred Ebb decided to rent Carnegie Hall for a concert. However, as Liza and Fred were always aware, a star cannot just do *another* show—it must be better and more spectacular than the previous one. They decided this would not be an ordinary one-night stand at the fabled Carnegie Hall. Instead, they booked the place for eleven nights, with Liza breaking all Carnegie Hall records for a run of performances by a single artist.

Tickets were $7.50 to $25 a seat—the top prices in Manhattan. By opening night, September 4, 1979, the entire run was completely sold out for the first time in Carnegie Hall history. The performance that night and the ten nights that followed justified the public enthusiasm.

Newsday's Jerry Parker wrote, "The show has three or four high points in which the power and excitement pouring out of Minnelli is almost frightening. She is terrific, maybe the greatest musical-hall artist going today. Are there any other performers these days who knock themselves out for an audience the way Liza does?"

Gannett's Jacques LeSourd declared: "The show is dynamite from start to finish. Liza galvanized the venerable hall in a way I have never seen. She dispenses enough controlled energy in two hours to power the entire metropolitan area for a decade. She glitters and dazzles in Halston sequins. It's a job splendidly well done and a truly memorable night."

And *New York Daily News* writer Patricia O'Haire offered, "As Liza begins to sing 'How Long Has This Been Going On?,' the musicians file in one by one and take their places on various platforms. From then on, energy, pure and simple, takes over. It's a dazzling display."

The show clearly achieved what Liza and Fred, who wrote, produced, and directed it, hoped to accomplish with the help of their talented staff and crew: choreographers Wayne Cilento and Ron Lewis, set designer Lawrence Miller, and production manager Mark Gero. They wanted the show to be sensationally new and, at the same time, vintage Liza so that it would rock Manhattan on its sophisticated heels. And that it did. In addition, they wanted a show nucleus they could take on the road just as they did cabaret concerts Liza and Fred created years before, beginning with the first at the Blue Room of the Shoreham Hotel.

Meanwhile, there was a man five years her junior interested in

Liza, but she was not initially drawn to him even though she thought he looked like her friend Robert De Niro. Mark Gero was a sculptor earning his living in the theater. He had worked backstage on *The Act* and was strongly attracted to Liza. He asked her out a number of times, but she always turned him down. It wasn't until *The Act* closed that they finally went out on an official date. After that Liza began hanging around with Mark either at Studio 54, along with her buddy Halston, or at meals. It was a natural connection since Mark, a man with dark, serious eyes and a classic long-nosed face, was also a theater brat whose father was an actor.

They continued to see each other even after *The Act* closed and after Fred Ebb and Liza decided she should go on a concert tour in 1978 and 1979. Mark joined her as stage manager so they saw each other daily as Liza returned to the London Palladium in November. They extended their European stay with a trip to Paris at Christmas, 1978. The following year Mark joined Liza on her trip to England where she opened at Covent Garden in *The Owl and the Pussycat* on July 23. After this she was off on her concert tour with Fred Ebb and Mark as stage manager. Mark and Liza decided to announce their engagement at a cast party when the tour reached New Orleans.

Some wondered why Liza was attracted to Gero because he was not a star in his field such as Bob Fosse, Martin Scorsese, Mikhail Baryshnikov, Halston, or Jack Haley. That, of course, may have been the attraction. He wouldn't compete for the limelight with Liza, and perhaps Liza was looking for a quieter private life where she could have the baby she had been thinking about for a long time.

Before getting married, however, Liza had to appear in a television show with Goldie Hawn entitled *Goldie and Liza Together*. The two stars had a lot in common with their show business backgrounds and public images. Liza said: "Goldie and I are two cartoon characters. She's the blonde airhead. But Goldie's as much an airhead as Einstein. I've worked with other women and it was tough, but it was different with Goldie. If there was something wrong with my dress, she would fix it. I know people who would have let me go on covered in lint. The basis of the show we did was to prove you don't have to be better than anyone else, you just have to be as good as you are."

Liza and Goldie became fast friends. Liza shared with Goldie the secret she was pregnant with Mark Gero's child. Goldie felt good about the personal relationship. "I'm so glad I did that special with her," she said. "Liza and my kids became buddies. I told her having children would be the most important, beautiful thing that would ever happen to her. Liza is so sweet."

The wedding took place December 4, 1979, in a small ceremony at St. Bartholomew's Episcopal Church in Manhattan. About two dozen friends attended. The pregnant bride arrived an hour late. She wore a chiffon Halston gown and the reception was held at Halston's house on East Sixty-third Street. Vincente gave his daughter away while Lorna served as matron of honor and Mark's brothers Jason and Jonathan were best men. Guests included Vincente's longtime girlfriend Lee Anderson, Andy Warhol, Elizabeth Taylor, Steve Rubell, and Faye Dunaway. Hundreds of fans waiting outside showered the couple with rice as they emerged from the church.

Liza was quite moved by this nuptial, her third. "Everyone else was supposed to cry, but I cried throughout my whole wedding!" she recalled. "It was so embarrassing. I went to say my vows and I sounded like Miss Piggy! I've been married before, but I've never been *married* before. Mark comes the closest to all the stuff I ever read about romance. Before Mark came along, I don't think I ever loved before."

They set up their new home in a fourteen-room Upper East Side apartment on Sixty-ninth street in New York's Yorkville district. It had white marble floors with black, silver, and red highlights and was decorated with art by Mark and Andy Warhol. Mark had returned to sculpting full-time and his work tended toward abstract marbles that fit in with the décor. The apartment featured a dramatic skyline view of the city and special touches, such as posters from Vincente Minnelli's movie successes, added to personalize the home.

Further decorating accents in bright colors and bold patterns were provided by Halston and colleague Tim MacDonald, including the broad-brush use of reds, zebra striped chairs, and white leather furniture in the card room, bar, and master bedroom. It was a splashy way to start their new life together in a home designed for entertaining, which they did with élan.

Sadly, Liza wouldn't carry their child to term. She was going to name the baby after Kay Thompson if it was a girl and after her brother Joey if it was a boy. Instead she underwent a painful miscarriage after she was rushed to New York Hospital-Cornell Medical Center with unbearable stomach pains. The heartrending event occurred just six days after her wedding. Liza lived by a feel-good philosophy, so she came out of the depression surprisingly quickly. She told friends it wasn't a disaster and there would be another time. Meanwhile, she went Christmas shopping.

A year later, at age thirty-five, she found out she was pregnant again. On October 4, 1980, she was rushed to Massachusetts General Hospital with painful stomach contractions. She had been in nearby Framingham doing a spot appearance with Joel Grey at a local club when the pains began. The following day she learned she was pregnant, but her doctors considered her a high-risk patient because of her previous miscarriage and because she was such an active performer. The physicians told Liza and Mark if they wanted to have the baby, Liza would have to forgo her life as a wild, onstage dancer for the next eight months. The two agreed. Liza really wanted the baby for many reasons, including what Goldie told her about the joy of motherhood.

Liza canceled her concerts for the rest of the year and went into restful seclusion at a home she purchased on Lake Tahoe. Then on New Year's Day 1981, Mark dashed to the Reno Hospital with Liza. The physicians who examined her concluded she needed some minor surgery because the fetus was not developing quite right. It turned into another terrible miscarriage, and 1981 dawned as a depressing time for Liza and Mark.

22

Arthur and Other Things

Professional success alleviated some of Liza's heartbreak. In the early part of 1980 she was featured in two television shows. The first was *Goldie and Liza Together* on February 19, 1980. It received pleasant—not rave—reviews.

John O'Connor wrote in the *New York Times,* "Two attractive, talented women have put together a nice show. Not spectacular, but nice."

The second special was a salute to musical theater, but seemed more a showcase for Mikhail Baryshnikov. *Baryshnikov on Broadway* aired April 24 with Liza making a guest appearance. Liza enjoyed appearing on this show with her former jet-set lover.

She said: "Misha and I talked about working together for years, but that TV special was our first real chance. When I think about it now, I realize what an unlikely combination we must have been. I bet lots of people tuned the show in just to see what the hell we were going to do! But Misha? A warm, gentle man. A genius. A hell of a dancer and a great human being."

Of this show, O'Connor wrote: "The show is a smash hit, a marvelously imaginative format. Miss Minnelli proves invaluable as guide, narrator and supporter. In fact, her name deserves to be in the title. Her singing is stirring—especially on 'Music That Makes Me Dance'—and her dancing is splendid. She performs with rare and admirable generosity. All concerned deserve a standing ovation."

Liza finished the television special with Misha and moved on to her next movie, which looked like it would be a winner. It was an engaging story about an indecisive, bumbling, millionaire drunk torn between marrying a snooty, rich, debutante bitch and a down-to-earth, kind waitress.

Engaging actors would play the main roles, including Sir John Gielgud as Hobson, the grumpy, crafty British butler; Jill Eikenberry as the boring debutante Susan Johnson; and Dudley Moore, the short comedian-musician with the tall girlfriends, as Arthur Bach, the bachelor millionaire. Liza was to play Linda Marolla, the pretty, pink-collar, salt-of-the-earth waitress. There were no songs to sing, but there were laughs to be made and that, along with the stellar cast, attracted Liza. She felt this would assure her a hit movie after three successive disasters.

As with every film, there were problems shooting *Arthur,* but one developed the production staff hadn't anticipated—Liza's fans. A number of scenes were shot around New York, and production crews expect there will always be a few spectators. However, the crew was totally unprepared for the idolizing Liza fans who filled the streets in New York. For Steve Gordon, the director and writer of the film, it was not only his first experience as a director, it was his first experience dealing with a charismatic star and her loyal adherents.

He recalled, "By mid-morning, we were surrounded by thousands of people. We became a tourist attraction. People would say, 'Let's visit the Plaza Hotel and the Statue of Liberty and, on the way back, let's stop at *Arthur.*'"

Shooting took place in the late summer of 1980 and it was hot and humid, but the weather made no difference. Spectators thronged around the set to be near Liza. "People would fall down laughing at Dudley," Gordon said with amazement, "but they wanted to reach out and touch Liza. It's as if some bit of her magic would rub off on them."

This enthusiasm for Liza was shared by both her costar and her director. Dudley Moore said: "It was easy to be in a good mood while making *Arthur* because I was usually around Liza. Her confidence attracted people." Gordon's assessment was, "I think she's wonderful, a great example of a giving actress. She gave Dudley the kind of comic relief he needed. Everything you think she is, she isn't. She knows nothing and then she knows everything."

After Liza finished shooting her scenes in the film, she went on a concert tour and came back in May 1981 for some pickup shots. *Arthur* was released in July.

Unfortunately, the reviewers were not as taken with *Arthur* as the stars and the crew, but the movie did well. David Ansen of *Newsweek* thought—as had others before the movie went into production—*Arthur* should have been a terrific film. He declared, "*Arthur* is not the best comedy of the season, which is a pity because it has the best comic team—Dudley Moore and Liza Minnelli. Liza is not to be blamed for the film's derailment; she never had a chance."

Stanley Kauffmann at the liberal *New Republic* disagreed with Ansen and thought Liza was clearly to blame for the film's failure to hit the right tone as a comedy. He wrote, "*Arthur* has spots of amusement, one of which is not Liza Minnelli's performance as a waitress. She manages to turn any moment, any place—a Queens kitchen, for instance—into Las Vegas show biz full of 'heart.'" And John Simon in the conservative *National Review* wrote: "Jill Eikenberry is an able, attractive actress, she was deliberately made to look as dreary as possible, but even so...she is a thousand times more preferable than Liza Minnelli. Miss Minnelli, though relatively restrained, still exudes her special brand of physical and spirited repulsiveness."

The *New Yorker*'s Pauline Kael, one of the most respected reviewers of the time, also criticized Liza's performance, which she saw as out of sync with the good work done by costars Dudley Moore and Sir John Gielgud. Her view was: "A larger idea that doesn't work is the casting of Liza Minnelli. Moore and Gielgud bounce off each other...they have common ground. But when Minnelli turns up, she doesn't bounce off anybody and there's no common ground under the three of them. I haven't a clue what Linda is supposed to be and I doubt if Minnelli had much of a clue. When she needs to be appealing, she's electrifying; her gamin eyes pop open as if she's just seen a ghost. Yet you feel Arthur would be better off marrying Hobson."

There had been rumors in the past about Liza doing drugs, particularly after her mother's funeral when she was on tranquilizers or when she was hanging around Halston, who was notorious for drug use. But Liza always denied any drug dependence, although she once smoked what she called "this funny stuff" and didn't like the reaction. Most of her chemical dependence, she said, consisted of chain-smoking Marlboros, drinking Grand Marnier and Coke, or knocking back bullshots. But perhaps some of her problems with *Arthur* stemmed from imitating the title character. It was often rumored Liza's drinking and drugs interfered with production.

Ironically but predictably in the relatively small environment of show business, Liza's path crossed again with ex-husband Peter Allen while she was making *Arthur.* In 1981 Peter wrote the theme for the movie in collaboration with Burt Bacharach, Carole Bayer Sager, and composer-singer Christopher Cross. The song, "Arthur's Theme," won the Oscar for Best Song. Peter's career continued with many successes and failures until his death from AIDS in 1992.

Soon after *Arthur* was released Liza went on a concert tour to Australia, Japan, and the Philippines. Poor reviews for the film may have also torpedoed Liza's chance to play Eva Peron in the movie version of the stage production *Evita,* as well as costing her a couple of other film roles in which she was interested. However, she did arrange to have Sam Cohn, an agent at International Creative Management, represent her. That kind of representation, appropriate for a star of her stature, would ensure her continued good roles and gigs even if she didn't get every one she wanted.

Her next big tour in Africa and Europe went well. It began in the fall of 1982 in a fairly unlikely place, Bophuthatswana, South Africa.

Americans might wonder why a star of Liza's dimensions would go into the African wilderness to entertain a bunch of elephants and giraffes, which is what they probably envisioned at the mention of the words "Bophuthatswana, South Africa." In fact, the place, called Sun City, is a giant resort and casino development like Las Vegas. Liza did eleven performances for $1 million with her traveling troupe of fourteen musicians and dancers. Then the troupe swung north into Europe for engagements in Paris, Milan, Rome, and Vienna.

23

1983—Tributes and Concerts

L iza's devotion to her father grew deeper as he grew older. On February 19, 1983, his eightieth birthday, she gave a reception for him at the Palm Springs Desert Museum. He was old and tired and had been fitted with a pacemaker in late January, but his life was enriched by his fourth wife Lee Anderson, who he married in 1980 in spite of his earlier conviction he was not suited for marriage. They courted a long time and she was loving and patient, so the marriage became the most serene Vincente would have. Everyone was convinced Lee's loving care extended Vincente's life.

A frequent visitor to their Crescent Drive home in Beverly Hills, Liza would spend at least one day a month with her father, jazzing up his life with the latest gossip and news about the world of show business and music. She also introduced Vincente to some of her hip friends, like Michael Jackson. His other daughter Christina, Tina Nina, by his second wife Georgette Magnani, lived in Mexico with her children Vincente and Xeminia, Vincente's only grandchildren. She would come to see Vincente from time to time, but she and Liza were never close—certainly not as close as Liza was with her mother's children, Lorna and Joey Luft.

Some people believed Liza was jealous of Tina Nina and did not want to acknowledge the father she cherished could possibly have sired another child. Tina Nina recalled, "Liza was much more at ease, much closer to Daddy than I was. She had her mother, and although Judy had her ups and downs, Liza put her on a pedestal. But Daddy was her stability and Liza was practically in love with him."

Several weeks after the Palm Springs tribute, Liza leavened her new concert tour with a tribute to her father's movies that ran almost half an hour. Fred Ebb also felt it was time to bring Judy into one of Liza's concerts. To convince Liza, he pointed to her living room display of awards—an Oscar, four Tonys, and countless others—and said, "It says Liza Minnelli on them, not Judy Garland. You've arrived. Now we can put some of her songs in your show. Maybe it's time you said thank you."

The show was called *By Myself,* and the reviewers were fervent in their criticism after it opened in Los Angeles at the Universal Amphitheater in April 1983. They wrote that Liza's electricity and energy overwhelmed the material and left no room for subtlety. The rock 'n' roll tempo, they declared, was inappropriate for songs taken from Vincente's musicals or for those made famous by her mother. As usual the public didn't care about the reviews and the perform-ances sold out.

In March 1983 Liza paid another tribute to her father at the Museum of Modern Art in Manhattan. While Vincente was too ill to make the cross-country trip to attend, he sent his loving daughter a telegram that was read to the 250 people attending, including Joan Bennett, Cheryl Tiegs, Kitty Carlisle, and Farrah Fawcett. It began, "My darling Liza, First of all, as your father, let me remind you to stand up straight and speak slowly."

The moment that topped the evening of cocktails, film clips, and clever speeches was the fabled Lillian Gish toasting Liza: "You're Vincente's greatest production!"

In May Liza took *By Myself* to one of her favorite venues—one that held the same place in Judy's heart—London. Except this time it wasn't the Palladium, it was the Apollo Victoria Theater. The audience loved her. This performance was followed by the Cannes

Film Festival where Liza—whose films are popular overseas regardless of whether they are disasters in America—was awarded a Distinguished Achievement Award.

Mark and Liza still wanted a baby despite two tragic miscarriages. By 1983 she was close to forty, and while adoption was a possibility, Liza had a different first choice: "I want a baby of my own before we adopt."

24

Recovery, Rejuvenation, and Release

T he year 1984 would be another turning point for Liza when she saved her own life without much help from others, including husband Mark Gero. This is an important area where Liza radically differs from her mother. Liza has the determination and strength to save herself when things go wrong. Liza had been rehearsing since the previous year for her role in *The Rink*, a musical with lyrics and music by her close friends Kander and Ebb. It opened on Broadway on February 9, 1984, at the Martin Beck Theater to less than enthusiastic reviews, but the backers kept it open.

Meanwhile, Liza and Mark's marriage was in trouble. Part of the reason was the strain of the unsuccessful pregnancies. Liza saw it as "a real bad period of not listening to each other." The two decided to separate to see if they could get themselves centered and then come back together. Liza seemed troubled. By the fifth month of *The Rink* she was missing performances, which was totally unlike the dedicated trouper Liza had become.

Liza wasn't sure herself what her problem was so she secretly had two doctors examine her to make sure she was not ill. They gave her a clean bill of physical health but concluded she was under a lot of emotional pressure trying to make *The Rink* a success. *The Rink* was a musical comedy about a daughter who returns to the family-owned roller-skating rink and then has to confront her troubled relationship with her mother. For Liza it had an autobiographical ring because of her relationship with her own mother.

Liza recognized the roles she had to play on stage and in life. "I have to be witty. I have to be glamorous, I have to be bubbly. Well, I tried to be those things for many, many years." To help her, doctors had offered the same remedy since her mother died, Valium.

During this time, Liza was haunted by the fear she would end up the way her mother did—an older, fading star deeply in debt and overdosing on pills. She often shared this fear with ex-husband Jack. Early in July she went to see the new muppet movie, *The Muppets Take Manhattan,* with some friends. The next night, July 11, she appeared in *The Rink* and as usual went out afterward to some nightclubs with her publicist Barry Landau.

They ended up at her apartment where she became upset over a swelling on her neck. She was convinced the swelling demanded immediate attention and early the next morning she went to her doctor's office. The doctor's careful approach was to take a biopsy. He injected a shot of local anesthetic and Liza went into convulsions. This incident convinced Liza she had taken too much Valium, booze, and other drugs.

Landau was with her at the time. "She was petrified," he said. That was the moment Liza decided she needed help.

Liza seemed to have learned from her mother's poor decisions. When Judy got into emotional or financial trouble, she created an aura of the helpless child and waited until someone stepped forward to help her, but as time passed, fewer were willing to do so. When Liza realized she was in trouble, she faced the problem and actively sought help. She decided to become clean and sober. Since the Betty Ford Center was the rage among rich celebrities, that's where she wanted to go. Barry Landau knew Mrs. Ford personally and telephoned her in Rancho Mirage, California.

Liza called her father so he wouldn't hear the news from someone else. While startled, Vincente was proud his daughter had the sense and the courage to confront her drug abuse.

Lee said, "Liza told her father she had to get help so she can continue living. She said she was trying to put her life back together and this was the only way. We were shocked and surprised by her decision, but we were also very impressed by her strength."

Stockard Channing replaced Liza in *The Rink* for the last few weeks of its run and Liza flew to California with Lorna to enter the Betty Ford Center. Newspaper headlines blossomed across the country:

DESPERATE LIZA BATTLES SAME PROBLEM OF PILLS AND BOOZE THAT KILLED HER MOM JUDY GARLAND.

Liza issued a dignified statement saying she had a problem, and like a grownup, she would take care of it. In reality, she was shaky and vulnerable when she arrived at the clinic in the Palm Springs desert, but she was welcomed by an understanding and caring staff. She was put into gentle isolation for the first five days until she could relax and get her bearings.

The concept behind Betty Ford's center is that people become chemically dependent because they are insulated from the real world and, more important, themselves. So all patients have to perform chores designed to put them back in touch with the real world. An important emotional-mental exercise is to write a long, honest letter to someone whose presence or absence, actions or omissions, left a mark on the patient's life. Not surprisingly, Liza chose to write Judy. Liza dealt with the death of her mother when it happened by being very busy with the funeral and immediately returning to shooting *Junie Moon*. She decided it was best to keep occupied rather than sit around mourning the death of a loved one.

Liza did not have a chance to tell Judy her feelings and settle whatever problems were between them. For one thing, Liza was always troubled by the fact that the world adored her mother but ignored her father, who was equally loving and talented. He certainly was easier to live with. At the end of his career, he was left with only one movie—starring his daughter—that was a disaster.

This made Liza feel all the more her father was never given the accolades he deserved. Finally, Liza had to say good-bye to Judy. At Betty Ford, she got the chance.

"I had one special thing to get rid of," she said. "I had to bury my mother. At last, I had never had the time—or taken the time—to mourn her or to really bury her, the sort of burial that doesn't take place in the ground but rather in the spirit. I was overprotective. I saw myself as my mother's mother. What I didn't know was that I loved her too much."

Liza found the help she needed and faced up to some of the decisions she had to make. Elizabeth Taylor visited in mid-July and pumped up Liza's self-respect. At the same time, Liza was thinking hard about her marriage to Mark and their separation. Even though he phoned frequently, she avoided talking to him and contemplated taking the legal steps toward divorce.

Her half sister Tina Nina spelled out some of the problems Liza was having with Mark: "Liza used to say Mark was protective and fatherly, but Lee told me Mark took advantage of her. She would say Liza worked like mad, worked her head off, while Mark would go to Lake Tahoe with his family and spend all his time playing tennis, poker and gambling."

Liza was also attracted to Gene Simmons of the rock group Kiss. In the end, Liza returned to Mark when she left the Ford facility. The time there apparently struck a responsive chord, helped free her of some demons, and let her talk frankly about her problems.

Yet in most of her disclosures about chemical dependency, Liza was usually careful to identify only those things that had some degree of social acceptance such as alcohol and prescription drugs.

In a *People* magazine interview about her use of prescription drugs, she denied she ever used illicit recreational drugs such as cocaine or heroin. She said, "I'd find myself getting dependent on safe Valium, so I'd switch to Librium. And all the time I was taking the Librium, I'd be telling myself, 'See, Liza, you are not dependent on Valium. You just quit it.' You fool yourself for years."

Liza has to be given full credit for recognizing her dependency and doing something about it. She became a fan of the Betty Ford method and urged others to avail themselves of it or some comparable program. She told an interviewer for the *London Daily Mail,* "I'd like people to know you don't have to face this alone—chemical dependency is an accepted disease and you can get help. With counseling, you can still go through withdrawal, but you won't have to go it alone."

The concept that she didn't have to get well by herself pervaded her thoughts during 1984 as she turned thirty-eight and tried to get a grip on herself and her life. Her marriage was still rocky, her career on cruise. She felt she had to do something professionally that would make an impact. In addition, she had gained thirty pounds, in part because she had stopped the chemical abuse.

She planned to appear with Charles Aznavour at an August 1984 benefit in Monte Carlo for the International Red Cross, but the extra weight concerned her. She decided to drop two things: the benefit and the pounds. She checked into a spa in Pompano Beach, Florida, and started to slim down, but she was still thinking about her marriage and her career. Friends were pleased she joined Alcoholics Anonymous after the Betty Ford experience but became troubled when she apparently stopped attending meetings. According to the *Boston Herald,* Liz Taylor chastised Liza for not faithfully attending AA. By March 2, 1985, it was reported Liza had checked herself into the Hazelden Clinic in Minnesota, another center famous for dealing with chemical abuse.

Liza demonstrated she was back on track personally and professionally when she launched a grueling twenty-six-city tour three months later. Her performances were dazzling. When it was over, she rewarded herself by returning to at least part of her old, glamorous life in New York, hanging around with singer Michael Jackson, whose gender preferences were not yet the focus of scandal. The old crowd had changed and its playpen, Studio 54, was closed.

All the while, Liza was looking for another vehicle for her talents. She found it in the tragic life story of a young woman struggling to save a son afflicted with muscular dystrophy. It was the kind of heartrending story that appealed to people who made movies for TV in the era of Oprah, Sally Jessy, and Donahue. Mary Lou Weisman, the woman whose true-life story it was, wrote a book and sold the rights to television. Her life intrigued Liza and she wanted to play Mary Lou. She made her usual energetic pitch to get the part, which she did. She spent a lot of time with the real Mary Lou to recreate her anger, pain, and frustration for the movie *A Time To Live*. It was broadcast October 28, 1985, and turned out well enough to win Liza another Golden Globe.

As 1985 wound down, however, other troubles erupted in Liza's life as she slipped back into old, self-destructive ways. Early the following year, she became what Betty Ford's staff refer to as a "retread," checking in to the clinic again for a refresher session. She may not have been successful the first time around, even with her stay at the Hazelden clinic, but Liza felt better about herself and felt she was making progress.

She confessed to an interviewer: "I think one of the biggest changes in my life is I'm not afraid like I used to be. I'm not afraid of anything anymore. I'm not afraid of meeting new people and that free-floating anxiety I used to always feel is gone and what a blessing. When you are very sick, you lose sight of faith."

With her renewed faith, Liza undertook a new and nostalgic engagement: an English tour, ending at the London Palladium. She stayed at the Savoy with Mark and their marriage seemed to reverse course and start mending. Liza's psyche was mending to the point she stopped biting her nails for the first time in her life.

While in London she even attended AA meetings. Another attendee was quoted as saying, "Liza stood up and told everyone about her problems in the past. It helped a lot of people there and gave them a lot of encouragement."

The English tour, which included Manchester, Brighton, and Birmingham, ended with a performance at the Palladium on March

7, 1986. From there Liza jetted to Atlantic City for a performance that would become a regular gig—appearing with Frank Sinatra. Later, they would team with Sammy Davis Jr. in concerts and on TV shows and set the audience on fire with their act. Sinatra was Judy's friend and knew Liza from the day of her birth. It excited Liza to be sharing the stage with this legend.

The Sinatra-Minnelli act held forth for almost a week at the beginning of May, and her life was looking better except for one dark cloud—the health of her beloved father Vincente. She undertook a series of American and European concert dates right after Atlantic City. When she reached Indianapolis, she received word her eighty-three-year-old father was seriously ill. Canceling concerts, she rushed to his side in Los Angeles. Vincente was suffering from Alzheimer's, but being near his wife and daughters had a soothing effect. Liza spent two days with her father assuring him he was going to get better and telling him her marriage was strong again and she and Mark hoped to have a baby.

By July 25 Liza felt he was holding his own and it was safe for her to catch a plane for her next concert date in France. Unfortunately, she was wrong. Vincente quietly slipped away that night after dinner while Liza was high above the Atlantic Ocean. The cause of death was a fatal combination of pneumonia and emphysema from all his years of smoking cigarettes.

Frank Sinatra is an odd mixture of personalities who helped his friend Liza when she most needed it. Sinatra is an extraordinary singing talent admired by millions of fans, but his personal life is another story. To the public he comes across as the tough guy in a world of smart alecks and alleged Mafia connections. Dubbed "the Chairman of the Board" by his "Rat Pack" sycophants like Sammy Davis Jr. and Dean Martin, he swaggers around living up to the title. He is notoriously rude to the press and to those who interfere with what he seems to regard as his royal domain. He publicly refers to women as "broads."

Yet in his private life, he tends to be fragile, withdrawn, and amazingly sensitive and loyal to his friends. He is an anonymous donor to charities and important causes and often helps friends when they can't take care of themselves, such as reportedly paying for Judy's mausoleum when no one else would or could.

Sinatra learned through the Hollywood grapevine of Vincente's death and knew Liza was unwittingly flying to Europe. He feared she would land at Nice, be surrounded by the media wolfpack, and learn of her father's death before she was prepared to cope with it. So he arranged a phone call to the Nice airport that would reach Liza before she could be confronted by the newshounds. Frank gently conveyed the sad news to her. Stunned her father was dead when she had just left him hours before, she managed a return flight to Los Angeles.

Liza was faced with yet another emotionally charged funeral exacerbated by the conflicting wishes of family members. Lee and Liza started planning the funeral services, but Tina Nina was not included because nobody told her Vincente was dead. Apparently it either slipped everyone's mind or they decided it would be better to wait until the details were worked out to make everything as quick and painless as possible for Tina Nina. "I discovered Lee and Liza were making plans for the funeral and I wasn't consulted," she said.

Then a flap arose, as it had with Judy's funeral, over final disposition of the body. Both Judy and Vincente wanted to be cremated. Tina Nina said Vincente left a note saying his ashes should be disposed of by the survivors as they saw fit. As with Judy's death, everyone was against cremation, and Lee and Liza wanted a funeral befitting the wonderful man Vincente had been. Tina Nina wanted to follow her father's wishes, but Liza wanted to follow the wishes of his survivors.

Tina Nina recalled, "I talked to Liza about it and reminded her Daddy hadn't wanted a funeral or any service at all. But she said Daddy's friends wanted that kind of a funeral and Lee, too, wanted a big funeral because Daddy was so important. I got the impression it was all just part of show business."

A tasteful and elegant funeral service was held at Forest Lawn Memorial Park five days after Vincente died. Beautifully landscaped and dotted with fine sculptures, murals, and other works of art, Forest Lawn is the resting place for many of Hollywood's most famous stars and one of the top three tourist attractions in Southern California. Vincente was not buried in Beverly Hills because nobody is buried in Beverly Hills—the city bans cemeteries.

The service took place in the chapel known as "the Wee Kirk of the Heather" with priest George O'Brien presiding. More than a hundred friends and family gathered to bid Vincente good-bye on his last journey. Stephen Harvey, a chronicler of Vincente's movies, described the setting: "It was one of those grand ceremonials Hollywood reserves for its departed greats. Three generations of show business notables crowded into the Forest Lawn chapel which uncannily resembled one of his own sets for *Brigadoon.*"

The mourners included stars and close friends. Both Kirk Douglas and Gregory Peck spoke. Douglas called Vincente a wonderful man with mysterious ways and Peck praised his artistic talent.

Harvey commented on Douglas's reference to the mystery of Vincente: "Douglas noted that despite all their years of collaboration and friendship, there remained a private core to Minnelli's nature which he could never quite penetrate. Which was just as well, for perhaps that secret place was where this director's art came from and Minnelli would have been the last person capable of explaining its mystery. His movies endure as both his own composite self-portrait and a glass that reflects the time and place that nurtured him. And, as Minnelli proclaimed in his last celluloid farewell, the mirror must be beautiful, too."

Eva Gabor related an event both mysterious and artistic which suggested the master director might actually be orchestrating a special effect at his own funeral. She recalled, "Vincente's favorite color was yellow and so he was dressed in a yellow blazer and buried in an open coffin. All of a sudden, a yellow butterfly flew out of his blazer pocket and flew over the congregation."

Of the family there, Liza seemed to have the toughest time. According to Tina Nina, "Before we got to the church, Liza whispered to me the funeral was so incredibly difficult for her to go through now as she was completely clean."

Once at the church, Liza collapsed, but Tina Nina held onto her and helped her stiffen her resolve so she could get through the ordeal. To Tina Nina and most others, it seemed a moving and dignified service—at least until it was over. Then, as they left for the graveside service, Liza and Tina Nina's limo stopped, Michael Jackson got in, and, according to Tina Nina, he and Liza began working out the details of a picture project they had in mind. Tina Nina could not grasp what was going on even after everyone adjourned to the Minnelli home in Beverly Hills for refreshments.

Tina Nina and Liza were together for a few days and confessed their mutual jealousy over their late father's attention and affection, but Tina Nina never got over the way the simple little funeral her father wanted was transformed into a Hollywood happening.

"The funeral was arranged like a big event," she said. "It was very hard for me knowing as I did Daddy didn't want there to be anything public at all. Yet, it ended up being like a show business party with personalities and stars and a buffet and drinks at the house afterward....My father was dead and I knew he hadn't wanted this."

Vincente's funeral offered an opportunity for various family members to get together again after long separations. Tina Nina had two children Liza had never met and Liza hadn't seen Tina Nina's mother, Vincente's second wife Georgette, for years. They tried to organize a family dinner with Liza and Mark, Lorna and her husband Jake, Sid Luft and his wife, and Georgette and Tina Nina. It was set for Le Dome on the Sunset Strip, "the" place for the Hollywood music crowd. Jake and Mark did not appear. The group had a civilized evening, after which Tina says Liza discarded her.

25

The Liza–Tina Nina Heir War

Before his death, Vincente cashed in and spent his MGM
pension, so at the end Liza was sending money to Vincente
and Lee and paying the mortgage on their house in Beverly
Hills. When Vincente died, the house was the only thing of value
left in his estate. It was worth between $2.5 million and $3 million.
After Vincente was gone, two of the three women closest to him, his
wife Lee and daughter Tina Nina, were broke. Liza was the only one
with income from her career. The money question became a major
issue within the family because for Lee and Tina it meant survival.

Vincente, for whatever reason—probably assuming her mother
and aunt could care for Tina Nina and her two children—left her
only $5,000. He left the Beverly Hills house to Liza on the condition
that Lee would live there as long as she wanted. The stage for
conflict between Liza and Tina Nina was set. Tina Nina reluctantly
took her stand by refusing to sign the documents that appointed
Liza executor of their father's estate.

"Liza told me, 'Don't worry about a thing, I will look after
you.'" Tina Nina said. "But I didn't believe her and I decided to
fight the will. Liza's attorney drew up Daddy's will but Daddy hadn't
signed it. He was unable to write and Lee was signing all letters for
him. Daddy couldn't write anymore and even on the phone, he
would black out and forget who he was talking to. Lee always picked

up the phone and spoke for him and answered all his letters for him. She was always there, translating for Daddy. Daddy and I could have communicated with our eyes or through touch or through a few words, but Lee never gave us the chance."

Tina Nina felt she had been frozen out of the family and Lee and Liza had formed a cabal against her. Money was not the only issue. She said: "I didn't question the will for the money. I questioned it because I wanted to do what Daddy wanted. And he always wanted Liza and me to share the house. Many times, my father told me, 'I want you to know that in my will, the house will be half for you and half for Liza.' Daddy wouldn't have just told me this, he said it for a reason and he said it many times. He knew I was in financial need and Liza didn't need money and my children were his only grandchildren."

It was a painful time for everyone concerned. Liza didn't want to hurt anybody and wanted to do what was right. Tina Nina felt she was right and that Lee, Liza, and Mark were ganging up on her as she fought for the benefit of herself and her two small children.

Tina Nina recalled: "Finally, we made an out-of-court settlement whereby my children were beneficiaries. It was nothing like I would have originally received. But I never blamed Liza because she was influenced by other people. There was always a power struggle between us. Liza was always jealous of me because all her life she wanted to be Vincente Minnelli's only daughter."

The legal case was settled, but things between the half sisters probably never will be.

Meanwhile, Liza turned her attention to other things, including her on-and-off marriage. She participated in a September 22, 1986, memorial to her father at New York's Museum of Modern Art. The tribute was put together by Martin Scorsese and Stephen Harvey, curator of the museum's film department. In 1989 the museum would publish Harvey's definitive book on Vincente's career, *Directed by Vincente Minnelli*. Harvey began the work in 1982, four years before Vincente's death, with the full cooperation of Vincente and the entire family.

Vincente made thirty-four films between 1943 and 1976, all for MGM. Most directors would have moved around to several different studios during their careers, but Vincente was under contract to MGM. As Harvey wrote, "Minnelli's pictures were among the studio's most prestigious and popular films....Minnelli's productions were acclaimed for their artistic cohesion...this was a gift of great value to the studio which lured him west."

Liza and Mark were paying more attention to each other and their marriage and she had returned to a clean and sober life. Then came a call from old friend Burt Reynolds about making another movie with him, *Rent-a-Cop*, to be filmed in Rome. Suitably enticed, Liza flew to Italy to get in front of the cameras after an absence of six years. The legal fight with Tina Nina was distracting, but Liza plowed ahead with the film. The weather was miserable— they were filming in December—and Liza was gobbling vitamin C to ward off colds, flus, and anything else that might bring her down.

When she finally finished the film at the end of February 1987, she flew back to Los Angeles to attend some parties, do a benefit, and appear on a couple of television shows, including another tribute to her father, *Minnelli on Minnelli*. She returned to New York in May to open her scheduled concert at Carnegie Hall. Again she mustered the key ingredients that made her concerts successful in the past, costumes by Halston and music by Kander and Ebb.

She had passed her fortieth birthday the year before and it was exhilarating to receive the kind of reviews this production brought her. It turned out to be a Carnegie Hall record breaker for the longest run by a solo performer. Liza shone for three weeks starting May 28, 1987, and the critics and audiences loved her. Then she went on a national tour in August, to the delight of adoring crowds.

Typical of the critical praise mixed with sentimental feelings about Liza was Liz Smith's observation, "The super comeback of a girl who never really went away but who experienced enough ups and downs to keep us fascinated for years. Onstage came the same youthful looking gaminlike, innocent, wide-eyed Liza we have always known and loved."

Critic and longtime Liza fan Clive Barnes wrote: "Liza Minnelli at 41 is A number-1, cream of the crop, king of the hill, top of the heap. She comes on in a shiny, spangly Halston miniskirt, her hair all moussed up in her customary pixie bouffant. She looks gorgeous, almost edible. Her eyes are black brilliance in a guileless doll's face of heartbreaking innocence, a vulnerability stretched by the scarlet gash of her mouth.

"Her beauty is as much of a child as a woman—it depends in part on character, on shifting expressions of trust, love, friendship and simple openness. It is a face you'd give your last penny to. It's a face where all the smiles have a subtext of tears and all the tears are washed away on a rainbow. The very real gaiety has a very real undertow of sadness. The face is a map of contradictions. Liza wears her vulnerability on her sleeves."

On August 9, Liza kicked off her national tour in Saratoga Springs and dazzled audiences around the country. In mid-November she flew to London to appear at the Royal Albert Hall. Several observers noted the absence of liquor revitalized her and her sexy wardrobe, designed to show off her great legs, flattered her even more. Jack Haley Jr., still a good friend, was delighted with the new Liza. "I've known her since she was fourteen. I've never seen her more happy. Liza's gift is her resilience, her knowledge and her experience." Her self-reliance was something her mother did not have.

On New Year's Day, 1988, *Rent-a-Cop* opened in theaters around the country. It paralleled the last movie she made with Burt, *Lucky Lady*. Making the movie was great fun, but the public reaction was tepid. In the meantime, Walter Yetnikoff, head of CBS Records, arranged a recording project for Liza involving an English group, the Pet Shop Boys. The recording, "Losing My Mind," became Liza's first hit since her single "You Are for Loving" from *Best Foot Forward* twenty-five years before.

After the not-so-great release of *Rent-a-Cop,* Liza appeared on television in a set of three plays, each written by a different playwright. The central theme was the line "Sam found out," and it was entitled *Sam Found Out: A Triple Play*. Of the three, one was written by Kander and Ebb as a brief musical. Reviewer Kay Gardella wrote, "Minnelli, who has proven over and over again she can handle heavy drama, light comedy and musicals as well, covers all bases here. Liza is absolutely first rate."

Later in 1988 Liza appeared in a television commercial written by Kander and Ebb—her first—for Estée Lauder. The ad agency account executive summarized why they wanted Liza: She was to New York what Edith Piaf was to Paris.

Meanwhile, Liza and another movie buddy, Dudley Moore, set out to film the sequel to *Arthur*. *Arthur II* picked up the story as millionaire Arthur Bach (Moore) and bride Linda (Liza) become victims of a vicious plot by the girlfriend Arthur left to marry Linda in the first movie. In this plot, Arthur loses all his money and becomes a drunk again while Linda turns out to be infertile. In the Hollywood ending Arthur returns to sobriety and they adopt a child. It was a wistful role for Liza. Unlike *Rent-a-Cop*, released about nine months earlier, *Arthur II* received good reviews and was successful at the box office. Though it had started poorly, the year finally went well.

Next Liza shifted back to the stage with a series of eleven concert appearances with Frank Sinatra and Sammy Davis Jr. Their trio, which would prove popular around the country, was originally Frank, Sammy, and Dean Martin, but when Martin became ill they substituted Liza. The Frank–Liza–Sammy combination became a standard show with all their inside patter and familiarity with each others' lines, jokes, and shtick. It was a real boost for Liza, too. She said, "I mean, can you imagine standing up there with two people you grew up with, your Uncle Frank and your Uncle Sammy and suddenly you're sharing the bill with them!"

Sadly, many of the men with whom Liza regularly worked and played were faltering because of age or illness. Sammy Davis Jr. developed throat cancer requiring an operation that would end his singing career. Sammy decided he would do it his way, singing to the end. Once when the sheet music didn't arrive in time, Sinatra canceled a concert ten minutes before the curtain was due to rise because he couldn't remember the lyrics. Halston was afflicted with AIDS.

Liza desperately wanted to have a baby and that desire was underscored when she saw Lorna with her two children, Jesse and Vanessa. It seemed to Liza some of the most important problems of her life would be cured if she could become pregnant or adopt a child. It would be maternally fulfilling and would keep her from being lonely. And it would, she thought, alter her relationship with Mark and turn two semi-independent people into a loving, close-knit family.

But the decision to adopt was not hers alone. She would have adopted a child in a minute, but Mark refused. So Liza had to become pregnant. In her usual forthright way, she wanted to make sure she was doing everything she could to complete her part of the deal. So she booked herself into the Omega Institute in Louisiana, a fertility clinic.

26

A Time of Changes

T he last few years had been a time of surprising, even alarming changes, for Liza and people around her. One of the most significant was revealed in January 1989 over dinner in New York between two brothers sharing a dark secret. One was Bob Frowick, a distinguished American career diplomat many of the other brother's friends didn't know existed. The other was one of the most revered fashion designers in America, Halston Frowick, known to most of the world simply as Halston. At dinner in 101, Halston told Bob he had tested positive for HIV, the virus that causes AIDS.

Bob was stunned his brother had let himself become infected with HIV through indiscriminate and unprotected sex and that he seemed so casual about it. Halston said with proper diet, rest, exercise, and the new drug AZT, he would survive. Buoying his spirits even more was the fashion industry's new appreciation of his work. A tribute in the April 21, 1989, *Women's Wear Daily* declared, "His clean-cut, all-American style showed up at every major New York collection. His spirit is everywhere."

Halston had been on an emotional roller coaster since his suspicious symptoms began appearing in November 1988. A few months later came another terrible blow: betrayal by a friend.

From 1976 on, Andy Warhol began keeping a diary of his

activities and those around him. The result was an 897-page book naming 1,366 celebrities with whom he spoke, partied, traveled, and did drugs. The diary was published in the spring of 1989 after Warhol's death. It would prove a disaster for Halston's public image because it contained more than two hundred references to Halston, including items about Halston's relationship with lover Victor Hugo, his drug habits, sexual orgies, and connections with other celebrities. It featured extensive references to Bianca Jagger and Liza, neither of whom came off well.

According to Steven Gaines, the revelations in Warhol's diaries were devastating to Halston: "As he watched the book race up the best-seller lists he became so angry with the Warhol estate for publishing it he dumped almost all his Warhols onto the market at wholesale prices so he would never have to see them again. What he didn't sell he gave away to the Des Moines Museum of Art....

"What little spirit he was able to muster in the face of his illness was destroyed along with the last shreds of his dignity. Soon after the publication of the Warhol diaries, his health began to deteriorate rapidly, and a month later he was rushed to New York Hospital for his first major AIDS hospitalization for an opportunistic pneumonia *Pneumocystis carinii*, complicated by Kaposi's sarcoma lesions in his lungs."

His brother rushed to the hospital and was astounded at how much worse Halston appeared since they had dined in January. "I was absolutely shocked to see what bad shape he was in," said Bob. "He had deteriorated greatly since January and I didn't think he'd survive more than a very short time. He'd lost weight, he was weak, and he could hardly breathe."

Miraculously, Halston recovered sufficiently to leave the hospital but returned again and again as AIDS took its toll. He decided he didn't want to die in New York, and in one of his stronger moments, flew to San Francisco. He had had no income for some months, but there was enough money from the sale of his art and other assets to keep him in comfort at the Mark Hopkins Hotel. He bought a Rolls-Royce Silver Cloud to tour the Bay Area nightclubs so he could enjoy what he undoubtedly knew were his last days.

Liza would call him from wherever she was to ask if he was okay. He would cheerfully assure her he was happy and in good spirits despite the specter of premature death that hung over him. Naturally, the *National Enquirer* made the most of the situation, running a cover story headlined:

LIZA IN SHOCK:
Her Designer Pal Halston Is Dying of AIDS."

Halston was so upset with this news leak he immediately checked out of the Mark Hopkins in his wheelchair and moved in with his sister in Santa Rosa.

He was soon back in the hospital at the Pacific Presbyterian Medical Center. As Steven Gaines described in *Simply Halston: The Untold Story:* "He was always dressed in silk pajamas, wearing a bright red Halston robe, and several times a day freshly pressed, fine linen sheets were put on his hospital bed. It was a pleasant enough room for a hospital, with a small sofa and a large window with a view of the San Francisco Bay and the Golden Gate Bridge in the distance, and on every table, as always, there were clay pots of white orchids." Within a short time, the suffering became hardly bearable and when the end came, it was a blessing. He died in his sleep March 26, 1990, at the age of 57, mourned by his family and missed by close friends such as Liza Minnelli.

As many stars as he helped and who claimed to be his friends, Liza was the only celebrity who attended Halston's simple funeral service at the Calvary Presbyterian Church on San Francisco's Fillmore Street. Ten weeks later, Liza hosted a memorial service at New York's Lincoln Center. Another friend of Halston's summed up Liza's relationship with him: "I remember her dedication to Halston was one of the most beautiful I've ever heard. She was a very loyal friend to him and when nearly everyone else abandoned Halston, Liza never did."

One of those who failed to appear was Halston's longtime lover and companion, Victor Hugo. Two months before Halston's death, Victor signed an agreement not to contest Halston's will, sell the story of their seventeen-year relationship, give interviews about him, or embarrass the family in any way. In exchange he received a six-figure inheritance. Victor spent the money, broke the contract, and betrayed the memory of his lover.

Liza remembered, "The last time I saw Halston was about five days before Thanksgiving." He was having an early holiday dinner with her at his New York home because he would celebrate the Thanksgiving Day with his family in Santa Rosa. Liza added, "I was saying *this* was so hard and *that* was so difficult and *that* was difficult."

Halston replied he had enjoyed a wonderful life filled with success, good friends, and all anyone could want. He shamed Liza into realizing how lucky she was. After dinner was over, they hugged and kissed goodnight, and he promised to be back with her for Christmas or New Year's.

She never saw him again.

Upsetting as the Warhol diaries proved to be, they described the lifestyle and environment in which Liza functioned during the end of the 1970s and through much of the 1980s. The diaries make clear why Peter Allen didn't want to stay with Liza and provide insight to what was going on in Liza's mind that she should be a part of this milieu.

The London *Economist* described the creation and scope of the diaries in a July 29, 1989, story: "Warhol began dictating his diaries in the late 1970s to keep track of expenses for tax purposes. He continued until his death in 1987. Beyond the costs of his taxis and paints, they record his frantic social round in the worlds of art, entertainment, politics, fashion and high society. All this is a backdrop to Warhol's real interest: the nefarious ways of celebrities."

Which, of course, is why characters such as Liza kept surfacing in the Warhol diaries. Warhol's style is bitch-in-heat, and it was as if he wanted to wreak vengeance against Liza, Bianca, Capote,

Halston, Rubell, and the rest. The diaries were similar in content to Truman Capote's *Answered Prayers,* in which he savaged New York society. Capote was shunned afterward because they didn't realize he was actually writing down all they did and said.

As the *Economist* wrote: "Warhol must have known he could never be a full member of the group he ran with in Manhattan. He was not chic enough, not good-looking. The urge to take its members down a peg, particularly when so much of their magic was achieved with mirrors, must have been irresistible. In doing so, Warhol dead has shattered the pop icons Warhol living created."

Oddly, Warhol hated phoniness and hypocrisy yet spent years amid the very people he despised. He was so obsessed by money that it colored his view of everything. He admitted in the diaries he didn't want to say too many unflattering things about Halston because Warhol and moviemaker Paul Morrissey owned a house in the Hamptons they rented to Halston, and he didn't want to upset a tenant paying $40,000 a month in rent. He once was offered $80,000 by someone else but turned it down because Halston furnished the place and kept it in perfect condition. Halston used to give Liza the use of the house so she could have trysts with various lovers, which Mark eventually discovered. In return, Mark mounted a subtle campaign to alienate Halston and Liza. He was able to convince Liza she should not wear a Halston dress to the Oscars, which in the narrow world of fashion was considered an enormous slap in Halston's face. For a time, this caused a dramatic cooling in Halston and Liza's friendship.

The Warhol diaries recorded how Bianca Jagger now had Halston's attention and affection. For example, there was this incident on January 3, 1978:

> Went to Halston's. Halston and Bianca were in the kitchen together cooking and he said he had so much energy he wanted to go dancing. He told me lots of gossip—he said the night before when the doorbell rang it was Liza Minnelli. Her life's very complicated now. Like she was

walking down the street with Jack Haley, her husband, and they'd run into Martin Scorsese, who she's now having an affair with, and Marty attacked her for also having an affair with Baryshnikov and Marty said, 'How could she?' This is going on with her husband standing there! And Halston said it was all true and he also said Jack Haley wasn't gay. You see? Halston said Jack likes Liza but what he really goes for is big, curvy blonde women. So, when the doorbell rang the night before, it was Liza in a hat pulled down so nobody would recognize her and she said to Halston, 'Give me every drug you've got.' So, he gave her coke, a few sticks of marijuana, a Valium, four Quaaludes and they were all wrapped in a tiny box. Then, a little figure in a white hat came up on the stoop and kissed Halston and it was Marty Scorsese. He'd been hiding around the corner.

Three and a half weeks later, Warhol was with Bianca at a party in New York's famous Dakota apartments, home to many celebrities, including John Lennon and Yoko Ono. When Bianca and Andy left, she wanted to stop at Halston's place to pick up something. Warhol wrote:

> When we got there, there was a pretty boy in a fur coat standing outside, and when we walked in, there was Liza Minnelli talking to Halston. She wanted to know if she and Baryshnikov—it was him outside—could spend some time at his place. So we weren't supposed to see this. And, it was so exciting to see two really famous people right there in front of you about to go make it with each other.

Time magazine assessed the Warhol diaries as a chronicle of the atmosphere in which people like Liza swam: "The book provides extraordinary insights into a man and an era. At that time, American nouveau cafe society reached its fullest flower, populated by the actors, rock stars, models and hangers-on of Manhattan's nighttime demimonde. Studio 54 was in its heyday, fueled by cocaine, a blatantly gay sensibility and very self-conscious attempts at decadence."

Halston died March 26, 1990. Soon more of Liza's good friends began to slip away. Sammy Davis Jr. died seven weeks later. The year 1990 also saw the end of Liza and Mark's marriage. Mark and Liza loved each other once, but he hated being in her shadow and often fled from her glamorous presence because people regarded him as "Mr. Liza." Also Mark did not become as successful and rich an artist as he had hoped. As Thanksgiving approached, Mark decided he didn't have a lot to be thankful for in their relationship and moved into his own place in Greenwich Village. By Christmas, the gossip columns reported Liza and Mark were no longer together.

Forty-four-year-old Liza trudged on as the professional performer she was in spite of her personal trauma, or perhaps because of it. To start the new year of 1991, she flew to Paris and spent the time with Charles Aznavour and his family, including his wife and their three children. It was a bittersweet time, but at least she wasn't alone for New Year's.

27

Grief in the Time of AIDS

L iza was forty-four and had begun to mellow. On the night she won her Oscar for *Cabaret*, her father gave Liza a gold butterfly pin which had belonged to her mother. She soon realized luck and happiness were things to be shared and not greedily grasped for one's self. So in March 1988, within days of Liza's forty-fifth birthday, she went to see her friend Sally Kirkland on the last day of shooting for Sally's film of *Melanie Rose* and gave her the gold butterfly for good luck.

The month after that, Liza became the second woman to receive the Friars Club's Lifetime Achievement Award (Lucille Ball was the first). At the Century Plaza Hotel testimonial dinner, a teary Liza stood looking around the room and said, "I can't tell you what it is like not only to receive an award like this, but to look around and to know that I have known all of these people all my life."

She was born into a talented, rich, warm fraternity she was now beginning to appreciate. For the 1990 Academy Awards, Karl Malden, president of the Academy, was determined to have Liza sing "Over the Rainbow," which she had never done in public. She refused despite Malden explaining a billion people would be watching her. Liza said "Rainbow" was her mother's song and nobody could sing it better than she did. At the Awards Diana Ross tried, but Liza was right. Liza still was reluctant to do any of her mother's signature songs although she would in time when she felt more comfortable with some of her memories and ghosts.

Meanwhile, she continued to attend AA meetings and hold onto the sober life. During a 1991 appearance before a French audience, Liza gave expression to her feelings in French when she talked about her mother and father and how much she owed them. "Please!" she told the audience. "Now, stop this! You always talk about my mother, my father and how my life belongs to them. I love them a lot and they are always with me, but now, I am a 45-year-old girl. I think it is time to say goodbye to the little Liza child."

Around this time her star was put on the Hollywood Walk of Fame.

Earlier in 1991, Julia Phillips's book *You'll Never Eat Lunch in This Town Again* appeared. Phillips wrote that Liza was on drugs when she attended the 1975 Golden Globe Awards. In a defensive salvo, Lorna declared: "The despicable opening sentence regarding Liza Minnelli at the 1975 Golden Globe Awards was completely inaccurate. My sister Liza did not even attend the show, because she was performing on Broadway. As a result I took her place on the awards show that year. This is just a sample of the fabrications Ms. Phillips has written. Maybe the $120,000 worth of cocaine Ms. Phillips admitted putting up her nose in only two months fogged her so-called photographic memory just a hair."

Liza discovered ex-husband Peter Allen was dying of AIDS so she went to him and tried to comfort him. Bruce Cudd, Peter's assistant, recalled, "Liza rallied around him. She really helped him get back in the swing of things so he wasn't sitting at home. She was real strong." They spent many of his last days together talking, remembering, partying out on the town as they had when they were together. The end came June 18, 1992.

"Peter was a wonderful man," Liza said afterward. "I knew he was ill and we stayed close, but no matter how much you prepare, it's still a shock."

After the deaths of Peter Allen and rock star Freddie Mercury, Liza began performing AIDS benefits for a variety of organizations such as the City of Angels and World AIDS Day. Later, Liza would tell *TV Guide* some of her feelings about losing young friends to AIDS, heart attacks, and cancer: "You just don't expect to lose people until you're like 60. And, some of these people passed away young with AIDS. That's just agony. [Peter Allen and I] were friends. We never should have married, because we were such great friends. And, Fosse was such a shock. With all those heart attacks, you expected him to go—but just not that particular day. And Gower [Champion] was a shock. But I think what was hardest was when Sammy [Davis Jr.] went. And Halston. And then Peter. I didn't know what to do except to move. Keep moving and keep talking about it."

Then, still another man left Liza's narrowing circle. Lorna decided after eighteen years of marriage to leave her husband, guitar player Jake Hooker, because she was in love with Colin Freedman, an English piano player.

Finally, Liza received the stunning news that old friend and lover from years past, Ben Vereen, had been hit by a speeding car as he walked late at night along the side of a Malibu road. He was in critical condition but recovered and months later returned to Broadway to play Ebenezer Scrooge in a production of the Charles Dickens classic, *A Christmas Carol*.

In June 1994 Liza was back on the road again touring, something she does well. The *Los Angeles Times* reported: "Liza leaves the States heading out for two sold-out concerts in Russia. When Liza is on tour, she travels with a small army, musicians, grips, personal assistants. She wants everyone to fly first class. [In answer] to someone who questioned her on what he considered an unnecessary extravagance, the great star's enormous eyes narrowed to slits, 'You mean, you think all these people who work like dogs for weeks and months on end, all over the world, helping me to do what I do, don't deserve to travel in comfort?'"

On December 17, 1994, forty-eight-year-old Liza entered Century City Hospital in Los Angeles for hip replacement surgery. This surprised many who didn't know she suffered from degenerative arthritis for ten years but continued to dance even as the pain grew worse. She had the same surgeon who operated on Elizabeth Taylor and Angela Lansbury. Two days before Christmas 1994, she returned home and started therapy after the metal replacement of her right hip.

"I feel so much better," she told reporters. "I never told anybody because I was ashamed of it. I don't know why. Also, you know, you start lying and people ask, 'What's the matter with your leg?' and you say, 'New shoes.' Now, I'll ring bells when I go through the airport. The operation went great and it is wonderful to be out of pain for the first time in five years. I will be on crutches for only six weeks and then I can do anything again."

By this time Liza decided to move back to Los Angeles and scheduled a new concert tour starting in March 1995. In April she announced she would play the lead in the movie *Torch: The Life and Times of Helen Morgan.* Morgan was a popular blues singer during the Roaring Twenties who became a speakeasy owner and got in trouble with the law.

Liza's first performance after the hip surgery was at the Cerritos Center for the Performing Arts in Orange County. The *Los Angeles Times* reviewer proclaimed: "Liza's back. And with a vengeance. Forget the much-publicized hip surgery. Forget the hiatus from performing. Forget the doubts about how both might impact her career. The opening concert of Liza Minnelli's five-night run was a brilliant confirmation of her world class skills.

"In fact, Minnelli's somewhat reduced mobility happily placed greater emphasis on her vocal and theatrical presentation. Instead of filling the stage with high-voltage, rapid-fire dance steps, she brought the focus in much closer via more subtle strutting, her classic, mime-like arm and hand movements and richly multilayered lyrical interpretations. The result was a far more intimate show than she has offered in past appearances—irrefutable evidence of Minnelli's return to the first rank of musical entertainment."

28

The Once and Future Liza

O n March 12, 1996, Liza celebrated her fiftieth birthday. She was overcoming a series of painful losses and reassessing her life. The painful losses included the deaths of people close to her such as her father, Halston, Peter Allen, and Sammy Davis Jr. The pain of these people leaving her life was such that she would be moved to tears just thinking about them long after they were gone.

As her mother did before her, she found temporary solace in frenetic activity that isolated her from having to think about those she lost. She found consolation working in Las Vegas, New York, Los Angeles—wherever there was a booking. She might have found solace with her husband Mark Gero, but he was no longer there. By 1991 Liza had divorced again. Actually, the marriage was dead by 1989 but that was not the time to arrange the interment. She was too busy preparing for her Radio City show *Stepping Out*, which is exactly what she planned to do. The show opened April 23, 1989, and was a success beyond every expectation, setting a Radio City box-office sales record of $3.8 million and launching her eighteen-city national tour.

Her enormously successful *Stepping Out* debut at Radio City Music Hall also brought her a new romance with Billy Stritch, her musical arranger for the show. Born in Sugarland, Texas, in 1962 and

part of the rock group Montgomery, Plant, and Stritch, Billy was
sixteen years younger than Liza. He wore a beard, mustache, and
glasses to make him look older than he was.

Billy and Liza connected during the show with the kind of
chemistry Liza always seems to generate around men. Billy was
playing at Bobo's on Forty-second Street when he and Liza found
each other. Every night after her show, she became part of Billy's
enthusiastic audience. They built their relationship with Liza
devoting herself to Billy as she does to each of her lovers. She even
sang several duets with him on his album. Liza's hit concert
Stepping Out was made into a film that became another instant blip,
quickly disappearing from America's consciousness.

Soon after, there was a flap in the American press when
columnist Liz Smith reported Liza and Billy were engaged in
Copenhagen. Liza was still married to Mark Gero. Liza called Smith
from Germany. While eating a sausage, Liza set Liz straight in a
friendly way, denying she and Billy Stritch were engaged. "We were
just kidding around in this jewelry store, buying rings and silly
things! A guy came up and asked if we were getting engaged. We
said 'no' but the European press printed it anyway. How can I be
engaged? I'm not even divorced yet."

On December 17, 1991, when Billy and Liza returned to the
States, Liza filed for divorce in Manhattan State Supreme Court.
The divorce was quickly granted, effective January 27, 1992, on the
grounds Mark Gero abandoned her November 1, 1990.

At this time, Liza began to understand something about
personal limits that would make her life easier. She said: "Once you
know what your limits are, it's like somebody giving you this
wonderful present. Once you are told, you can do anything in the
world except this, you go, 'cool, that's great.' Today I value the
philosophy of one day at a time [that she learned at the Betty Ford
Clinic and AA]—take it easy. The only person I ever let down was
myself. I let myself down, so you fix that. And you can! You just fix
it!"

At fifty Liza has achieved a lot professionally and personally.

Looking back on where she has been and what she has done, she offered this evaluation: "I have the only friend I'll ever need, ME. People want to put me into their grinder; they want to shred me so they can get to my bones. They bone-picked Mama, but they're not going to bone-pick me. Everyone thinks I'm as frantic as a Ping-Pong ball. Well, I'm *not* crazy and, as long as I'm around, I can be my own protector."

She can be her own woman, too. She lives in New York and is still part of the nightlife there. In May 1996 Liza appeared in the gossip columns again with her antics at Ingrid Casares's trendy night spot and pan-sexual hangout, Liquid. As reported by *New York* magazine, "The frenetic chanteuse began dancing onstage as fast as she could." And this was without the benefit of drink. She took over the disc jockey's booth and spent the next hours fiddling with the light and smoke machines and playing disco numbers. It was exactly the sort of kid-in-the-candy-store behavior Halston used to display at Studio 54. Liza said, "Bianca did it at Studio 54 and Liza's going to do it at Liquid."

On April 9, 1996, the *National Enquirer* reported Liza was headed for an early grave just like their mother and she and Lorna were not speaking. The story immediately prompted Liza to telephone her sister in Las Vegas to assure her everything was all right. Lorna was in Vegas at the MGM Grand with fiancé Colin Freedman and her children, opening a Don Rickles act that centered around his turning seventy. Liza's call prompted Lorna to tell *USA Today* columnist Jeannie Williams she was surprised because Liza had not called in more than a year.

Liza opened her new stage production at Bally's in Las Vegas May 26, 1996. This Las Vegas appearance was built on the release of her latest record album, *Gently*, which is anchored deep in her past and the songs of a generation ago. They include such standards as "Embraceable You," "I Got Lost in His Arms," "It Had to Be You," and "In the Wee Small Hours of the Morning." These melodies have strong memories for Liza.

She said, "Usually the songs I'm drawn to are about what I

hope to be like. At their best, they are strong, unsentimental and relentlessly cheerful. The songs on this album, in truth, are much more what I'm really like: sentimental, romantic and sometimes foolish. I usually don't sing these songs out loud."

The genesis of the *Gently* album was a drive down Sunset Boulevard in west Los Angeles along what is known as the Strip. She was listening to Johnny Mathis singing "Chances Are" and getting an instant high at the pleasure of it. Impulsively and typically Liza, she pulled into the next record store she spotted, dashed in, and asked for their "romantic" section. That brought blank stares from the clerks. It was then she decided she had to make an album of all those great romantic songs once sung by her buddies Sinatra, Sammy Davis, and the rest she knew growing up in New York and Hollywood. The album marked the end of almost two years in which Liza was mostly out of circulation except for a few concerts.

Thinking of the album, Liza said, "I thought, 'Oh, man, I remember this song so clearly.' And I recalled getting my first kiss to it. So I thought, 'Well, I've got to make one of those [romantic] albums. I felt it would be fun to do it very simply, just piano, bass and drums.

"You get to a certain point where, as opposed to swinging on the rafters and doing high kicks, you just make a statement that I'm really glad I'm alive and here are some really good songs I grew up with." Liza wants to move from the spotlight to directing, a desire inspired by her father, of whom she said, "I got from my father a sense of the overall. When I do a show, I don't just think from the singer's point of view. I think from the audience's point of view and about the whole picture and the effect the evening will have."

Several movies are in the making about Studio 54 where she, Halston, Andy Warhol, and Bianca Jagger used to hang out. One is directed by the former assistant doorman, Al Corley, who went on to become an actor on TV's *Dynasty*. Corley recalled, "It was the best running show on Broadway. Sexual mores were broken down. People had fun." Corley expects to release his film in the spring of 1997 and beat everyone else to the punch.

Other Studio 54 films in the making include one by New Line done with the cooperation of the club's cofounder, Ian Schrager. New Line president Michael DeLuca said, "I would only do the one with Ian because he has the rights to the name. All these other ones are, like, Studio 54 inspired."

There are several other potential movie projects, including a film based on Steven Gaines's biography of Halston, which includes a lot of material about Liza. However, no film about Studio 54 will probably be filmed at the site of the legendary nightclub since the club has now become a virtual-reality family entertainment center called Cyberdome.

On July 3, 1996, Liza and Dudley Moore began a cross-country tour in Holmdel, New Jersey, to coincide with the fifteenth anniversary of *Arthur*. Tour coordinator Ed Kasses said, "It's got the same appeal as *Tony Bennett Unplugged*." The tour included a fifty-five-piece orchestra with Liza singing songs from her *Gently* album and Dudley performing jazz numbers and old standards. At the end, they performed "Arthur's Theme" together.

Everyone agreed Liza looked well at the 1996 Tony Awards when she and Bernadette Peters opened the show with a duet of "The Show Must Go On" and later presented the Best Lead Actress in a Musical award to Donna Murphy. She followed that with a European concert tour. The most recent romantic development in Liza's life is rumored to be the twenty-five-year-old Australian actor Simon Crocker, who moved into her Los Angeles home early in 1996.

"I fight to be Liza Minnelli onstage and I fight to be Liza Minnelli offstage," she once said. "God gave me a talent and I'm not going to spit in His eye. People are trying to prove history repeats itself. But Mama always told me history doesn't have to repeat itself. Mama always complained and fell apart on the job. Well, I'm not like that. I have different goals than Mama did. For me, living is having peace of mind. I don't think Mama ever had that."

Finally, Liza is able to sing Judy's songs as a tribute to her incandescent mother without feeling awkward or trying to pass herself off as Judy. She is now able to say to the world—and more important, to herself—"Mama was marvelous and here is what she sang, but I am Liza...her daughter and proud of it."

Judy is remembered in other ways, too. The Arts & Entertainment channel broadcast a two-hour documentary devoted to her in December 1996, while Capitol Records released a seven-CD boxed set of her recordings in November.

Liza has also come to terms with her physical appearance as her mother never could. Occasionally, a critic will make some hurtful remark about Liza's appearance, but most people think Liza is a long-legged, attractive performer.

While still doubtful about herself, Liza said: "The longer someone knows me, the better I look. But in all honesty, if you compare me with your average beauty, I just ain't it. If I was spectacular looking, maybe I wouldn't be able to act so well. Still, beauty is what's inside and at least I don't have to worry about staying beautiful for my fans."

In some ways, Liza is like Bette Midler, who struggled to achieve and now that she is a star, has matured and become domesticated. A major difference between them is Bette has her little girl Sophie, while Liza was never able to have the child she always wanted.

Liza has proven she's not just Judy Garland's daughter, yet she is the child of Vincente and Judy. An interviewer once tried to quote Liza saying what her mother and father each gave her, but garbled the quote. Liza corrected it: "The way they quoted me was, 'My father gave me my dreams, but my mother my drive.' And that's not what I said. I said, 'My mother gave me my drive...which is the basic way you know I am, but my father gave me my dream...my father taught me nothing was impossible, nothing was out of the question. There's always a way to accomplish something."

Liza exalts in life now. "This is such a wonderful time in my life. I wake up in the morning and say: 'Oh, my God, it's still here. Everything's still fine. Thank you, God!"

Index